Help My Unbelief!

Help My Unbelief!

Doubt, Faith, and the Gospel of Mark

J. TIMOTHY ALLEN

RESOURCE *Publications* • Eugene, Oregon

HELP MY UNBELIEF!
Doubt, Faith, and the Gospel of Mark

Copyright © 2017 J. Timothy Allen. All rights reserved. Except for brief quotations in critical publications or reviews, no part of this book may be reproduced in any manner without prior written permission from the publisher. Write: Permissions, Wipf and Stock Publishers, 199 W. 8th Ave., Suite 3, Eugene, OR 97401.

Resource Publications
An Imprint of Wipf and Stock Publishers
199 W. 8th Ave., Suite 3
Eugene, OR 97401

www.wipfandstock.com

PAPERBACK ISBN: 978-1-5326-0037-1
HARDCOVER ISBN: 978-1-5326-0039-5
EBOOK ISBN: 978-1-5326-0038-8

Manufactured in the U.S.A. JULY 10, 2017

Scripture quotations marked (NIV) are taken from the Holy Bible, New International Version®, NIV®. Copyright © 1973, 1978, 1984, 2011 by Biblica, Inc.™ Used by permission of Zondervan. All rights reserved worldwide. www.zondervan.com The "NIV" and "New International Version" are trademarks registered in the United States Patent and Trademark Office by Biblica, Inc.™

New Revised Standard Version Bible, copyright 1989, Division of Christian Education of the National Council of the Churches of Christ in the United States of America. Used by permission. All rights reserved.

For my brother Mark,
for obvious reasons.

Contents

Introduction | ix

1. Who Am I? | 1
2. Help My Unbelief! | 21
3. Who Are My Mother and My Brothers? | 40
4. Jesus as Teacher | 65
5. Miracle Worker or Demon Possessed? | 98
6. The Cloud of Unknowing | 129
7. Who Do You Say That I Am? | 146

Bibliography | 161

Introduction

IN 2004 I COMPLETED my doctoral studies with the Graduate Theological Foundation. Years of undergraduate and graduate work came to fruition that special day in May when I received my degree. Then I endured what grad students everywhere experience after the culmination of their studies: depression. What does one do now that one has accomplished all that was dreamed of?

The depression worsened and in 2006 I faced a night of suicide. Reaching for the gun I wrestled with whatever Entity that was pushing me toward the end of life. At that moment I did not ponder the great theological debates surrounding the virgin birth of Christ nor did I take comfort in the literal seven days of creation. Perhaps I should have taken refuge in the physical resurrection of Jesus and the resulting conquest of death but that did not occur to me at the time. Neither was the immanent return of Jesus foremost in my mind. Instead, I uttered a simple prayer: "Help me!"

I survived the night.

Ever since that night I have come out with what country singer Steve Earle calls "a brand new plan." The old theologies did not make sense to me anymore. Suddenly contradictions in the Bible seemed much more important than the Apostle's Creed. Inconsistencies in biblical theology bothered me. I became frustrated with the Church and its petty arguments and squabbles. The superficiality of contemporary services was annoying. And born-again-Christian-know-it-alls have no idea what they are talking about. Certainly there is more to Christianity than this? To put it simply, there are a lot of hurting people out there and the worries over the jots and

Introduction

tittles of the faith are not really that important when one is hungry, homeless and marginalized, not to mention contemplating suicide.

In my New Testament class I used the Gospel of Mark as the starting point to get a handle on the man Jesus. In my reading of that gospel I began to realize that something was amiss here. While we are taught to put together all the gospels into one harmonized account of Jesus' life what if we took Mark as the only account of Jesus' life, as was the case until ten years after it was written when Matthew and Luke came along. What did people think of Jesus based solely on the Gospel of Mark?

Second, in my background readings I began encountering histories that were not as sympathetic with Christian beliefs as were the courses I took while in seminary. Now I learned of the major and embarrassing battles over theology that took place. Much of the theology of the early Church was based more on satisfying Roman emperors and power-thirsty bishops and corrupt popes than it was from the Holy Spirit. Suddenly the Church did not seem as nice as it was in my seminary days.

Third, it became apparent to me that the decade preceding the writing of Mark was filled with danger, fear, confusion and dashed hopes. Judaism was torn by factions, including the Jews who claimed Jesus was the Messiah. The early believers were upset that Jesus had not returned as predicted by the Savior himself. Persecutions by maniacal Roman emperors led to defections from the faith. Battles between Jews and Jews who believed in Jesus were destroying the faithful. Suddenly it was disheartening and even dangerous to be a Christian. On top of that, the ever-present threat of Roman destruction of Jerusalem loomed over the roofs of the Temple and the homes of the Jews.

With all of this in mind, as I reread Mark suddenly it seemed as though the author was addressing the doubts and confusions of the people. Episodes in the gospel seemed to be addressing tough questions. And one of the questions seemed to be at the very base of the Christian faith: was Jesus resurrected from the tomb? The original ending of Mark, unlike the other three gospels, has no resurrection appearance by Jesus. Instead, the reader is instructed to go to Galilee where he or she would meet Jesus again.

Questions abound in the Gospel of Mark and perhaps these questions were on the lips of the confused and fearful readers of the first gospel.
Today questions abound in the minds of some of the faithful. Is the virgin birth of Jesus really relevant? Does it matter if I believe in the immanent return of Christ? Were the miracles real or mythical? Is there more than

INTRODUCTION

one way to salvation? What do we make of other religions? On and on the questions go. The response of the Church: dodge the import of the questions by requiring simple and unwavering faith to the creeds and tenets of the faith. But, many people are asking these questions because they do follow this dogma and they have found it to be wanting in logic and lacking in spiritual peace.

So, this book is for the intelligent, discerning Christians, the people who are asking the tough questions but are being ignored by the Church. We want to keep reading our Bibles and attending our communions and worshiping our Lord. But, we need some scriptural guidance in our doubting quest for faith. As we will see, doubt was a major component of the faith before the Church condemned it. And, maybe it is time to put healthy doubt back into the mainstream of faith. That is what this book is about.

1

Who Am I?

My Soul Thirsts for God.

(Ps 42:2 NRSV)

IT SEEMS THAT MANY Christians live in a time of doubt and confusion today. Things don't make sense, the old ways are missed, the current ways are displeasing and the future looks increasingly bleak. Faith diminishes amid trite evangelical contemporary services, divisive fundamentalist politics and tired mainline creedal faiths. Christians who once believed in the old, old story now find the story to be indeed old, tottering or even dead. Milk is served for infants in the faith, bread and wine for the old faithful, but the table seems empty for some. Where does one go for a filling dinner when all that is served are happy meals or recipes from yellowed cookbooks?

Some are asking: if this is Christianity, then who am I?

In a thought-provoking study, the Barna Group examines why people are leaving the church. They are not leaving the faith: indeed, most are very spiritual, they are committed to Christian values, and religious faith is important for them. Yet they also tend to be "independent and self-reliant." Many read their Bibles and pray regularly. At the same time, those not attending church are not necessarily "overly impressed by the pedigree, history, or importance of the Bible." More and more, young people, tired of simplistic faith, are dropping out of church because they have doubts and questions that the church is simply not answering. "Churches that are unwelcoming to young adults' doubts and questions are equally unwelcoming to older adults' doubts and questions." They, too, are tired of what Barna-Group describes as shallow church experiences.[1]

Steve Weinberg provides an upsetting term for these faithful doubters. At the end of his review of Gina Welsh's new book *In the Land of Believers: An Outsider's Extraordinary Journey into the Heart of an Evangelical Church* in the local paper he described himself as "an evangelical agnostic who sometimes attends mainstream churches." If ever there was a Christian oxymoron this was one. How can a person be an evangelical agnostic?[2]

For some Christians this appellation is not so odd. Clandestine discussions often elicit brave admissions of disdain. Here are some I have heard: "I don't know if I really believe in God anymore." Or, "I don't care if Jesus was born of a virgin." Or, "I repeat the Nicene Creed in the liturgy but I don't believe half of it." Or, "I don't care what the Bible says, I refuse to believe that." The fact that these and other similar lines come from laity and ministers alike reveals a gaping and widening chasm in the faith.

What exactly is going on? Why are long time-believers suddenly coming out of the faith closet to admit that centuries of theological proofs and statements and tenets of faith are either unacceptable, out of date, out of touch with today's issues or just plain insufficient for their faith? If the traditions are so unsatisfying why do they bother still going to church? The answers spiral from a nucleus of doubt. But, a doubting faith is not new. Christians have doubted for centuries, ever since Jesus died and his disciples began planting house churches in the Mediterranean, Africa, the Middle East and even the Far East. But pastors, the laity and theologians typically decry a lack of faith. Doubts are the devil's breeding grounds, they extoll, therefore those who doubt are not real Christians.

I have heard many state that those who doubt are not true Christians. Some of this is based on faulty interpretations of scripture. In James 1:6 the believer is warned that one who doubts "is like a wave of the sea, blown and tossed by the wind" (NIV). But in this verse the prohibition against doubting is for those who are asking for wisdom. This is a very specific issue. Likewise Romans 14:23, where the believer is warned not to doubt *in regards to dietary issues*. In Matthew 21:21 Jesus points out that doubts are bad but the context is prayer, specifically praying for something to happen. Why bother praying if you are already doubting? For some Christians, their

---

1. Barna and Kinnamon, *Churchless*, 41, 57, 59, 95–96, quotes from respectively 44, 77 and 105.

2. Weinberg, "Author Goes Undercover."

doubts have nothing to do with asking for wisdom or eating restrictions or getting their prayers answered. In fact it could be said that their wisdom has led to their doubts. That is what James Fowler suggests in his book *Stages of Faith*. As one matures in spiritual matters one sees the inherent holes in religious tenets. Once spotted, these contradictions can only lead to doubts about the integrity of the faith. In this case, Fowler argues, doubt is actually a sign of deepening faith![3] The small letter of Jude reminds Christians "Be merciful to those who doubt" (Jude 22 NIV). This demonstrates that many in the early church still doubted.

There are two religious phenomena moving at the same time in Christianity today. First, there is what I will call the Da Vinci Code phenomenon. Most people were introduced to the criticisms of the Catholic Church when Dan Brown's novel—which suggests the Catholic Church has covered up and even lied about the historical Jesus—was published some years ago. This was the popular version of the criticisms against Christianity but non-church historians, some New Testament scholars and a few early church historians have leveled strong and persuasive arguments against many of the respected traditions and long-held beliefs of Christians. Many within Christianity, generally, but not exclusive to, those of conservative background and faith, have decried these works and even claimed these authors were on a vendetta against Christianity. Maybe so but, perhaps Christians should instead use these academic and popular critiques as a catalyst for an extensive and long-overdue reevaluation of the faith. Facts are facts. If these historians are correct then we should listen to them. The Bible says the truth shall make us free (John 8:32) but many Christians, rather than furtively exploring these new facts and claims, simply dismiss them with the same trite brushoffs or the tired theologies of old.

The second trend is less visible but it is slowly coming to light. It runs like a quiet brook alongside of this flooding critique of Christianity. Simply put: a growing number of Christians today are annoyed of the mega-church mentality or bored with the tedium of out of date mainline theologies. These long-time loyal Christians are asking tough questions, many of them inspired by the criticisms noted above, but the Church is ignoring them. Instead, the Church simply reasserts the age-old dictum of believe without doubt. Never question the faith! While the world progresses the Church retreats and demands strict adherence to its laws, much like a military dictator who tolerates no dissension in the ranks.

---

3. James Fowler, *Stages*, 31.

Where does a loyal yet disappointed Christian look for answers? Where does one turn for nurture? Why not go to a book of the Bible that has quite a few questions? Robert M. Fowler examined the Gospel of Mark and discovered that it has "approximately 116 questions." Why so many questions in the shortest gospel in the New Testament? We will see that in the times of Mark's writing significant questions were being raised by an increasingly skeptical faithful. Perhaps Mark's gospel can be a source of renewed faith for those who are filled with doubts and questions today. My contention is that Christians can find solid answers to the current criticisms and remain loyal to their faith if they learn how to interpret their scriptures in new ways. Faith and doubt go hand in hand and the Gospel of Mark shows how the two can work together in the life of a Christian.[4]

In 2007 the religious world was shocked to hear that Mother Teresa, the Saint of Calcutta, had strong doubts about whether God cared for her or even existed at all. A new book, edited by Father Brian Kolodiejchuk, appeared on the market. Father Kolodiejchuk knew Mother Teresa for over twenty years and is the priest responsible for collecting the necessary documentation for the beatification of this selfless nun. He gathered her letters and writings in order to reveal to the world her enduring faith throughout her spiritual journey. What he found, though, was almost the very opposite. Readers and admirers who revered Mother Teresa as the epitome of faith and sacrifice were surprised to read that this tireless woman who unselfishly gave her whole life to the service of the poor and exiled of India experienced many episodes of doubt. These spiritual pains were so intense that, as her life of ministry came to a close, she increasingly questioned the existence of God. Could Mother Teresa, the symbol of sacrificial faith for this generation, also be a model for doubt?[5]

Mother Teresa doubted God, but like many unchurched or frustrated people in the pews today, she continued her religious rituals and praxis. For example, she prayed, but only out of a sense of her vocational duty. "I don't pray any longer.—I utter community prayers . . . I no longer pray.—My soul is no longer with You." She lamented "How terrible it is to be without God—no prayer—no faith—no love.—The only thing that still remains—is the conviction that the work is his." Caught within this spiritual paradox, what she called Hell, she lived within the two extremes of longing for God and refusing this God who seemed to have left her behind to a life of silence.

---

4. Robert M. Fowler, "In the Boat With Jesus," 245.
5. Kolodiejchuk, *Mother Teresa*.

Who Am I?

Although this sister of light lived in a world of darkness she persevered in her work and thousands of the poor and dying in India received the love that she longed to give to a god who seemed more and more absent and uncaring as she aged in her ministry. In the face of this black hole of faith it is telling that her doubts led to the soothing of souls, the salving of wounds, healing in times of sickness and love in the time of lonely death. Despite her inability to adhere to the strict teachings of dogma she still lived out her faith in acts of love and justice. To put it succinctly, she *did* her faith.[6]

Mother Teresa's doubt is not an aberration. The Bible overflows with people who doubted God and God's will. An aging Abraham, having been promised a life of blessing through land, children and reputation, voiced serious doubts that God would ever give children to him. Sarah, his aged wife, laughed in disbelief when told that she would bear a child (Gen 12 and 15). Moses, the one who gave us the Old Testament Law that led to what is today called Judaism, doubted that God would give him the strength to lead the Israelites out of the land of Egypt (Exod 3 and 6:12—7:7). King David and other poets, as evinced all throughout the Psalms, sang about doubts. Ecclesiastes, the book that looks at the vanities of life, reveals that "the meaning of life is not found in the macro-assumptions one holds, but in the way one manages life's micro-significances." In other words, the Solomonic wisdom of pithy proverbs and "Do good and God will bless" theology is tossed aside as deeper questions of the faith are explored.[7]

In the early Church Paul, a zealous Jew, questioned his calling ("Who are you, Lord?) but still persevered in his ministry while plagued with numerous hardships and a serious health problem (Acts 9; 2 Cor 11:16—12:10). Staring straight at a resurrected Jesus Mary Magdalene did not believe it was him (John 20). Some of the disciples, with Jesus standing in their midst and eating fish, expressed doubts (Luke 24). Perhaps most surprising of all, Jesus, son of God, proclaimed his doubts about God's plan for his life when he prayed for God to take the cup of death from him. It was not to be and, as he hung on the cross, he cried out, in the ultimate, haunting, expression of doubt, "My God, my God, why have you forsaken me?" (Mark 14:36; 15:34 NRSV)

If doubts permeate the Bible's great characters, then why should Christians be afraid of doubts?

---

6. Ibid., 245, 250, 270.
7. Horne, *Proverbs-Ecclesiastes*, 375.

Doubt is a major issue in religious news around us today. Several atheistic writers have claimed that all religions are bogus, infantile, psychotic and thus are destroying our world. Chanting the mantra of Neitzche's declaration that God is dead, these authors defy anyone to give credible rational evidence for God. This movement, called "scientism" (not to be confused with Scientology), calls for the choice between religion and science. Its main practitioners consist of Oxford biologist Richard Dawkins, the noted Carl Sagan, Sam Harris, and Christopher Hitchens among others. If science is the new religion these are its priests.

It is easy to dismiss these people as fundamentalistic scientists and rationalists, as noted religion author Karen Armstrong deftly does, but such a judgment might be a bit premature. Sam Harris' *The End of Faith* is indeed simplistic and his assessments of and dismissal of religions is too quick but he has many valid points that should be addressed by the religious community. His argument is quite profound: *faith* is killing us. People's blind faith in their sacred books is leading them to draw dangerous lines and kill those who cross them. Or, in a stab at the liberal religious left, he points out that those who give up the major tenets of their scriptures, that is, those who water down their faith in hopes of diversity, political correctness, and multiculturalism, have sold out their religion altogether. In his view, that makes them worse than fundamentalists who stick to the literal scriptures at all costs. He argues that irrational faith must be replaced with a reason that knows the difference between ancient superstition and modern reality, reason that knows when blind adherence to a doctrine of "kill the infidels" must be defied in order to live in harmony with our neighbors.[8] When analyzed impartially, Harris' assessment is a very fair synopsis of Jesus' thought and teachings! Jesus took on the pharisaical fundamentalists of his day while reminding the liberals that the Law was still to be observed. Jesus, like Harris, was not against faith, just unreasonable faith. And today some Christians are stating the same.

How has the religious establishment responded? A barrage of *rationalistic* defenses of God and religion rather than an honest conversation with the "enemy." Here is one example.

Timothy Keller's book, *The Reason for God: Belief in an Age of Skepticism*, is a *New York Times* bestseller and an excellent apologetic (defense) of the Christian faith. Keller's theology makes sense. He deftly answers the questions of today's skeptics, especially the young ones. His skills in logic

---

8. Armstrong, *Case*, xvi; Harris, *The End of Faith*.

and his fatherly blunt, yet loving, responses to people's questions about God and the Christian church are a welcome alternative to the harsh and divisive fundamentalism or the watered down liberalism that drives people away from a potential life in the Church. The fact that his other works are a veritable industry in evangelical circles and Christian bookstores indicates its appeal for readers and his success suggests a hunger among Americans today for a substantive faith far removed from fundamental absolutes or relative platitudes.[9]

His book, however, does not meet the needs of some long-time Christians who find that the old ways of the faith are just not meeting their spiritual needs and that the ministers of today do not understand these needs at all. First, as noted throughout the book, his arguments are for thirty-something skeptics. Most of these are college-educated and intelligent. They are skeptical of the faith claims of Christians and wonder why choose Christianity over the other available religions. Keller is quite adept at answering their questions. But, these are people new to the faith and those barely familiar with the Christian religion, not old-timers who have lost the will to believe in their old church and its doctrines.

Second, the questions of these young people are those of young minds and reveal a minimal life in the faith. Why just one religion? How can a good God allow suffering? Why has the Church caused so much injustice? Has science disproved religion? Is the Bible the literal word of God? These are superficial, popular questions that reveal little knowledge of the deeper questions of a spiritual life. These are not the questions being asked by many of those who have lived long in the Christian faith.

Third, in order to answer these questions, Keller then understandably resorts back to the basics of the faith: how we know of God; the problem of sin; the gospel story; the importance of the cross; the reality of the resurrection; and the loving life of faith in God. His answers are deftly crafted and his theology is predictable. And, his chapter entitled "The (True) Story of the Cross" is excellent, perhaps the best interpretation of the role of the cross in the beliefs of Christians available today.

Fourth, Keller rather naively states that all Christians believe the statements of the creeds and this is where he is indicative of many pastors and theologians today. Some Christians, certainly not the majority of them, do not believe or do not focus their faith on these basic tenets of the Church. As noted above, there is a lot of new information available that raises

9. Keller, *Reason for God*.

serious questions about the integrity of the Church and how these creeds and theologies were established. Keller dismisses these new works by citing *the novelist Anne Rice*? Several years ago Rice recently returned to her Catholic faith but Keller seems unaware that, after encountering its harsh creeds and faith demands, she left the Church. She retained her allegiance to Jesus but dropped the appellation of "Christian" from her faith life. As Rice's "reconversion" demonstrates, some Christians want more than just simplistic creedal liturgy and illogical theology such as the doctrine of the Holy Trinity or the doctrine of predestination.[10] Is Keller aware of the spate of new books questioning how the creeds came about in the first place?

Fifth, Keller is quite the logician and can out-argue his opponents. His evaluation of skeptical comments is keen and he is knowledgeable enough of both rational thought and the Christian faith to answer his skeptics. But as any logician knows, any logical argument can be taken apart by another logical argument. And, if a premise or two or three of the argument is proved wrong, then the argument falls apart. And one can pick apart some of Keller's arguments as noted above. So, the bottom line here is, yet again, one person logically, rationally, argues against another. Stalemate. Again.

While Keller approaches the theological issues, another popular pastor, Craig Groeschel, examines the practical life of the Christian in his book *The Christian Atheist*. Groeschel is pastor of LifeChurch.tv, an organization that has multiple campuses around the United States and globally with Church Online. After pastoring for several years he noticed that he had become a "Christian atheist." That is, one who did the faith but did not fully know God. The book is basically an autobiographical faith journey back to a more God-centered Christian life.[11]

One look at the reviews of Goeschel's arguments and we can see many of the current critiques of today's Church. John Gibbs wrote a positive review:

> The book examines a number of ways in which Christians fail to act consistently with their stated beliefs: not really knowing God, remaining ashamed of your past, being unsure of God's love for you, not believing in prayer, not trusting that God is fair, failing to forgive, not believing that you can change, clinging to worry,

---

10. Keller, *Reason for God*, 102; Bass, *Christianity*, 20–21.
11. Groeschel, *Christian Atheist*.

Who Am I?

pursuing happiness at any cost, trusting more in money than in God, not sharing your faith, and not being part of the church.[12]

But, a few dissented from this and multiple other positive reviews. Mike Pettengill wrote:

> There is not great substance to the book, but it is not heretical. The topics that are covered are important issues we should all be discussing, but the lack of depth and substance are disappointing. The author seems almost afraid to commit to strict or definitive standards. While the Bible is black and white, Groeschel doesn't seem to have a desire to be so absolute.
>
> It appears the audience for this book would not be the well-studied Christian, but instead the seeker or the sleepy pew sitter. There are many more books you should read before this one.[13]

Those with substantive critical reviews of Groeschel's book echoed the same sentiments. Daphne Huffman's opinion is typical: "I was disappointed with this book. I didn't find it to be very deep or helpful. It did talk about the issue of 'Christian atheism' and was clearly written, but I didn't find any new insights in it." C. Clingerman sums it up very well: "Topics are covered on surface only. No depth. Not good writing. Perhaps better suited for new believer."[14]

There are many positive comments such as "simple" or "just what we need" from the majority of readers. Out of 114 reviews listed on Amazon.com's page for this book, 77% gave it a 5 star rating, 14% a 4-star, and 10% gave it three stars or less. And this might be a fair estimate of the percentage of discerning Christians who want more than the usual fare for their Christian sustenance. There is a lot of Christian fluff out in Christian bookstores today. Where does the learned, experienced and critical Christian go to read deeper into the faith?

One more recent author deserves mention as well: young evangelical YouTube sensation Jefferson Bethke's book and video series *Jesus > Religion*. His poem "Why I Hate Religion But Love Jesus" went viral and has over 25 million hits. This exuberant, fatherless youngster (early twenties when he wrote the book) is relatively new to Christianity, having lived a hellion's

---

12. Gibbs, "A Challenging Call."
13. Pettengill, "The Author Seems Afraid to Commit to Biblical Absolutes."
14. Huffman, "I Was Disappointed With This Book;" Clingerman, "ok on the surface."

life, faked Christianity, lived a so-so Christian life and then found "true" Christianity in a relatively short span of time. He relates a past life of porn, stealing, sex, drinking and other sins and lives with the realization that his mother is lesbian. Despite all these strikes he is now a devoted Christian and new husband (four months when he wrote the book)[15]

His observations are keen and witty and worth the read. He excoriates what he calls the "subculture of Christianity." Bethke exposes Christian fundamentalism, has no words of comfort for the "spiritual people" and in some ways even sounds like a liberal Christian ("People don't go to hell because they are gay"). He is also a therapist's dream because within his thoughts are still the guilt of past sins and anyone mature in the faith can see through his "party" mentality.[16]

While observant in many ways and quick with a biblical retort to many of the ills within today's popular Christianity Bethke seems to think that Christians only attend contemporary worship and listen to Christian music. Still, his observations are fun if a bit innocent. He seems to have a predilection for Bible stories about adultery and an obsession with proving that Christians can drink beer and get tattoos. There is nothing in the Bible explicitly against drinking beer. He is correct here. Proverbs 31 even encourages the king to get the poor drunk so that they don't know how bad off they are. But any wise person with years in the Church would recall the prohibition against tattoos in Leviticus 19:28. And this reveals the problem inherent in Bethke's somewhat juvenile approach. He seems quite witty yet incredibly naïve at times. His book is great for social media types but not good for those whose doubts are spurred by years of reflecting on the contradictions of the faith.

For example, Bethke seems obsessed with the story of the Samaritan woman at the well who had many husbands. He alludes to it numerous times throughout his book and calls it one of his favorite stories in the Bible.[17] Evangelicals who interpret the story blame the woman for the divorces. In the NIV Study Bible we are told in a note that, "the woman's life had been exceedingly immoral."[18] Likewise, Bethke blames the woman for her "promiscuity" and notes that she divorced her five husbands and lived in sin with another.

15. Bethke, *Jesus*.
16. Ibid., 6, 69.
17. Ibid., 70.
18. NIV Study Bible, 1771.

Who Am I?

This conclusion might be based on the passage in Deuteronomy 24:1–4 where a man can divorce his wife for "displeasing" him (NIV). It is not clear what "displease" means and later rabbis spilled much ink interpreting the term. Of course infidelity was one interpretation but one rabbi even suggested that it could mean ruining the dinner. By the time of Jesus Jews were following the Roman precedent of allowing women to divorce their husbands but the Samaritans were more strict and may have followed the law to the letter in Deuteronomy which says that men can divorce their wives, not the other way around.

Modern day Christians with deeper sensitivities would quickly point out that the story deserves more than a sexist, indeed misogynistic interpretation. Maybe her past husbands were immoral and simply wanted another woman. Maybe they were horrible husbands. Maybe she was a tempestuous wife and her husbands divorced her for that reason alone, not adultery. Maybe she could not produce children, an embarrassment for a Middle Eastern family. There is nothing explicitly promiscuous in the story. There is every possibility that a woman who has been divorced five times by men would not want to marry anymore and instead has chosen to live with a man. There is also the possibility that the two were in betrothal in which they could legally and religiously live together before their marriage. There are deeper issues here than just a sinful and lusty woman and discerning Christians would appreciate a more in-depth exploration of this topic rather than the brisk assumption that she was promiscuous.[19]

Bethke, who otherwise exhibits a good knowledge of the Bible and its background, seems ignorant of these deeper questions. He indeed exhibits what evangelical scholar Mark Noll describes as the "scandal of the evangelical mind," an inattentiveness to the larger details of the liberal arts, history and even theology. "Unlike their spiritual ancestors, modern evangelicals have not pursued comprehensive thinking under God or sought a mind shaped to its furthest reaches by Christian perspectives." Some Christians want more than just the simplistic, rote interpretations that demonstrate no will to explore the matter further.[20]

Another example deserves exploration as well. People deep in the faith have pondered the conundrum of suffering. If God has created weal and woe, as Isaiah 45:7 states specifically and as many Psalms agree, then one has to at some point at least ponder why God allows us to suffer. A

---

19. Goodman, *Rome and Jerusalem*, 215–217; Jeffers, *Greco-Roman*, 244–247.
20. Noll, *Scandal*, 4.

logical step from this is that God is punishing us for something and many Christians have uttered this belief and the Bible is full of stories where punishments are meted out for past sins. Biblically speaking, there is ample evidence that God punishes the sinner, or even the innocent as the Book of Job so beautifully yet painfully points out. Bethke, however states unequivocally that "Suffering is never from God" and "when you are suffering, God is not punishing you." This is because God already punished Jesus and thus there is no more punishment.[21] This seems just a bit simplistic.

While looking like a reformed Christian with a new set of clothes Bethke falls back into the old wineskin of idolizing scripture. His overwhelming attention upon Jesus makes one wonder if God has been tossed aside. Citing scriptures, even if done in a new way, is still telling people they have to believe in a certain way according to "the script." What if we dared to go outside of the Church, literally out of doors to find God and faith again? That is what writer, teacher and former Episcopalian priest Barbara Brown Taylor did when she left the confines of the Episcopal Church. In many ways her assessments of Christians and the Church are similar to Bethke's but there is a sagely element and a refreshing vitality to her open-ended observations and conclusions that only years of reflection can bring about. She writes, "After twenty years of serving Mother Church at the altar, I have pitched my tent in the yard, using much of what she taught me to make a way in the world." Again, sober sagacity rather than youthful exuberance leads to greater truths and some Christians want this on a weekly basis.[22]

There is a crevasse here that church theologians, apologists, and pastors are not trying to bridge. To put it simply, the church is spending its time answering childish questions, feeding milk to the young and then burping them as well. The apostle Paul saw this phenomenon in his days of ministry and he noted that some still were not ready for the solid food of advanced faith (1 Cor 3:2). In the meantime, many are asking tough questions yet when they explore the complicated issues they are treated as children and pointed right back to the ABCs of the faith. But, rather than spelling the faith quite well, discerning Christians want to parse the words of faith. And, as anyone knows who has had to translate from one language to another, words have many different meanings depending on their context. Some Christians today want to explore these connotations and contexts. Instead they are told to sit in their pews and memorize this,

21. Bethke, *Jesus*, 119, 122.
22. Taylor, *Leaving Church*, 222.

repeat rote lessons from yesterday, and say the creeds or just praise Jesus with hands raised. As the writer to the Hebrews noted, "solid food is for the mature, for those whose faculties have been trained by practice to distinguish good from evil" (Heb 5:14)

Within this either/or scenario people either believe or disbelieve. Either God is chucked away or is cuddled like a baby doll. If one just loves Jesus enough and accepts that all is forgiven then Christianity will be saved from bad religious behaviors. There is no middle ground. The consequences? People blindly put their faith in a deity or savior they have never fully explored, questioned, doubted, nor even contemplated deeply, thus they don't really know what or who it is they worship. Their faith does indeed seem simplistic, naïve and childish. This is what Thomas E. Bergler describes as the "juvenilization of American Christianity." He writes that "it should not be surprising to find that many Americans have an inarticulate faith characterized by moralistic, therapeutic deism." He concludes that, while such juvenilization has "revitalized American Christianity" it has come "at the cost of leaving many individuals mired in spiritual immaturity."[23] How can you know that which you have not questioned? Rather than leaving the idea of God and the person of Jesus open for constant scrutiny and interrogation the Trinity has been closed off in a closet with dusty faith and doctrines. When the door is periodically opened in a fit of revivalistic housecleaning, a tumble of junk falls on the floor.

This situation is not new. And it is this very same approach that ruined the infant Church according to some scholars. Historian Charles Freeman argues that the early Church left its true roots when it succumbed to the reductionism of creeds and rational theologies. Early Church theologians brought their preconceived beliefs about atonement, salvation, the deity of Christ, the resurrection, the Trinity, and various notions about God in general, to the scriptures for justification rather than the other way around. Instead of paying attention to the diversity of Christian communities throughout the fading Roman Empire a small cadre of select bishops (often chosen by unscrupulous emperors and vice versa) demanded absolute adherence to, and belief in, the simple tenets of one faith, one baptism and, eventually, one major creed. In essence, there was no room for doubts. A few centuries later, as the church turned to reason, specifically the philosophy of Aristotle, it left behind the cold superstition of the so-called Dark

23. Bergler, *Juvenilization*, 220, 225.

Ages to begin its love affair with scientific rational processes that led to extended proofs of the faith. While these proofs "settled" theological matters they also led to dismay among some of the faithful who desired more spirituality and less doctrine from its leaders. Because of this emphasis on reason the fruitful region of doubt has been cordoned off.[24]

With this legacy behind them, Christians must believe in _____ because it has been logically proven. Or, they must believe in _____ because the church leader said so. Such fundamental dogmatism from both the left and right has been questioned by Karen Armstrong who demonstrates that the Church's focus on *logos*, reason, as opposed to *mythos*, story, is, in her estimation, the cause of the problems within Christianity today[25] The old, old story of Jesus has been reduced down to cold hard facts.

Part of this trend away from a narrow-minded dogmatism—which denies any room for doubt, any room to wander, and assumes that faith is a one way street rather than a meandering walk through the region called Life—has led to a predictable exodus from the basic tenets of Christian faith. Noted writer Sue Monk Kidd is an example of such doubt. This dutiful Baptist woman realized one day that the church she had faithfully given her life to had not been truthful to her. Feeling the pangs of feminism deep within herself she wondered "Did I dare step over the boundaries church and convention had drawn for women?" One of those conventions was a simple phrase heard over and over again: the God of Abraham. Why not the God of Sarah, Abraham's wife? In her quest to find the answers to her new and childlike questions the only answers she found in the church were the ones that had led to her questions. She concluded that, for the Church and the faithful, "leaving the circle of orthodoxy means leaving the realm of truth . . . giving up a world where everything is neat and safe."[26]

Doesn't the very idea of religion require a will to accept boundaries and live within them? One of the definitions of religion is "to restrain; to tie back." What happens when the boundaries of faith are questioned? Acclaimed writer, retreat leader and Franciscan priest Richard Rohr is informative here. Those who are truly centered in God understand which boundaries are necessary and which are restrictive. Only through the inward struggles of faith, the "dark night of the soul" as it is described, can one discern the proper boundaries. "Both maintaining and surrendering

---

24. Freeman, *Closing*; likewise, Rubenstein, *Aristotle's Children*.
25. Armstrong, *Case*.
26. Kidd, *Dance*, 33, 76.

Who Am I?

boundaries ironically require an 'obedience,' because they require listening to a Voice beyond their own . . . they are always *free to obey* but they might also *disobey* the expectations of the church and state to obey who-they-are-in-God."[27] This sounds very much like the person of Jesus as presented in the gospels but you would not know it based on how today's churches promote their legalistic theologies.

It is a shame that a loyal Christian woman had to leave the church to find, explore and affirm the feminine part of her life that God gave her. Did her church leaders not know that, within the Bible, there are passages that affirm the feminine ideal, the feminine mystique? Writers such as Elisabeth Moltman-Wendel, Carol Meyers, Carla Ricci, and Claudia Camp, among many others, have published works exploring the feminine in both biblical, ancient Near Eastern and Greco-Roman cultures. Surely church leaders are aware of archeological evidence that demonstrates the significant role of women in the church before the New Testament writings emerged such as that discovered by Karen Jo Torjesen? What of all the female saints throughout the Church's history? The Church *does* know but rather than look into its past, the past that is not just enshrined in its scripture but is also known in other texts, contexts, and artifacts, it prefers the circle of orthodoxy rather than the whole truth. The creeds and doctrines of old that are repeated and blindly memorized do not and will not speak of these issues until they are readdressed by the church today.[28]

Is this trend of doubt a spiral down to unbelief? Not necessarily so. Noted theologian of the New Testament Marcus Borg describes his own journey of belief in Jesus. He recalls his initial faith in Jesus, the divinely begotten Son of God. Puzzled by inconsistent doctrines of God—how could God be everywhere but only in Heaven?—he slowly moved away from a belief in God. Introduced to the scholarly study of religion in a Lutheran college, his quest for answers was initiated. While in seminary he began to see that the difference between the Jesus of history and the resurrected Christ of salvation was a theological invention of the Church. Indeed, in Borg's estimation, the Jesus of history would not recognize the person behind such theological acclamations of faith. Eventually, after a time of agnosticism and even atheism, he began to have mystical experiences that led to a new understanding of Jesus. Instead of belief in the numerous doctrinal tenets

---

27. Rohr, *Everything*, 24–25.

28. Moltman-Wendel, *Women*; Meyers, *Discovering*; Ricci, *Mary*; Camp, *Wisdom*; Torensen, *Women*.

of the faith he saw relationship as the key to a religious life. His doubts led from a naïve and blind faith in tedious theological understandings of Jesus Christ to a renewed relationship with the historical Jesus.[29]

Noted author and now former Episcopal priest Barbara Brown Taylor experienced the same doubts. She reflects on why people say "I am spiritual but not religious." She notes that "Plenty of them are satisfied, too, even as they confess that they are sometimes lonely." Tired of the insistence that God and enlightenment can only be found in the Church proper and through extensive belief of doctrines and facts, she now realizes that God can be found in the everyday as well. She is not the first person to come to this realization. Still, despite her exit from official church work she continues to examine the Christian scriptures for the interpretation and understanding of her faith. Recalling the words of Jesus as instituted in the sacrament of communion, she reminds us that Jesus did not say "*believe* this in remembrance of me" but instead "*do* this in remembrance of me." She then sums up her revelation noting that the "last thing any of us needs is more information about God . . . Not more *about* God. *More God.*"[30]

Acclaimed author and Benedictine Sister Joan Chittister also follows this line of faithful, yet doubtful, faith. She adds a cultural twist to the fray when she points out that the previous generation, fresh out of World War II, based itself on blind obedience to dictums. As if all were in the military, no one questioned authority. Instead, there was a dogged faith in the control and demands of authorities, both church and government. Along with this, answers were allowed only when questioned but no one could question the questions. But with the present generation, "all the givens of life have melted into mist. We live in a new world now." The result, she writes, is "individual isolation." We want answers but that implies disturbing questions which the authorities—parents, police, priests, presidents—don't want to deal with. What to do? Her suggestion is that "We look at all the absolutes and we begin to question them. One at a time; incident by incident; issue by issue: we question them all." The goal? The cultivation of wisdom rather than the practice of obedience.[31]

Part of the problem today is simple. In the Old Testament the dominant and easiest to understand theology is this: do good and God will bless;

---

29. Borg, *Meeting*, 3–15.
30. Taylor, *Altar*, xii, 45.
31. Chittister, *Called*, xvi–xvii, 4, 124.

do bad and God will curse. This basic concept permeates nearly all of the whole Old Testament. But two books deviate from this theology and it is no coincidence that many preachers leave these wisdom books out of their preaching plans. In the book of Job, the exemplar of this doctrine is the victim of every possible tragedy despite that fact that he lived a blameless life. Why? The book questions (and questions and questions) the very backbone of Old Testament theology only to conclude that it is all bunk: God can do anything God likes anytime God likes to anyone God likes or dislikes because God is God. So much for "do good and God will bless."

Along with this belief in doing good is a complementary belief: the sign of God's blessing is wealth. After all, if one does good then one is blessed and one sign of blessing is the wealth God has bestowed upon the faithful. The writer of Ecclesiastes, in the voice of the very wealthy King Solomon, looks back at his life of luxury and notes that it was all chasing after the wind. He had accrued everything in life only to learn that it amounted to nothing like contentment and peace. Wisdom, toil, wealth—all of the accepted ways of respect in the Old Testament world—are reduced to naught. Eat, drink and live is his new mantra. But along with this comes an odd theology, what I label as "dichotomies of faith."

Today believers say that war is either wrong (liberals) or war is necessary (conservatives). But Ecclesiastes says there are times for both! Indeed, there are times to kill (!) and times to heal (those who were injured but not killed?). There are times for war and times for peace. How can these be put together? In the either/or world of facts and simplistic rational belief they cannot be put together. Both/and works better but our churches today do not preach or teach this. Instead, it is this way or that way. But, some disagree with this dichotomy and long for a faith that embraces the doubt-ridden land between absolutes. Discussing the dilemma for today's Christians who want to be both religious and spiritual, Diana Butler Bass reminds us of the "energy of *and*."[32] Although the context here is different, the point is the same: when we finally "get it" and are able to incorporate the both/ands of Ecclesiastes then we have achieved the proper perspective on life through the impossibilities of opposites.

Thus, there are problems within the Church and these are leading some to have serious doubts about their faith. While a few leave for other religious ventures or for no religious life at all others wish to remain within the

---

32. Bass, *Christianity*, 91.

fold. *Doing* the work of God, for them, is more important than believing in man-made theologies and fundamental facts specifically chosen as proof for faith.

These are indeed conflicted times for Christians of all stripes. But it was the same for Christians two thousand years ago. Out of that period of chaos a person named Mark wrote a book. Perhaps it can fill the void that many doubting Christians are staring at today.

There are several assumptions that underlie this work. First, I focus on the *initial* readers of the gospel. Most perhaps had little to no knowledge of Jesus at all, thus they would have to compare him to what they already knew about gods and rituals and religion in general, from paganistic Roman religions to the monotheism of the Jews. Readers outside of the Jewish or Christian-Jewish faith would have naturally compared Jesus and the rituals accompanying his worship to their own gods and pagan rituals. Those familiar with the writings of Paul or the teachings of the various apostles and other itinerants did not know of the details of Jesus as presented by Mark and the other gospels because they had not been written yet. How did these first listeners and readers of Mark respond to the evangelist's story?

Next, the most reliable manuscripts we have end with Mark 16:8 where the women who discovered the empty grave are terrified. A man dressed in a white robe informs them that Jesus has gone to Galilee and that they should tell the disciples to meet him there. The frightened women flee the scene. And that is where and how Mark ends his story. The verses after this in our Bibles today were added later. This mysterious and frightening episode leads directly to questions of doubt: Where is Jesus, what happened to his body, would he really show up in Galilee as he said? Based on this manuscript record, the Gospel of Mark is open-ended, raising two questions for the reader: who do you think Jesus is and what do you think Jesus is? This ending implies doubts among Mark's readership, if not Mark himself, and it forces them and, consequently us, to think through the various depictions of Jesus that Mark provides.

Third, many scholars assume that Mark wrote his gospel for a Christian readership. David Rhoads and Donald Michie are typical of these scholars today. They argue that Mark wrote his narrative so that the reader and listener would be inspired to go out and teach the story of Jesus. In essence, it is assumed that the first century reader and listener is a faithful follower of

Who Am I?

Christ.[33] And this is also the typical assumption of modern readers of Mark today: early Christians of the first century read this book to become more enlightened and inspired followers of God through Jesus the Christ.

But this ignores an important point: as will be argued in the following chapters, how Christian were these readers? Oddly enough, Michie and Rhoads note that a Roman soldier, Syrian peasant, Jewish nationalist, or moderate Pharisee would have been readers of this story, but then these scholars settle on a "sympathetic" reader who is aligned with Christianity. Elizabeth Struthers Malbon's recent study of Mark goes a little further noting that Mark's book can be understood both by Jewish and Gentile audiences. This observation agrees with that of Rodney Stark who demonstrates that the main recipients of the gospel message in the first century were rather affluent *Jews*.[34] The Book of Acts 13:5 and 14:1 verifies this. Paul went to the synagogues first to preach the gospel. If the Jews were not receptive then he presented his message to the Gentiles. These were non-Christians, non-Jewish Romans who worshiped and prayed to numerous pagan deities. Thus, Mark's readers ran the spectrum from Jew to Christian Jew to Gentile Christian to Gentile pagan. And this conclusion agrees with that of Mary Ann Tolbert who suggests that Mark follows the style of popular Hellenistic writings read by all kinds of people much as different people read novels today.[35] In other words, Mark's gospel would have been received and heard as any other book about the gods of that time.

Along with this, the permanent divide between Jews and Christians was not fully made until several centuries later. This means that Mark's gospel would have been read and heard by many doubtful Jews who had to be convinced that Jesus was son of God as well as doubtful Christians who, by the sixties of the Common Era and because of the delayed parousia, were less convinced that Jesus was the Messiah. If Christianity was in such turmoil, as will be explained below, then many of Mark's readers in general would have been full of doubts as to who and what Jesus was. Not only that, but they would also have been rethinking their membership in this very conflicted sect of Judaism.

One final assumption: Mark initially wrote his gospel for a Roman audience. As Alan Culpepper demonstrates, the matter of who Mark wrote for

33. Rhoads and Michie, *Mark As Story*, "Conclusion."

34. Malbom, *Mark's Jesus*; Stark, *Cities*.

35. Tolbert, *Sowing the Gospel: Mark's World in Literary-Historical Perspective*, 70–79, as cited in R. Alan Culpepper, *Mark*, 17.

has been debated but the stronger evidence points toward Rome. If so, and I believe it is, then Mark's audience was composed of people of all stripes heavily influenced by the Greco-Roman and Jewish cultures of their day.[36]

Last, I agree with William Lane's argument that Mark was written in the late 60's CE. This was a time of intense persecution of Christians as the maniacal Roman Emperor Nero blamed the Christians for the burning of Rome (which was done by Nero and his thugs) and which led to cruel persecutions of Christians as well. The story of a persecuted Jesus would have resonated with Roman listeners and readers who were faced with the question of whether to follow or keep following Christ in such deadly times.[37] Some scholars, noting that Mark seemed to have awareness of the destruction of the Temple in Jerusalem (chapter 13), which occurred in 70 CE, suggest that Mark was written after that date. But anyone with solid knowledge of the tempestuous times in Jerusalem and the increasing tension between Jews and Romans could have easily foreseen that the Temple would be destroyed and the city of Jerusalem demolished by the Romans. If the Old Testament prophets like Isaiah and Jeremiah could read between the political lines and predict the fall of Israel and Judah then certainly Mark could have understood the inevitable would happen to an increasingly politically unstable place such as Jerusalem in the 60s CE.

With this in mind, modern readers of Mark's gospel should assume, if they can, the attitude of the very first readers and hearers of Mark. "Who is Jesus?" should be the underlying question as they encountered the story of Jesus, the Son of God, for the first time. They should study the gospel with doubts in mind. As we will see, unbelief permeated Mark's world. Thus, the story in Mark 9 where Jesus encounters the man whose son has many demons becomes a major focal point for the gospel. The disciples could not exorcise the demon and the father was desperate. We can hear his plea for help when he asks, "If you can do anything . . . " Jesus fires back that anything is possible to those who believe. The man responds like many people do today: "I believe! Help my unbelief!"

---

36. Ibid., 25–29.
37. Lane, *Mark*, 17–21.

2

Help My Unbelief!

Be merciful to those who doubt.
(Jude 22 NIV)

Scholars have long pointed out that Mark chapter 8 is the turning point of the Gospel. From chapter one up to chapter eight the identity of Jesus has not been understood. From the outset Mark presents him as a mysterious stranger who appears out of nowhere to be baptized by John the Baptist. As will be seen this action implies that Jesus is a disciple of John. This seems to be the case because after Mark reports the Baptist's death Jesus then begins his ministry just as any protégé would do out of respect for his mentor. From this point forward, however, Jesus is an enigma for those around him. Mark presents him as a healer, then a miracle worker, then a teacher. The religious teachers from Jerusalem see him as a threat to Judaism just as were Jewish upstarts appearing everywhere during this period. Jesus' followers see him as the cure for all the evils and oppressions of the Jewish and Roman culture around them but every peripatetic guru was esteemed the same way. The Romans worried that he might start a rebellion. As Mark presents Jesus' disciples, however, they do not have a clue who he really is.

So with the skill of an excellent writer the author of Mark's gospel, in chapter eight of sixteen chapters, has Jesus stop and ask the disciples point blank who the people—Roman leaders; Jewish theologians; the crowds who follow him—think he is. The answer is a compendium of Jewish expectations. Some say he is John the Baptist returned from the grave in some form. Others believe he is Elijah who never died and thus was technically still "alive." Still others proffered the generic answer: he is one of the ancient prophets. All of these replies reflect the ancient belief in some form of resurrection of important and revered figures and these answers would have been expected. These answers also reveal that the idea of resurrection was simply accepted by people in Jesus' day as very possible and even likely for esteemed figures. Then Jesus' right hand disciple, Peter, offers an opinion: Jesus is the Christ, meaning the Anointed One. Ah, finally one of his disciples understands who Jesus is. But does he?

Jesus quickly, indeed *strongly*, instructs his disciples not to tell anyone about this. He then goes on to teach the disciples in three episodes (8:31–33; 9:30–32; 10:32–34) that he must suffer persecution, be killed, and then rise again. Peter, aghast at the first prediction, rebukes Jesus for saying this. From Peter's Jewish point of view, this is nonsense. How can the Christ, the Messiah, endure such treatment? The long-awaited Messiah was to be a great military hero. He was not supposed to die. Surely Peter's assessment of Jesus is correct. How can Jesus say this?

Jesus then rebukes Peter. He basically says, "Get out of my sight, Satan!" implying that Satan, aka Peter, was getting in his way by standing in front of him.[1] Peter does not understand that Jesus must undergo such persecution in order to fulfill what he believes is God's plan for him. Indeed, Peter does not understand anything about Jesus at this point. Neither do any of the disciples. This raises an important question: do Mark's readers understand who Jesus is at this point in the story?

The word "rebuke" is a very strong word in Greek. It means "rebuke," "reprove," "censure," "speak seriously," and "warn." It also can have the sense of "punish." It is used in Mark when Jesus commands the demons to desist, when Jesus warns the disciples not to tell anyone that he is the Christ, and here when Jesus reproves Peter. William Lane notes that the term is so strong it embarrassed later New Testament interpreters so that in several early manuscripts of Mark the word was changed to mean, "Jesus spoke to him."[2] It is probably safe to say here that in this episode Jesus is *very* indignant with Peter if not downright angry.

After this confrontation Jesus and his disciples then head directly to Jerusalem where Jesus' prophecy about his impending persecution will

---

1. Anderson, *Mark*, 217.
2. Lane, *Mark*, 295.

come true. The disciples follow along, clearly believing something about Jesus—why else would they continue to follow after such dire predictions?—but not understanding exactly what the "something" was. They embody the very epitome of Mark's gospel: belief yet unbelief.

However, right in the middle of the Gospel of Mark there is another episode where this paradox is succinctly summarized. In chapter 9, just after the amazing transfiguration of Jesus high on a mountain and just before his second prediction of his passion, a man brings his demon-possessed son to Jesus' disciples. Tired from many years of guarding and rescuing his boy from the destructive wiles of the demons, the father seeks out the disciples and asks them to exorcize the demons from his child. The father was disappointed: Jesus' disciples could not cast out the demons. At the height of the father's despair and utter exasperation Jesus appears and asks the boy's father what he wants. The man explains that he brought his son to these disciples so that he might be healed however the disciples could not produce the cure. Frustrated with his disciples Jesus moans "You unbelieving generation, how long shall I stay with you. How long shall I put up with you?" (Mark 9:19 NIV) We can sense the embarrassment of the disciples, the impatience of Jesus, and the uncomfortable rise in tension of all those around.

"If you can do anything," the father replies, "take pity on us and help us." Jesus answers rather incredulously, "'If you can?'" He then tells the father that anything is possible to one who believes. The man instantly responds, "I do believe!" but then fires back the words that many Christians yearn to speak but are so afraid to say: "Help me overcome my unbelief!" (Mark 9:22–24 NIV) Jesus then performs the miracle. To me, this may be the decisive "middle point" of the Gospel of Mark.

Recent scholarship has raised doubts among the faithful about the veracity of the Church's claims to the life of Jesus as proclaimed in the creeds. Charles Freeman's history of the rise of faith at the expense of reason in the early centuries of the Christian Church demonstrates that faith in certain approved creeds overruled the reason of the early believers. He is puzzled that, while other religions in the Roman era were quite content to have varying spiritual views within their faith, Christianity insisted on one coherent and consistent understanding of its beliefs. The emerging orthodox leaders, chosen by the Emperors of the fourth century in particular, molded an orthodox faith that suited the needs of a failing Roman Empire. They hoped that, if they could unify Christianity—which in itself was still in theological and creedal disarray—then they could unify an increasingly disintegrating Roman Empire. These selected Christian leaders shaped their biblical exegesis to fit their interpretation of the life of Christ as declared in the new creeds. Faith was based on strict belief in what had been chosen as the correct understanding of Jesus. Freeman concludes, "The effect, of course, was to make reasoned and open debate on theological matters increasingly difficult." The troubles for the Church both then and now, Freeman points out, come "from the determination to make 'certain' statements about God."[3]

This "quest for certainty" is the basis for many of the religious wars and battles of today according to atheist Sam Harris. Angry about the religious irrationality that spawned 9/11 Harris takes on the three monotheistic faiths that are the causes of such destruction. Criticizing the faith that emerges from both the fundamentalist literalistic and metaphorical interpretations of scriptures he excoriates those whose "belief in, and life orientation toward, certain historical and metaphorical propositions" [in their scriptures] supersedes all reason. He makes a distinction between this world faith—belief that the bridge will hold as the train goes over it—and next world faith—where the truth of one's faith *then* will be proven. Confused that "most religions have merely canonized a few products of ancient ignorance and derangement and passed them down to us as though they were primordial truths," he sarcastically concludes that we "are even now killing ourselves over ancient literature." In essence, the freedom to believe is a myth, Harris argues, because if you don't believe the way I do then I have religious justification to kill you.[4] While Harris has been criticized as fundamentalistic and simplistic in his scientific interpretation of other religious systems, as noted in the previous chapter, his point is an excellent observation of our times: a twisted understanding of faith in many religions is indeed maiming our world.

Each of these trends suggests doubts among the Church, scholarship, and public culture, but that is a good thing. It seems then, that, within the triangle of these three examples, we should rethink faith and belief. Karen Armstrong does just this in her book *The Case for God* where she makes a poignant argument about belief and this passage is an important point for her case. She notes that other religions do not put a heavy emphasis on belief as in "I adhere to a system of doctrines or commands." If one studies

---

3. Freeman, *Closing*, 198, 336–337.
4. Harris, *End of Faith*, 72, 51 respectively.

the major religions this fact will become apparent. Hindus, Buddhists, Taoists and Confucianists all emphasize following various life principles rather than adherence to a strict code, creed, or set of dogmatic rules and legalisms. There is little philosophical, theological, historical wrangling over the jots and tittles of their ancient texts and beliefs in these religions. Instead, ritual and ethical lifestyle are the standards. As for the monotheistic faiths, however, it is not so simplistic. Judaism has always focused on the study of the Torah and conservative Jews especially embody this today. But the ends of this means is to interpret the laws of God for ethical living. One loves God through the study of the Torah in order to love her neighbor. While there is much angst within Islam concerning the interpretation of the Quran over issues of *jihad* the overall tenets of Islam as learned in the Five Pillars is to live an ethical life manifest in helping others.

This said, Armstrong is puzzled why Christians dwell on such an interpretation of "belief." Referring to the Greek understanding of the term *pistis*, "belief," she reminds us that it means trust, loyalty, engagement, commitment. But, the word actually has more connotations than these. Faithfulness, reliability, solemn promise or oath, proof, pledge, trust, and confidence are also definitions of *pistis*. Still, her argument is that, based on the ancient understanding of this word and how it is used in the Bible, there is no sense that one must believe in a *dogmatic* fact. "Jesus was not asking people to 'believe' in his divinity, because he was making no such claim. He was asking for commitment." Armstrong points out that this understanding was preferred by St. Jerome when he translated the New Testament into Latin and, based on the use of the word "belief" in the Old English of King James' time, the sense of loyalty and commitment was the true definition of this venerated translation. It was only after the seventeenth century that the word "believe" assumed its modern and formal sense of compliance with creeds and doctrines as witnessed in the statement "I believe in the Nicene Creed."[5]

Based on what my students say, what some Christian writers are complaining about, and how I observe many people acting, it seems that some people are tired of trying to follow commands and creeds and dogma and doctrines that are complex and contradictory and confusing. Here is a sarcastic example from one of my students of the rational results of today's theological inconsistencies.

---

5. Armstrong, *Case*, 87.

"God so loved humanity that He impregnated a woman with Himself so that He could be born into His own creation, to grow up, to be sacrificed to Himself because it was necessary to punish Himself in order to appease Himself enough to persuade Himself to forgive the people He created in the first place for behaving in accordance with the sinful natures with which He endowed us in the first place. Up there on the cross, He cried out to Himself to ask why He had forsaken Himself and to beg Himself to forgive these people, for they knew not that they sacrificed Him to Himself in perfect accordance with His perfect plan to pay Himself off for our debt to Him which He decided we owed Him in the first place. Then He died, spent the weekend away, rose from the grave and ascended into Heaven to reunite with Himself and to spend the rest of eternity sitting at His own right hand."[6]

This example, while humorous, lampoons the results of what many Christians are taught today. Others, aware of such inconsistencies, want to be encouraged to *do* their faith rather than be scolded for not remaining compliant with theological quibblings that make no sense to anybody but denominational theologians and philosophical biblical scholars. They believe, but they want help with their unbelief. They believe in Jesus' teachings. It is remaining loyal to Christ in the heat of life and what it holds that is difficult. With the plethora of books criticizing the beliefs and questioning the veracity of Christian claims, doubts are now rising amongst the faithful. And all the minutia of doctrines and creeds and dogma does not help them at all.

And I think that the writer of Mark understood this sentiment very well. Doubts permeated the 60s CE just before Mark wrote his book.

If we cull the wisdom of the mystics we will find that unbelief and belief are polar opposites in the life of faith and yet the paradoxical gap in between is where we find God. In the above story in Mark doubt was in the company of faith when the miracle was performed. Perhaps, as exemplified in the life of Mother Teresa, doubts, tethered with faith, bring about miracles, healing, wholeness. Doubts, it seems, are the very substance of faith. Thus the man who approached Jesus and proclaimed, "I believe, help my unbelief!" may very well be the best example of how a believer should live the life of faith. Would that today's church would encourage a life lived in this liminal land of doubts.

---

6. By permission, Michael Starling, Axia College of the University of Phoenix, 3/02/11.

Christians today turn to the Bible, specifically the New Testament, for faith and assurance, for edification and religious training, for spirituality and hope. For today's Christians who attend church regularly, religiously read their Bibles, and studiously (if sometimes boringly) sit through Sunday School or weekly Bible studies, reading the Bible is more about looking for nuggets of faithful gold than critically examining the text. And this is understandable: scriptures are primarily for faith, not academic scrutiny. But this search for answers must be tempered with a sobering reminder that most Christians read back into the Bible what they already know. For example, Mark begins his story about Jesus with a seemingly obvious and therefore plain proclamation: The beginning of the gospel of Jesus Christ, the son of God. Today's readers of Mark's gospel, unwittingly led by what scholars call a harmonized understanding of the story of Jesus, read the Gospel of Mark with Matthew and Luke's birth stories in mind, or they think of Jesus in terms of John's preexistent *logos*. When they read the first verse of Mark they instinctively put the verses, ideas, plot, theology and characters of the other gospels together with what they read in Mark. They *assume* the preexistent presence of Jesus with God and *assume* that he was born to the Virgin Mary and laid in a manger in Bethlehem.

Mark, however, was written probably a decade before Matthew and Luke, and at least two decades before the gospel of John. Therefore, readers in Mark's day did not have the luxury of knowledge that today's Christians have. Mark does not provide his reader with a quaint, if dangerous and exotic, tale of Jesus' birth, so his initial readers know nothing of Jesus' life before he was baptized by John. Until Mathew and Luke wrote their gospels, the theological life of Jesus did not include the narrative of a virginal birth. The very idea of a supernatural birth was apparently unknown in the early church community. Paul does not mention it: he focuses instead on the resurrection of Jesus. The other letter writers in the New Testament do not consider Jesus' birth at all. Thus, for Mark and his readers the birth of Jesus was not important for the story of this man. Mark's readers would have to consider Jesus as Mark presented him instead of understanding him as the aggregate of four gospel accounts mentally and theologically edited into one man.

If we are to understand the Gospel of Mark then we must first understand the author.

Traditionally scholars have placed Mark in the region of Palestine. This is where he was from and where he grew up. He was not one of the original disciples therefore he learned his information about Jesus from the disciples. It is even not clear among some that Mark even wrote the gospel that bears his name. The earliest manuscripts of the gospel do not include his name. However, a very strong tradition says that Mark was taught by Peter and then Mark wrote down the story of Jesus.

Thomas Oden, however, offers a different version of Mark's life that, while controversial, provides more information about this enigmatic person. This biography centers around the traditions from Africa concerning Mark's birth and life. These details will be very important for our discussion.

African traditions relate that Mark was born ca. 5–15 CE in Cyrene in modern day Libya. The city was a place of refuge, first for Greeks beginning around six hundred BCE and Jewish refugees arrived there three hundred years before Jesus was born. Soon the Jews were part of the African people and culture. In essence, they were Africans. Many of the Jews became multilingual prosperous traders and merchants. The Jewish populations grew and many were apocalyptic in faith, looking for the Messiah.

Mark's family included his father Aristopolus and his mother, Mary. They were respected people from the tribe of Levi. They went to Jerusalem for the major Jewish festal celebrations each year and this ability to afford such trips suggests some wealth.

Just before the time of Jesus civil unrest brought trouble to the Cyrenains. Running from the brigandage and wars, Jews fled the divided city and headed for Palestine and Jerusalem. According to African traditions, Mark's family fled to Palestine and settled in Jerusalem somewhere between 20–30 CE. Sometime later Mark and his mother joined the emerging Christian movement. In Jerusalem, according to Acts 12, the family had a house that probably included an upper room since Mary offered a room for Jesus and his disciples. After Jesus was crucified he worked among the disciples and traveled with his cousin Barnabas and the apostle Paul in the period of 34–60 CE. From 61–63 CE Mark laid the foundation for the church in Cyrene and then survived the burning of Rome by the insane Emperor Nero in 64 CE. Mark attended Paul and Peter in Rome where he no doubt learned the story of Jesus from Peter. Peter and Paul were martyred in Rome in 67–68 CE. While in Alexandria Mark was martyred in 68 CE.[7]

In sum, Mark's family was African and Jewish, of the significant tribe of Levi, of some wealth, multilingual, most likely had connections throughout the Mediterranean, and, because of the history of the city and the civil

---

7. Oden, *African Memory*, ch. 1 and 37–41.

wars in their day, they knew firsthand the fears and anxieties of tumultuous times. But, when they fled the terrible unrest of Cyrene for Jerusalem they left the pan of their home for the fire of first century Palestine. Mark traveled with the Apostle Paul throughout the Mediterranean, was with Peter and Paul in Rome, survived destruction in Rome but succumbed to martyrdom in 68 CE. Somewhere after his visit with Peter, as will be spelled out below, Mark wrote his gospel. And, it could be argued that, since Paul and Peter were martyred, Mark knew his time was imminent.

So, having met Mark the author, another question arises: Why did Mark write this gospel? Around 120–140 CE Papias wrote that Mark learned his information about Jesus from Peter, the disciple closest to Jesus. There is also much evidence that Mark learned his theology of Jesus from the apostle Paul. Papias noted that Mark did not write a chronologically correct story of Jesus' life. Instead he wrote a theological story about Jesus. In simple terms, Mark wrote his story of Jesus not for historical accuracy but to meet a particular need for his readers and the early church. And this leads us to the second question: What was this need?

In order to answer this question, we must fully understand the Greco-Roman, Jewish and Christian setting that influenced and inspired Mark to write this account of Jesus' life. Scholars of all stripes argue that Mark was written sometime in the 60s CE or shortly after this decade. This time was rife with doubts in the Christian and Jewish communities and I argue that Mark may have been addressing these doubts in his gospel. The basic assumption of this study is that the Gospel of Mark was written for the doubters of his time. If that is the case, then it is a most appropriate book for doubters of today.

Most Christians today assume, incorrectly, that the Church has always been settled on the matter of Jesus' identity. This is not the case. In the last few decades there has been a surge of scholarly works pointing out that early Christians were not sure about the true identity of Jesus until well into the fourth and fifth centuries. Several works of these include Marta Sordi's *The Christians and the Roman Empire*, Bart Ehrman's *Lost Christianities* (one of many books he has written challenging the legitimacy of the Church's claims about Jesus' life), L. Michael White's *From Jesus to Christianity*, James Tabor's *The Jesus Dynasty* and Richard E. Rubenstien's *When Jesus Became God*. After reading such studies two reactions generally follow: students of the Bible and church history are often shocked that early church theologians did not agree about who and what Jesus was while those who have always held the Church in suspicious eyes nodded and said "I thought so." What is discovered by readers today is that, in the early centuries of Christendom, the identity of Jesus was much in question. What becomes apparent to modern students of the Bible and Christianity today is that many Christians in the first century CE had not fully separated themselves from Judaism in these times and some Christians even interpreted Jesus through the lenses of Greco-Roman and Egyptian religions, thus adding more confusion to the emerging theologies of Jesus and his life.

With this knowledge today some Christians and people interested in the history of religion are intrigued by these debates. If we look at the book of Mark we can see the very crux of the matter as it played out in the 60s of the Christian era. Scholars of Mark point out consistently that the writer paints Jesus' disciples as ones who are totally ignorant of who Jesus is. In today's terms, they just don't get it. In story after story in the first eight chapters of Mark the disciples misinterpret Jesus and what he is teaching and preaching. Mark addressed these doubts and leaves his readers with a big question of faith in chapter 8 where Jesus finally turned and asked the disciples "who do people think I am?" The rest of the book is filled with incidents that demonstrate one answer to this question. But what answer did the book of Mark point to? One answer is shocking: there were certain Christian communities who used the gospel of Mark to argue that Jesus was *not* really the Christ.[8] This note is clear proof that not all Christians who read Mark walked away from the gospel believing that Jesus was the Christ, the Son of God which is how Mark began his gospel.

In the first century of the Christian era the person of Jesus was not in doubt. The Jews of Judea certainly knew of him and several historians—Josephus, a Jew, and Roman historians Pliny the Younger, Seutonius, and Tacitus—chronicled his existence. According to the Gospel of Mark, nearly all witnesses of Jesus did not understand what he was about nor why he interpreted the Law of Moses as he did but they saw him and heard him and wondered about him and a few even listened to him and believed what he preached and taught. Among these believers and the ones to come, the *fact* of Jesus was not in doubt, but *what* Jesus was had not been fully understood because it had not been fully explained. Was he the son of God or was he just a man? Was he the long-awaited Messiah or just another Messiah

---

8. Ehrman, *Misquoting Jesus*, 35.

wannabe? The adopted son of God, or The Son of God? And, for some, which god was he the son of?

The early believers also wrangled over what Jesus taught and how to interpret it. Did he intend for his followers to retain their Jewish heritage and rituals of faith, as the followers of Jesus in Jerusalem insisted (see Acts 11:1–18; ch. 15) and as the epistle of James emphasizes? Or, were they to drop all ties to Judaism and begin an entirely new religion, as the apostle Paul argued (Acts 15; Gal 2:11–16)? One issue that was germane to the argument centered around the rituals of Judaism. Jewish Christians insisted that rituals such as circumcision and the consumption of kosher foods should be continued among the new believers. Gentile Christians did not see the relevance of such rituals. Paul, the once devout Jew, took the side of the Gentiles while Peter, James and John remained loyal to the tenets of the Jewish faith. Divisions such as these among the believers could not help but lead to doubts about the life and teachings of Jesus. Did he support the Jewish interpretation or the Gentilic theology?

Each side doubted that the other's beliefs and explanations reflected what Jesus taught. But what if the other side was right? Along with this, the Jews who claimed Jesus was the Messiah were torn over the definition of and theology of their savior. What exactly was a Messiah supposed to be? A mighty warrior in the lineage of David or a meek and humble shepherd guiding the sheep of God? These divisions led to doubts that threatened to destroy the fledgling church.

Thus, as the emerging group of believers became a religious sect within Judaism, *who* and *what* Jesus was became points of intense and sometimes divisive theological contention among the faithful and their leaders as well as their persecutors. *Who* and *what* Jesus was, however, would not be "decided" until the fourth and fifth centuries and even beyond as creeds and "official" theology was developed and narrowed down. Until then, the early believers had to decide for themselves who Jesus the Christ was. Various teachers taught their own interpretations of Jesus' life and ministry and competition arose between these teachers (2 Pet 2). It seems that various regions around the Mediterranean Sea, at various times, had their own notions of Jesus' identity. Paul preached the resurrected Jesus while Matthew presents Jesus as a teacher who stays close to Judaism. Luke presents a more Gentilic Jesus but John gives a philosophical version of Jesus. Because of these competing theologies doubts and mistrust permeated the early churches and believers were torn between teachers and teachings. Their confusion was compounded further in that there were other "Messiahs." Mark calls them false Messiahs (ch. 13) and the apostle Paul constantly fought against their preaching. The confusion did not end in the first century. Gospels from the Middle Eastern portion of the Roman Empire portrayed very different depictions of Jesus than those writings from the Greek and Roman areas of the Northern Mediterranean.[9] These Middle Eastern writings deviated far from the more sober accounts of Jesus as found in the four gospels in the New Testament. It is very telling that gospels from the upper, predominately *Roman* Mediterranean—Matthew, Mark, Luke and John—were selected over those from the Middle East and Egypt to be in the New Testament.

In the time period of Jesus, as James Jeffers notes, the educated and wealthy were having serious doubts about gods in general. Temples were built in honor of the gods by the wealthy to display their power but religion was reduced to public rituals observed with no conviction. In the first century of the Christian era Romans observed the cult of the emperor where leaders were considered godlike. Three examples from the 60s CE are Emperor Nero, who was called *kyrios* (Greek for "Lord") and Vespasian and his son Titus who were called "savior." In the 90s CE Domitian, another son of Vespasian, required all people of the Roman Empire to call him lord and god. Humans depicted as gods also raised the question of the necessity of the cosmic deities. These ideas led to serious doubts among the common folk about celestial gods in general. Who was, and what exactly made up, a god anyway?[10]

As Bart Ehrman also notes, it was the wealthy and educated Roman converts who were responsible for writing and reading and often copying the texts that we now call the New Testament.[11] While they were no doubt Christian in faith they were still part of this Roman culture. Elite Roman citizens were well-educated and aware of the stories of the pagan gods. When they converted to the religion of one God they were taking a large step away from their former culture of paganism and polytheism. Just how far did they step away? Was Jesus just one of many gods for them? Did they see him as a person who, like their Emperor, became a god? When the Roman Emperor Constantine went to war in 312 CE he prayed to the gods for a sign of victory. Seeing a cross in the sky he assumed that the Christian

---

9. Ehrman, *Lost Christianities*, throughout.
10. Jeffers, *Greco-Roman*, 100–101.
11. Ehrman, *Misquoting Jesus*, ch. 1.

god was assuring victory. After he won the battle he honored this god by making Christianity a legal religion in the Roman Empire. In other words, how much of their cultural interpretation of religion did educated Romans bring with them when they converted to the new sect of Christianity? If we are to fully understand the book of Mark, not to mention the different theological presentations of Jesus in the other three Gospels, then we must take these issues into account. Doubt permeated the Roman and, therefore, Christian communities. Thus, we must approach Mark as his contemporary readers and listeners did, as skeptics, seekers, doubters, ones who simply are not sure about gods in general, not to mention their sons. What did they make of this person named Jesus?

Doubts surrounded the early years of those who proclaimed Jesus was the Messiah, in Greek known as the Christ. The years after Jesus died were tense politically and religiously in the Roman Empire. In Jerusalem, the Jews were divided. Sadducees competed with Pharisees over the interpretation of the Torah. Zealots planned guerilla attacks on unsuspecting Roman soldiers. Many Jews watered down the strict standards of Jewish faith in order to melt into the culture of Rome. The ascetic Essenes withdrew altogether from their Jewish friends and family to the Dead Sea wilderness retreat known as Qumran. They believed that the Jews in Jerusalem had deviated from the true faith altogether. Herodians were Jews who were sympathetic with the Roman culture and politics and did not mind forsaking some of their Jewish beliefs in order to get along with the Romans. Mark's recollection of Jesus prophesying that brothers and sisters and parents and children will turn on each other was very much on the mark considering the tense climate in the Jewish world (Mark 13).

Within this fragmented Judaism another division was emerging, a splinter group of about 120 Jews (Acts 1:15) who began teaching that Jesus was the long-awaited Messiah based on their various experiences and observations of this man. Their experiences were later written down in many different documents, some of which now comprise the New Testament. The problem, as revealed in these documents, was the early Christian writings were not consistent in their descriptions of the risen Jesus. For example, some suggested that his post-resurrection appearances were apparitional. In Luke 24:13–32, a resurrected Jesus catches up with two believers, one of whom was named Cleopas. Jesus talks with them and then eats dinner with them and, when he broke bread and blessed it, perhaps in the style of the

Last Supper, the two recognized him. Then Jesus immediately, mysteriously, disappeared. In two episodes in John 20 disciples in closed rooms suddenly were confronted with Jesus. How did he get in the closed room? Was he a ghost? Other stories described appearances where Jesus is clearly a physical person (Luke 24:36–43; John 21). Notice that both Luke and John record two different descriptions of Jesus' resurrected appearances, bodily and ghostly. There was no consistent Christian doctrine to settle the theological issues surrounding Jesus' physical appearance. Indeed, it was because of these conflicting accounts that later church theologians formulated their long theological and irrational proofs of Jesus' dual existence as the Son of God, in spirit, and the man Jesus, in flesh. Until then, the early believers struggled with the gospel accounts and their conflicting descriptions of the resurrected Jesus. These struggles led to doubts about who and what he was. And these stories are indicative of the early theological divisions of Jesus' followers.

As the early believers spread their fascinating message, parts of the story diverged from other accounts. Confusion ran amok among the faithful and sides were drawn as to which teacher's interpretation was correct. Paul was quite aware that competing stories of Jesus' life were circulated about the Mediterranean Sea by competing "apostles." Among these stories were various interpretations of Jesus' earthly and resurrected existence. Peter, the heir apparent to Jesus, warned about false teachers among the faithful (2 Pet 2) but it was the apostle Paul who provided the most information about these various gospels and stories about Jesus. In 1 Corinthians Paul writes that in Cloe's house church some believers claimed to follow Christ while some followed Paul and others followed Cephas while other believers trusted Apollos' teachings (1 Cor 1:10–12; 3:1–4). An emerging hierarchy of apostleship arose within the ranks of the early churches and this implies that some teachers were seen as more authoritative than others. Paul, in 2 Corinthians 11, battles against the notion that he is inferior to the "super apostles," most likely Peter, James and John. Along with this problem, Paul warns that some traveled about the Roman empire preaching different interpretations of Jesus and that some preachers were offering different spirits to their adherents (2 Cor 11:4–6). Which of these teachers should one believe? Which spirit was the correct one? How would one discern the true spirit? Doubts ran rampant in the early churches.

This confusion was indicative of the great disparity of beliefs that permeated the early Church. If church leaders could not agree about Jesus, and various teachers were spreading different and conflicting stories about Jesus, then doubts as to who and what he was would rise among the faithful and the curious as to who he really was. To simplify the issue greatly, some believers said Jesus was just a man who lived and taught great things; others said he "appeared" (as in "seemed to be") on earth after his resurrection; some taught that he was a man who, after he died, was resurrected in some form and became the adopted son of God at that time; while others proclaimed that Jesus was God from the beginning of time, came to earth in the form of a man, lived and taught and died, and was resurrected physically and rose to heaven to resume his place there as the son of God.

The early Christian hymn in Philippians 2:5–11 reflects the last interpretation and, several centuries later, this theology eventually became the official understanding of the church. Today this theology is recited by many Christians every week in the form of the Apostle's Creed or the Nicene Creed. But from the first century through the fourth and fifth centuries, this and other theories of Jesus circulated throughout the Christian world. Doubt was everywhere, yet somehow Christianity survived and thrived.

The witnesses of the resurrected Jesus formed small *ekklesias* (the Greek word from which we get "church"). These meetings began as house churches but when these various house churches gathered together it was called an *ekklesia*, basically the whole church. Home churches featured common meals and oral presentations of the story of Jesus. There was a Roman cultural, social and economic factor here that must be considered. Guilds and funeral associations revered a particular deity. When these associations met they shared a common potluck meal where libations were offered to the patron deity.[12] When Paul and Mark described the meetings of house churches and their common meals and their recollections of Jesus, their particular deity, this ritual would not have raised an eyebrow in the first century. Were the Christians a guild? There is indication that the Thessalonians certainly acted like a guild or funeral association. They certainly talked about death, the death of Jesus as well as the death of their own brothers and sisters.[13]

One problem arose, however. From these meetings emerged stories and first-hand oral accounts that suggested Jesus was executed as a religious and political insurrectionist who had resurrected and was coming again to initiate a new Kingdom. Such political preaching arising from

12. Collins, *Faces*, ch. 2.
13. Bridges, *1&2 Thessalonians*, 9–10.

these believing Jews threatened the very existence of an already fragmented and increasingly militant Jewish community because it seemed a political challenge to the power and jurisdiction of Rome. Something had to be done to quell this preaching before it brought the scorn and persecution of Roman legions upon the Jews.

Shortly after Jesus died (ca. 33 CE) some Jews took it upon themselves to persecute those who claimed Jesus was the Messiah. Paul, in Galatians 1 and 1 Corinthians 15 recalls his zealous pursuit of the early Christians. New Testament scholars have generally dismissed this on the basis that Jews did not have such jurisdiction but Paula Fredrikson reconstructs this time period and points out that if Paul were an officer of the synagogue court he would have been responsible for keeping order within his community at Damascus. Paul, ever the over-zealous Jew and aware of the divisions and temptations within the Jewish population of his day, was simply trying to save his synagogue and his Jewish family from the errant divisions caused by those who claimed that Jesus was the messiah.[14] The logic of the issue is illuminating: if Jesus' followers caused much dissension among the Jewish population, then the Jews might revolt against the new sect soon to be called Christians. If the Jews fought amongst themselves then the scorn of the Roman leaders, who were very leery of the Jews anyway, would come down hard on the ever-persecuted people of God.

With this inter-Jewish persecution two things happened. First, a rift in Judaism began that eventually led to the formation of the Christian Church. But in the 30s CE, Jews who believed in Christ were not recognized by the Romans as a legitimate Jewish religion. However, as Marta Sordi has demonstrated, the Romans basically left the rift to be decided by the Jews. Indeed, Tiberius wanted to make the Christian faith a legal religion *in Judea* but was overruled. Still, the believers in Jesus were initially left to their own devices within their parent faith of Judaism. Ironically and then tragically, they were persecuted by their own Jewish friends and Saul (as he was known then) was one of these persecutors.[15]

Second, as the Jewish community split over the issue of Jesus, Acts 6 reveals that a second fault line was developing among those who believed Jesus was the long-awaited Messiah. Hellenists, Gentiles who attended Jewish synagogue services and converted into the Jewish faith, were scorned by the minority of orthodox Jerusalem Jews who likewise proclaimed Jesus

---

14. Fredrikson, *Jesus*, 153–156.
15. Sordi, *Christians*, ch. 1.

their Messiah. Thus these Hellenists left the mother city of Jerusalem and its virulent legalistic Judaism for the more tolerant coastal cities of the Mediterranean to continue their faith. Some of these believers scattered around in the land of Israel (Galilee, Judea, Samaria) and perpetuated their more open-minded beliefs.

By about 34 CE tensions calmed down for the Jewish-Christians. Saul, the self-proclaimed persecutor of the Jewish-Christians, was converted while traveling down the Damascus Road. Taking the name Paul, he then lived with the Jewish community in Damascus that was most likely led by Peter. In cities such as Antioch the emerging break between Jewish-Christians and Jews was solidified as believers in Jesus were now labeled Christians, followers of Christ, for the first time. As Gentiles were added to the Antiochean church, leaders in the church in Jerusalem, who insisted that Jesus meant for his followers to keep Jewish laws and customs, began to distance themselves from them.

As if this was not enough division and confusion, a series of political events added more fuel to the already burning fires. During emperor Caligula's reign (37–41 CE) Jewish attacks against the Romans increased. Because of this, Jewish Christians and Gentile Christians became incensed and called for attacks against their militant Jewish siblings. These battles led to mistrust between Gentile Christians because their associations with the militant Jews as well as Jewish Christians might bring down the wrath of the Romans upon them. All Jewish groups feared repercussions from the battles between Jewish zealots and the Roman army in Jerusalem.

To make matters worse, in Jerusalem Roman Emperor Caligula set out to place a statue of Jupiter in the Temple, an act which incensed the Jews and incited further revolutionary attacks and ideologies. This may very well have been the "abomination of desolation" that Mark describes in chapter 13. Along with this, Herod Agrippa was made king over the Galilean region and he generally favored the Jews over the Gentiles. Thus, toleration for Gentile Christians, and those who preached to them, ended during Herod Agrippa's reign. After Agrippa's death in 44 CE the Christians were tolerated by the Romans until 62 CE. The only persecutions of the Christians in this time were by the Jews who saw them as a heretical sect. 1 Thessalonians 2:14–16, written around 50–51 CE, succinctly describes the situation. Paul very bluntly recalls how the Christians were persecuted by "your own countrymen" the Jews. Family was killing family.

Within this turmoil between Jews and Jewish Christians were even further divisions between the fledgling Christians. One point of contention, and therefore, cause of increasing doubts, was the return (parousia) of Jesus. In Mark 13 Jesus states that, after his death and resurrection, he will return soon and Jesus, as presented in the other New Testament gospels, was very adamant about his impending return. This event, according to Jesus' teaching, was immanent. But by the 60s CE, roughly a generation after Jesus' prediction of this return, the Messiah had not returned and this delayed parousia instilled doubts within the Christian community. Was Jesus just another delusional prophet? Was he yet another misdirected Jewish fanatic? Yet another confused Messiah? If so, were his teachings also suspect? Maybe he really was a blasphemous rogue Jew as the Jewish leaders claimed.

Paul, in the earliest Christian writing we have, advises his friends in Thessalonica that "according to his own word" Jesus will return and will gather up those believers who have died in the interim (1 Thess 4:13—5:11). The very fact that Paul had to address the issue of a delayed return of Christ reveals that doubts permeated the gatherings of Christians. The apostle Peter was also aware of the Christians' concerns over the delayed parousia. His first letter addresses this matter obliquely, noting that the waiting Christians are suffering for a purpose: suffering produces refinement, thus their faith is being tested by these trials, both Roman, Jewish and intra-Christian. He ends his letter with a note of mixed blessing: after you have suffered a little while God will restore you (1 Pet 5:10). Since the first letter of Peter did not sooth the worries of his constituents his second letter (written either shortly after the first or near the end of the first century by a "disciple" of Peter) explicitly tackles the delayed return of Jesus. In chapter three Peter notes that "scoffers" will say, "Where is this coming of the Lord?" Peter then explains the delay with a convenient theological reminder that a day for humans might be a thousand years in God's eyes, and, vice versa, a day in God's time might be like a thousand human years. "The Lord is not slow in keeping his promise," Peter then advises (2 Pet 3:9 NIV). For this study we should keep in mind the tradition that says Mark was taught by both Peter and Paul. Surely he was more than aware of the spiritual anxieties of the Christians about the return of Jesus.

The climax of this boiling cauldron of politics and religion came in the mid 60s CE. The somewhat maniacal emperor Nero set fire to a district in Rome that mostly included low-income tenants. Of the fourteen districts in Rome, ten were totally or partially destroyed. Rumors abounded that Nero set the fires, possibly to get rid of the poor and their slums, to provide room for a new palace for himself. In order to deflect this rising criticism, Nero blamed the Christians and began a period of intense persecution of the believers. Suddenly it was dangerous to be an openly professing Christian. Christians were covered with skins of wild animals and fed to dogs or were crucified and then burned as torches at night's end. Church tradition records that Paul and Peter were martyred in this time. In the 60s Rome now officially viewed Christianity as a very separate and dangerous religion from that of Judaism. Given the other ills enumerated above, some Christians no doubt questioned why they should remain loyal to a faith that increasingly was troublesome socially, theologically, and politically, if not life-threatening.

At the same time, Jews in Jerusalem were organizing to oust the Romans from their holy city. Brigandage was rampant as the frustrated poor broke into and robbed the homes of the rich, the result of a social and political battle where the Jews fought more amongst themselves than with the Romans. The war was more about control of the Jewish people where aristocrats fought against peasants, high priests against politicos. This impending war between Jews and Romans commenced in 66CE and came to a dramatic, destructive and decisive end in 70 CE. In Jerusalem the Jews' beloved Temple was destroyed and the Jews were finally quashed by the military hero Vespasian. This terrible and devastating defeat convinced many Jewish Christians to separate themselves from their Jewish families altogether to avoid more persecutions by association. In the ultimate act of blasphemy, Vespasian's son Titus placed the Roman standards in the most sacred of Jewish places, the Temple, demonstrating the victory of the Roman gods over the Jewish god.[16]

The apocalyptic chapter of Mark 13 describes in fantastical imagery the very scenes enumerated above. Just as Jesus in Mark predicts, in the 60s CE Christianity was anything but unified. However, the break from Judaism was not complete, Christians themselves could not agree on what rituals to follow, false teachers abounded, there were disappointments about the veracity of Jesus' teachings and predictions, the believers could not agree on how Jesus appeared after his resurrection, some taught that Christianity was a branch of Judaism while others insisted that it was a new religious sect, and some of their brothers and sisters in Christ were being persecuted. How could one not doubt in this time period? It was in this confused setting that Mark wrote his gospel.

16. Cohen, "Judaism," 57–66.

3

Who Are My Mother and My Brothers?

Your brothers, your own family—even they have betrayed you . . .
(JER 12:6 NIV)

IT IS HARD TO leave family. Folks who are religious have two families: family of origin and family of faith. Both of them are intertwined. Some may move away and so leave their families behind but, unless estranged, family still exists. When some move away, however, religious ties may be undone. It is difficult to change churches and especially denominations. But, even if we don't move away, sometimes the filial bonds of one's home church must be broken. The church may move away from its "original" ideas and beliefs. The denomination may switch theological stances. New people join and soon "take over" the church. Sometimes both family and church are tied together so that when one member of the family changes theological persuasions—say, from conservative to liberal or Protestant to Catholic, or even Christian to Buddhist—then both family and church affiliation are broken. When Jesus began his ministry he broke away from both family and the religious persuasion that he grew up in. That might be a model for some Christians today.

As we have already seen, there is a growing minority of Christians who are increasingly disgruntled with today's religion. Born into a family that lived in the Church, like my family, it was difficult to distinguish between the two. Soon, though, one of the children became dissatisfied with the family of the church (and, possibly with their own family who gave their allegiance to the old church). The search for a new religious family and home was begun but the prospects were not good. Overall, the churches they try do not fulfill their spiritual needs just as their old home church did not.

For example, when they tried the contemporary church movement with its house bands and karaoke on the screens and sound bite preaching all captured on jumbotrons by the magic of media production, the deep and powerful mystery of Christ was reduced to therapy and the Oprah style of pop Christianity. Emotionalism replaced contemplative introspection. Jesus is a buddy. God the Creator is reduced to a mantra in a chorus that drones on for minutes until the band leader decides that the Spirit has come down upon the service. Sometimes the theology is so trite, so irrelevant to today's critical questions that disappointment is the only nugget taken home from the service.

On the other extreme, some may visit a more liberal congregation in hopes of a more satisfying worship experience. But, the hope may be overshadowed by diversity and ecumenism, an overemphasis of "green" or the plights of homosexuals or the latest political flap. Jesus may be reduced to just another religious figure, placed on the shelf with Buddha, Gandhi, Confucius, or a modern religious guru such as Thich Nhat Hanh or Dwayne Dyer. These are all worthy teachers who have great insights that a Christian might want to use to supplement their faith in Jesus. The book *Living Buddha, Living Christ* by Thich Nhat Hanh is an example from this side. Some of the comparisons between Jesus and the Buddha are quite illuminating but the Jesus portrayed in the book is a bit watered down. Isn't Jesus more than just a later reincarnation of the Buddha?[1]

And, caught in the fray are some Christians who, as Mick Jagger sings, can't get no satisfaction. Or, to put it in the more staid and spiritually sober words of U2, they still haven't found what they're looking for.

One of the orthodox (both liberal and conservative) criticisms of such folks is that they do not know what they are looking for. Somewhere between the old religion and New Age spirituality these disgruntled family members wander about. The reason many wander about is very simple. They just wish the Church would grow up.

Instead, the Church wrangles and wallows over endless theological battles and draws up either/or lines of battle. Conservative versus liberal,

---

1. Hanh, *Living Buddha*, throughout.

pro-gay or anti-homosexual. When will the millennium occur? Is it pre-, post-, or a-millennium? Must I believe absolutely that every verse in the Bible is historically accurate or should I take the Bible passages with a salty grain of relative interpretation? Why is the Virgin Birth or the physical resurrection of Jesus the litmus test to see if one is indeed a Christian or not? Have those who disagree about global warming or read a conservative translation of the Bible turned their backs on their liberal friends? Each side criticizes the other, proof-texting their ideologies with the Bible verses that justify their beliefs. What is really apparent, however, is that all too often neither side really knows their Bible at all. How can they cite some verses from the Bible when others contradict them altogether? When calls for ecumenical love and understanding are heard each side takes its ball and gloves and goes home.

Just grow up already.

Jesus understood this very well. "If a house is divided against itself, that house cannot stand" (Mark 3:32). Best to move on. But, where does one go?

For those caught in the cracks, there are only four options. Leave the church altogether; continue going to church out of a sense of shear loyalty; join those who go through the buffet line of today's religious diets; or keep looking. Either way, family, both filial and religious, have been lost and the list of the lonely is growing.

What does the Gospel of Mark have to say about family? Sometimes you have to leave family in order to find a new one. Jesus left his family for another. Jesus also left behind his traditional Jewish culture and religion as he plowed new fields of religious thought for a new generation. His life can be an example for all of those who are looking for a new church family.

Nearly all scholars agree that Mark wrote for the Christians in the city of Rome. If we look at the "family" of believers in Rome we see a house much afflicted and divided. There had been a large population of Jews in the city for over two centuries and as many as thirteen synagogues were constructed there by the time of Jesus. These synagogues were home to Jews and Jewish Christians some time after the death of Jesus. In 49 CE Emperor Claudius expelled the Jews for public disorder, specifically, arguing quite strongly about a certain Chrestos, that is, Christ. This expulsion affected Jews who believed in Jesus, including Aquila and Priscilla, who left for Corinth and later entertained the apostle Paul (Acts 18). After Claudius, Nero became the emperor of Rome and allowed Jews to return to the city.

Who Are My Mother and My Brothers?

It was then that Priscilla and Aquila returned to their home. But, tensions were still high between the locals and the returning Jews, who were characterized as beggars, fortune-tellers, lazy, superstitious, and sexually promiscuous.[2]

With the expulsion of Jews and Jewish Christians, the Gentile Christians were left on their own in Rome. When the Jews and thus Jewish Christians returned they met with a strong Gentile Christian base who were now used to taking care of themselves, including slackening adherence to strict Jewish customs such as dietary restrictions and circumcision. Still, there were divisions even among the Gentile Christians. Roman Christians, Jewish and Gentile, covered the gamut from strict Jewish legalists to libertarian followers of Jesus. The followers of Christ worshiped in at least five small house churches mentioned by Paul in Romans 16. There were no doubt more that Paul did not list. The main reason Paul wrote to the Romans was to stitch back together a very divided church split between Jewish and Gentile Christianity.[3]

Much like Christians today, the Roman Christian family was divided and argued over customs and traditions and rules and regulations. How does one put the family back together? Mark points us to Jesus as an example.

Family is an important part of Jewish culture. The Old Testament presents lineages and genealogies throughout its pages. In the New Testament Matthew and Luke give the lineage of Jesus and the Apostle Paul, never one to miss an opportunity to state his credentials, also let his readers know of his Jewish pedigree. When members of churches and others questioned his credentials, he quickly cited his storied background. Furthermore, fathers taught their sons a craft and the basics of education. The mother taught the children morality and nurtured them throughout childhood. The firstborn received a double portion of the inheritance. Children were expected to honor and take care of their elders. Who a person was in the Jewish society of Jesus' day rested upon the reputation of the family. Honor was an important value. What the child did reflected upon the family. An errant child brought shame upon the family. Marcus Borg points out that conventional wisdom was conveyed in the family. Family, wealth, honor, and religious practices were the mediated traditions taught in the family. If we are to fully

---

2. Talbert, *Romans*, 5–6; Keck, *Romans*, 29.
3. Talbert, *Romans*, 8–12.

understand Jesus then we have to examine and figure out who his family was.[4]

So, who was Jesus' family? How did they shape his life?

We begin with the harmonized life of Jesus. Recall that Mark is the first gospel written. Matthew, Luke and John came later. Matthew and Luke have Jesus' birth stories and genealogies. They repeat stories of Jesus' ascension to heaven thus implying that Jesus was God's Son. The Gospel of John dwells on this last point: Jesus, the Word of God, was God. These themes and theologies are rigid beliefs for many and well-known for others today. Jesus was God's Son, born through the Virgin Mary, who was engaged to a man named Joseph and Jesus had brothers and sisters. While the curious details of this scenario have provided fodder for many a theologian and Church apologist—was Joseph married to another woman before Mary?; how did Mary really become pregnant?; was she a virgin before and after the birth of Jesus?—most people understand that these are the basic details of Jesus' family.

However, if the later literature of the Roman and Jewish world is indicative of the interpretations of Jesus in the first century CE, this version of Jesus' origins and family is very suspect. For many years scholars have neglected these extra-biblical sources claiming that they were not reliable or were too radical to be accepted as authentic. And, indeed, they are radical! But recent scholarship has pointed out, correctly, that if we are to fully comprehend the story of Jesus then we cannot ignore these historical documents. Myths and legends of old often have their basis and genesis in facts. Christians must reconsider their faith in light of these documents. Many Christians are aware of and are reading these other writings. At the very least they will decide that these sources are nonsense and unreliable for the life of faith. At the most, they will have to reconsider their long-held beliefs. And that might be a good thing. We have excellent examples in the New Testament of those who did reconsider their faith: Jesus and Paul quickly come to mind.

Christians and non-Christians such as Jews and those loyal to the Greco-Roman religions as well as adherents to the Eastern Mystery religions told stories that ran counter to the bucolic and theologically correct versions we read in the New Testament gospels today. Indeed, it is telling as well as shocking that certain groups of Christians actually used the book of Mark to support their claim that Jesus was not the Christ, thus implying

---

4. Borg, "Jesus," 70.

that he was just a man.⁵ These claims against the traditional story of Jesus' birth and family came under serious scrutiny in the first and second centuries. One persistent rumor emerged in the first century, possibly from the grandson of Jesus' younger brother Judas (not to be confused with Judas who handed over Jesus to the Roman and Jewish authorities) whose name was Jacob. He was a follower of Jesus and, when sharing his religious beliefs with others, he often ended his teachings with the phrase "in the name of Jesus the son of Panteri." Similar stories were told by the Jewish Rabbis, one involving a dispute with others about a "Jesus son of Panter" who could heal a snake-bitten person.⁶ What did this cryptic phrase mean?

Celsus, writing about 175 CE, made extensive use of Jewish anti-Christian polemic as he attacked the heretical group then known as Christians. He claimed that a poor Jesus made up the story of his virgin birth. His mother, according to Celsus, was convicted of adultery and dismissed by her fiancé only to give birth to her bastard son whose father was Panthera (or, Pantera), a Roman soldier. Jewish writings of this time period and later relate the same story. James Tabor notes that the gospels were often very kind to Roman soldiers (see Luke 3:14, 7:9; Acts 10:1–2) and it is quite telling that in the book of Mark, it is a Roman Centurion who finally makes the proclamation that Jesus is the Son of God. There is further evidence of one Roman soldier named Pantera who hailed from Sidon, a city where Jesus' sermons and teachings were well-attended and respected. In Mark 7:24 Jesus retreats to a house on the border of Tyre and Sidon but he could not escape the crowds.⁷ Is Mark secretly telling us something important?

When placed against the traditional teachings of Jesus' lineage and parentage as promulgated by the church we have to face some tough questions. Is there any truth to these rather fantastic facts? Have we been deceived by centuries of theological cover up? Was there a scandalous incident relating to Jesus' birth? These questions of faith lead to even more questions. We have to wonder when these stories began, where was their place of origin, what their purpose was. Were such stories in existence just after Jesus' death? Did many people question Jesus' background, his legitimacy, and his family's reputation? If the stories above carried any shred of truth then the reputation of Mary, mother of Jesus comes into question. Was she raped by a Roman soldier? If so, did Joseph remain loyal to her

---

5. Ehrman, *Misquoting Jesus*, 35.
6. Tabor, *Jesus Dynasty*, 64; see also Freund, *Digging*, 174–177.
7. Tabor, *Jesus Dynasty*, 64–72; Van Voorst, *Jesus*, chs. 2–3.

through this crisis? Or, did Mary have relations with an itinerant solider who left her pregnant? Would this explain the question of whether Joseph was the "real" father of Jesus or whether he had been married before and then married Mary who came with a child name Jesus?

Of course the previous points sound heretical and outlandish. But, that is because we have the hindsight of Matthew and Luke to point our heads to the virgin birth. Respected evangelical scholar Thomas Oden's *The African Memory of Mark* presents a unique approach to interpreting the first gospel. He argues that the people of Africa, where Mark hailed from, told stories about Jesus and Mark's recollection of him that often differed from those of the gospels. While he uses this information to bolster the claim that Mark's gospel is true to the core of Christian teachings, indeed, should be placed before the theologies of the other gospels, he also presents evidence that could very well be used to suggest that Mark collected material that directly contradicted that of the later gospels. In other words, Mark may be telling a story that was altered later to fit an emerging version of Jesus within the emerging church. "Since today the Gospel of Mark is widely regarded as the first Gospel written. It must have been circulating while some other original eyewitnesses were still living. Thus Mark's Gospel would not have been taken seriously by contemporary eyewitnesses if it had differed widely from other contemporary recollections of Jesus." In other words, before Mark had been altered by Matthew, Luke and John it must have been accepted as true. Would the sources that were outside of the Gospel of Mark and even outside of the Christian faith have been based on the above information?[8]

If all of these questions lead back to the negative stories about Jesus' heritage, then Jesus clearly could not be a great religious leader because of his suspicious background. Or could he? Since the Old Testament is full of stories where the least or the worst became the chosen steward of God, would it matter if any of these scenarios about Jesus' life were proven to be true? Don't we preach that God can take a mess of a life and turn it into a life of exemplary faith?

On the other side of these questions is a completely different evaluation of Jesus' lineage and parental background. James Tabor makes a compelling case that Jesus was of royal lineage. The genealogy of both Matthew and Luke indicate that he was of kingly heritage, indeed, descended from King David himself. Jesus' hometown, Nazareth, was known as a place

---

8. Oden, *African Memory*, 75.

Who Are My Mother and My Brothers?

where the royal family settled. Jesus was royalty? Is that why the wise men sought him?[9]

With these broad questions in mind, it is rather curious that Mark presents very little in the way of information about Jesus' family and origins. There is no romantic birth story; that would come later in the gospels of Matthew and Luke. In the earliest manuscripts of Mark there is no mention of Jesus' father. Mark only has two scenes where Jesus' family is introduced—3:34–35 and 6:3—and these only name Mary and Jesus' brothers and sisters. The problem for readers of Mark's gospel then and today is the definition of "family." Should it be interpreted in a biological way: Jesus was born from parents? Is it more metaphysical: Jesus is the son of a god or Son of God? Or, is it theological: Jesus, son of God, of the royal lineage of David, was born of a virgin?

It is universally recognized by Christians, indeed it is the very tenet of their faith, that Jesus was the long-awaited Messiah as anticipated by the Jews. The Jews of Jesus' day did not expect that this Messiah was to be a divine savior. In fact, the very opposite was believed: the much anticipated messiah descended from King David would be an ordinary, if perhaps privileged, man. According to the Psalms he would be a son of God just as the very human King David was praised as a son of God. Karen Armstrong reminds us that the Apostle Paul never called Jesus "God" instead preferring the title "son of God." When we remember Paul's self-proclaimed Jewish heritage and rabbinical background and brief yet very zealous Jewish persecution of Christians and vast knowledge of the Jewish scriptures, then this title can only mean that Jesus, in the eyes of the very early church, embodied the powers of God but was not considered God himself. Just as King David was lionized as the embodiment of God on the throne of Israel, so Jesus would be deemed the very human embodiment of God on earth.[10] With this background in mind, we can now begin to examine Jesus' biological family.

The first mention of Jesus "family" in the gospel of Mark is in the introductory verse: "The beginning of the gospel of Jesus Christ, the Son of God." Christians today assume that Jesus is the very Son of God. But for Mark's readers and listeners the phrase "son of God" had many connotations. Is Jesus literally the son of God? It seems that in this introductory verse Mark is presenting titles of Jesus: Jesus was his name, Christ was his

---

9. Tabor, *Jesus Dynasty*, ch. 2.
10. Armstrong, *History*, 80–83.

post-resurrection title, and Son of God was the phrase of faith among the Christian faithful. From this introduction Mark is describing Jesus the man as the resurrected Christ who was proclaimed the Son of God, but, *whose son was he?*

In order to understand Mark we must start with the earliest manuscript that we have of this gospel and it does not have the phrase "Son of God." This indicates that this descriptive phrase of faith was not important for Mark. Other later manuscripts do include the phrase, and this means either that copyists inserted "son of God" into the manuscripts, most likely to conform to the later emerging theology that depicted Jesus as the Son of God, or that later theologians had a different manuscript before them (manuscripts were often copied by various people and then passed on. The potential for errors or changes in theological descriptions was very high). The omission is curious because the idea of Jesus as son of God is found in Romans 1:3 which was written before Mark.[11] If Mark was aware of Paul's theology, then why would Mark exclude the phrase in his opening lines? It is even more interesting that the phrase is found throughout Mark's gospel, but it is voiced by everybody but the believers. If Mark's first manuscript really did leave out the descriptive phrase "son of God" in the opening list of titles and then placed the phrase on the lips of non-Christians, was he making a point that Jesus was not the son of God for believers? Or, was he commenting on the theological battles in the early church, pointing out the ironic tragedy that the believers could not agree on who Jesus was while the unbelievers understood clearly who and what Jesus was? One can see how the titles of Jesus, or the lack thereof, in the book of Mark, may have led to more doubts for his readers. No wonder some readers used Mark to disprove that Jesus was the Christ!

Throughout Christian history theologians have taken this appellation to mean uniquely that Jesus was the literal Son of God. This is evident if today's readers look at how the phrase is presented in modern translations: "Son of God" rather than "son of God" or "son of god." But readers and listeners in Mark's day would not have been so fast to make this conclusion. The phrase was quite common in the time of Jesus in the Greco-Roman world.

We have to remember that Mark's readers, as well as those of Matthew and Luke, grew up in the Greco-Roman world. If educated, they would have been familiar with Homer's *Iliad* and *Odyssey* and Virgil's *Aeneid*.

---

11. Culpepper, *Mark*, 43.

Who Are My Mother and My Brothers?

Even if not educated, they would know the stories of the Greek and Roman deities. Many heroes and lesser deities were the sons and daughters of the gods. Some were the progeny of a god/goddess and a human. In Roman times Hercules comes to mind instantly. He was the son of Jupiter (in Greek, Zeus) and the female mortal Alcmene. Aeneas was the son of the human Prince Priam (or Anchises) and the goddess Venus. It would not have stretched the imaginations of readers of Matthew and Luke if they read that Jesus was the son of God and the mortal Mary.

Many important and powerful people were considered "sons of god." Emperors who lived exemplary lives were proclaimed "a son of a god" after their death. Great military leaders were also given this title. Alexander the Great, Caesar Augustus, Nero, and Vespasian were considered sons of god. Calling someone "son of god" was not a unique idea in Roman culture. Indeed, the early church father Justin Martyr, who wrote a defense of Christianity in the mid-second century, listed several heroes of the Roman culture who were considered sons of god like Jesus: Hermes, Asclepius, Dionysus, Heracles, the Dioscuri, Perseus, Bellerophon, Ariadne, along with deceased emperors. Gregory Riley concludes that, "Christians . . . are saying nothing essentially different about Jesus the 'Son of God' from what the Greek and Roman poets had said about their 'sons of the gods.'"[12] So, the big question for readers of Mark then and now is, what did this phrase mean to Mark's first readers?

Recall that Mark had no gospels to model his writing on. Dennis McDonald, in his provocative book *The Homeric Epics and the Gospel of Mark* makes the bold claim that Mark, having no gospel template to guide him in his story of Jesus, used what was available in his time to model his plot: the epics of Homer. This assertion would seem quite apropos but it questions the long-held Christian tradition that Mark was guided by the Spirit of God to create a new genre of religious writing: a gospel. McDonald's evidence is not exactly perfect, but his observations provide some light on the topic at hand. For the ancient poet Homer, though his protagonist Odysseus was a mortal, he was described numerous times as born of Zeus. Also, Homer says that Odysseus was like a god. McDonald explains that, "When Homer likened heroes to gods, he had in mind physical beauty, not moral or spiritual qualities or divine parentage; even so, Homer's Hellenistic readers sometimes viewed Odysseus, as they did other heroes, as superhuman."[13]

12. Riley, *One Jesus*, 71–73.
13. McDonald, *Homeric Epics*, 16.

Closer to the time of Mark is Virgil's *The Aeneid*, the great tale of the travel of Aeneas from the devastation of Troy to the founding of triumphant Rome. Modeled after Homer's *Iliad* and *Odyssey*, the book was the authorized national epic that described the birth of Rome. Virgil's tale relates the triumphs and travails of Aeneas who is the son of the Goddess Venus and the human Anchises. Since the story was well known in Roman culture, the figure of a mortal as the son of a deity and a mortal would not have been unreasonable to Mark's readers. Along with this, Roman readers knew of Ovid's *Metamorphoses* and its interminable appearances of deities in human form. If Jesus was a son of a god, then his appearance on earth would likewise not have raised many eyebrows.

We must also keep in mind that many who heard Mark or read it were from a Jewish context as well. King David, a mere mortal, was called a son of God. Was Jesus just another son of God?

So, in Mark's book, did his readers understand Jesus as the heroic son of a god, a son of God, or, *the* Son of God? This was an important question for Mark's readers who lived long before later church theology declared Jesus as the Son of God, the Christ.

In several strategic places in Mark's gospel Jesus is proclaimed Son of God. After Jesus' baptism the heavens open up and a voice (ostensibly God since most gods lived in the heavens) acknowledges Jesus as his son (1:11). While demons know who Jesus is, such as those in Mark 1:24 who say that Jesus is the Holy One of God, the disciples throughout the gospel do not make the connection about Jesus being God's Son. For example, when Jesus asks the disciples who the crowds think he is, they respond with Elijah, John the Baptist, or one of the other prophets from Israel's past. Then Peter exclaims that Jesus is the long awaited Jewish Messiah (Mark 8:27–30). Did this mean that Jesus was a son of God?

Some scholars such as Morna Hooker claim that Peter fully understood the meaning of the term "messiah" and that Mark's readers surely would have understood the term, yet this assertion ignores the fact that, at this time, Jews and Jews who became Christians, were still wrangling over the exact meaning of the term.[14] Along with this, as noted in the last chapter, Jews dispersed about the Mediterranean and thus heavily influenced by Roman myths and culture, were the majority of the readers of the gospel in the first century and Jews of this time had a totally different understanding of messiah than did the Christians. The Hebrew prophets foretold of a

---

14. Hooker, *Mark*, 203.

messiah coming one day and the Jews had great expectations of this person. According to the *Psalms of Solomon*, a book popular in Jesus' day, written between the Old and New Testament periods, this messiah would be a descendant of King David. He would restore the Temple to its original lofty stature, cleanse the Holy City of Jerusalem of its occupiers, such as the Greeks and Romans, and rid Judaism of apostate believers. This great leader would then be a righteous king of the Jews. The messiah figures, in other words, would be humans who often led parties of believers in revolt against the persecutors of Jews. (To this day, as many a Jewish novel insists, Jewish mothers hope their daughters will be one who gives birth to the long-awaited messiah.) For Jews, the messiah was to be a military hero who would oust the Roman occupiers out of the holy city of Jerusalem. Since Mark does not portray Jesus as this warrior it was easy for Mark's readers to conclude that Jesus was anything but the Messiah.

Adding to this confusion was the fact that there were many such militaristic "messiahs" in early Judaism, including Judas Maccabee of the 160s BCE, another Judas in 6 CE, a Jesus son of Ananias in 62 CE, Menahem in 66 CE, and Simon son of Giorus who led the Jewish revolt against the Romans in 66–70 CE. The Jewish historian Josephus, writing in the late first century CE, did not call these people "messiah" but instead described them as pseudo prophets, charlatans, impostors, and deceivers.[15] If some Jews of his day thought so little of these revolutionaries, Mark's paucity of information of Jesus' origins did not help at all. Readers of Mark's gospel, unsure of who Jesus is, might have made the same evaluation. For example, the Jesus of the gospels could have very well been easily confused with the Jesus son of Ananias, especially since Mark does not include a birth story that would date Jesus and he only mentions Jesus' mother and siblings in his gospel (Mark 6:2–3). Since no father is credited with Jesus' birth, Jesus could very well be confused with the "son of" Ananias.

For Mark's readers, then, having Peter, a Jew, call Jesus a "messiah" was nothing new; it could be quite confusing and some might also take it as derogatory. As the literature of the Christians developed the definition of messiah was not consistent. What exactly did Peter mean when he called Jesus "messiah"? Indeed, for Mark's readers the term could be understood in a negative way. Was Jesus just another zealous upstart in a long line of failed messiahs, raising the hopes of desperate Jews only to see them fall?

---

15. Goodman, *Rome and Jerusalem*, 397.

Matthew, who follows Mark's outline, may have sensed the problem with this phrase. He changed the response of Peter in the story to a more precise "You are the Christ, the Son of the living God" (Matt 16:13–16). Still, even this depiction could be misleading. It can be interpreted as a man who emerged as the Messiah and thus was considered a son of God, as King David was a millennium before. In the Gospel of John, written later than the Gospel of Matthew, the writer states emphatically that Jesus is God from the very beginning of time. Thus, it seems that the early Christian theology evolved from Jesus as a man who was deemed a son of a god (as in the gospel of Mark) to the Son of God (Matthew), to God Himself (John).

Ironically, the characters in Mark's gospel who proclaim Jesus as a son of God are the very ones that the readers would deem suspicious as witnesses. Why should their word be taken as true? When Jesus threatens to exorcise the demons in a man they exclaim that Jesus is the Holy One of God (Mark 1:24). In Mark 3 the reader encounters evil spirits proclaiming that Jesus is the Son of God. In a similar story demons proclaim Jesus as Son of the Most High God (5:7). After forgiving a person of his sins, the witnesses of this absolution cry out, "Who can forgive sins but God alone" (Mark 2:1–7). One answer for Jews was obvious if blasphemous: Jesus must be God because only God can forgive sins. But for the Gentile readers of Mark's day the matter was not that clear: many deities were revered in the Roman world. Without any further clarification the reader would ask which god in the Roman cultural pantheon was Jesus equated with? Ironically, the only one who seems to understand Jesus in the book of Mark is a Roman soldier who, after Jesus died on the cross, exclaimed, "Surely this man is a son of God" (15:39). But, how would a Roman reader of Mark interpret a Roman soldier's claim of Jesus as a son of God?

The phrase "son of god" in this passage, however, can be read two ways, as modern translations of the Bible point out in footnotes. The NRSV translates this as, "Truly this man was God's Son" but adds in a note that the phrase is really, "a son of God." Likewise, the NIV has "Surely this man was the Son of God" but likewise clarifies with a note "a son" of God. Translators of this passage today, such as Alan Culpepper, Christianize it to read, not a son of God but the Son of God. Indeed, D. E. Nineham writes "the centurion's words meant not *a son of god* but *"the* son of God." Hugh Anderson asserts that, "it is barely conceivable that Mark has in mind here anything else but a full and authentic Christian acknowledgment of Jesus as *'the'* Son of God." From this side of the Christian faith it might be barely conceivable

Who Are My Mother and My Brothers?

but before the Church "proved" that Jesus was the Son of God the matter would have been open for debate. But Culpepper also notes that in the Book of Mark Jesus never uses this title for himself. Instead, he prefers the title "Son of Man."[16] If Jesus, according to Mark, who was taught by Peter, the man closest to Jesus, claimed only that Jesus was the son of Man, then did Mark mean that the centurion only claimed that Jesus was a son of a god? That would be an appropriate remark for a pagan, polytheistic Roman centurion to make. And, many new Christians came from this pagan, polytheistic culture.

Another point of confusion is that, after the brief theological and prophetic introduction in Mark 1:1, the author writes that Jesus appeared on the scene as a full-grown man. In Mark 1:9 we read, "In that time Jesus came from Nazareth in Galilee and was baptized by John in the Jordan." Thus, the readers of Mark are instantly presented with a question. Where did Jesus come from and who is he? This type of introduction was not uncommon in Mark's day. Greco-Roman biographers sometimes introduced their character without any details about their birth or early years.[17] However, biographers in Jesus' day generally gave some details about the familial and geographic origins of their heroes. Stories about heroes included a narrative about their divine origins, generally a male god mating with a virgin female earthling.[18] For Mark, then, the lack of details about Jesus' origins imply that, for Mark, these were not important for his story, for his theology, and, consequently, not deemed important for his readers. Since Mark does not introduce Jesus with the normal heroic roots of divine birth, is he implying that Jesus was just an ordinary man who was *declared* a son of god as some Christian groups later did, or was viewed similarly as the *adopted* son of God? In these cases God would have adopted or declared Jesus as the son of God either at his baptism or after his resurrection.[19]

Judging from the first Christian writings we have, Jesus' birth may not have been important in the days of the early church either. Jesus' humble human origins are emphasized when Paul, in Galatians 4:4, says that, when the time was right, God sent his Son, born of a woman. Both the NIV and NRSV capitalize son in this verse. But the capitalization of "son" can be questioned here as well. In this passage Paul notes that humans can also

---

16. Culpepper, *Mark*, 564; Nineham, *Mark*, 430; Anderson, *Mark*, 348.
17. Burridge, *What Are The Gospels?*, 201.
18. Riley, *One Jesus*, 39.
19. Jenkins, *Jesus Wars*, 43–48.

become sons of God, heirs to God. Did Paul mean for translators to capitalize "son"? Are we all Sons and Daughters of God? When examined in this context, Paul certainly could have understood Jesus as a son of God.

Paul, according to Calvin Roetzel, wrote to the Galatians probably between 52–56 CE, a full decade at least before Mark was written.[20] Paul did not have the gospels of Matthew and Luke to read about the virgin birth of Jesus because they were written two or more decades later. Those who interpret this verse as the virgin birth are reading into it the birth narratives from these later gospels. In Galatians 4 Paul is more likely indicating that Jesus, like any great man or philosopher or emperor, was sent from heaven for the good of the people at the most appropriate time.

In a later epistle, however, Paul cites a common Christian hymn in Philippians 2:5–11, what is called today the Christ Hymn. Here in this much-debated and explored passage Paul notes that Jesus gave up his divinity to be "born in the likeness of man" but there is no mention or explanation of how Jesus did this. Had Paul known about the important detail of the virgin birth surely he would have emphasized it somewhere in his writings. Instead, we only get oblique references to Jesus' origins in Paul's letters. And, if Mark had this writing available and interpreted it as though Jesus was divine but then gave up this divinity to come to earth, why did he leave out such an important point? The only conclusion we have from this lack of birth information in Mark was that there was nothing special about Jesus' birth. He was an ordinary man. Later Ebionites made this same claim and today some Christians agree.

Judging from the epistles written by Paul, which scholars date from about 48 CE to the late 50s, the main point about Jesus' life was his death, burial, and resurrection. We must remember that Paul saw the resurrected Jesus in a vision and that was his main selling point for his evangelistic message. Raymond Brown, in his extensive commentary on the birth narratives in Matthew and Luke, notes that the preaching in Acts focused on the death and resurrection of Jesus. He points out that Acts 2:23, 32; 3:14–15; 4:10; 10:39–40 all demonstrate the centrality of the death and resurrection in the early preaching of the church. Indeed, Brown concludes that Acts 10:37–41 is quite similar to the outline of Mark's gospel and it appears in John's gospel as well. Brown concludes that, "the birth of Jesus had not yet been seen in the same salvific light as the death and resurrection." In other words, the

---

20. Roetzel, *Letters of Paul*, 96.

birth of Jesus was not important in the earliest and most reliable preaching of the gospel message.[21]

For early Christians the return of Jesus, which was apparently delayed, thus causing some consternation among the awaiting believers, was the main point of interest. Paul and Peter both address the doubts caused by this delay and try to comfort their fellow believers but nowhere in their consolations and resulting theology do they mention a virgin birth for Jesus. Where Jesus came from was not important; *when* and even *if* he was returning were the burning issues for their day.

So, where did he come from? Mark mentions that, at the time of his baptism, he came from Nazareth. In Mark 14:67 a maid of the high priest confronts Peter, who has abandoned Jesus, and asks if he is an associate of Jesus the Nazarene. Culpepper observes that this implies contempt for Jesus and his home town.[22] At the end of the gospel, when an empty tomb is discovered by frightened women, they are told that Jesus of Nazareth is no longer in the tomb but has gone to Galilee. This association with Nazareth is found only in the gospels and the book of Acts and it appears to be another title of Jesus. Mark notes that demons call out "what do you want with us, Jesus of Nazareth?" (1:24). The phrase "Jesus of Nazareth" also appears in Mark 10:47. This phrase occurs as a title in fourteen other verses in the gospels and Acts (Matt 21:11; 26:17; Luke 4:34; 18:37; 24:19; John 1:45; 18:5, 7; 19:19; Acts 2:22; 3:6; 4:10; 6:14; 10:38; 22:8; 26:9). Clearly the early traditions associated him with Nazareth. What would this mean to the readers and listeners of Mark's gospel?

Matthew, perhaps writing in the early 80s CE, recalls that Jesus was born to the virgin Mary and her betrothed Joseph *in Bethlehem* (note that a named father is now part of the story). Then, after surviving the death threats of Herod and a harrowing flight to Egypt, they were led by a dream to settle in the town of Nazareth in the region of Galilee (Matt 1:18—2:23). Luke, written a few years after Matthew, expands the Nazareth origins somewhat, telling the reader that Jesus' parents lived in Nazareth before he was born in Bethlehem (Luke 1:26). Both Matthew and Luke provide genealogies for Jesus' parents, ostensibly to verify the origins of his mother and father. John's Gospel, probably written in the late 90s CE, notes that Jesus was from Nazareth (not born in Bethlehem!) but he then adds a condescending note: Nazareth was a place of ill repute according to Jesus' disciple

---

21. Brown, *Birth*, 26–28, quote from 28.
22. Culpepper, *Mark*, 523.

Nathanael, who asks, "Can anything good come from Nazareth?" (John 1:46) This comment in John's gospel, written perhaps thirty years later than the Gospel of Mark, reveals a lingering doubt about the reputation of Jesus' birthplace and thus of Jesus' reputation as well. Nazareth did not have a good reputation. Crossan and Reed put it even more bluntly: Nazareth "was absolutely insignificant."[23]

For Mark's readers a question arises: how can a great man, indeed one proclaimed as son of God, come from a place of such low reputation? Doubts of Jesus' origins, from his birth to his hometown, plagued the early believers in the first century and Mark's readers may have been aware of the reputation of Nazareth or, given the obscurity of the place, they may not have known anything about it at all. Richard Freund adds a more sobering thought: Jesus may not have been as important then as we have made him today. As we have seen, the name "Jesus" was quite common in that day. What sets Mark's Jesus apart from all the others? Surely not his place of origin, the bad place known as Nazareth?[24]

What was wrong with Nazareth? Reza Aslan adds more mystery to the confusion. He points out that Nazareth in the time of Jesus was a small village, possibly of a hundred Jewish families consisting of illiterate peasants, farmers and workers who lived in small mud huts. He concludes that it is "an inconsequential place." As an uneducated, lower-class woodworker such as Joseph or Jesus, there was not much to do in Nazareth. Indeed, the best work was available in nearby Sepphoris, "a sophisticated urban metropolis" filled with rich, cosmopolitan Jews. The city was under reconstruction as a major Roman city.[25] Can a son of god come from a small, obscure desolate village?

Interestingly, Aslan goes on to argue that Jesus was the product of Nazareth, which was situated in a hotbed of insurrectionary activity. Acting on the oppression of his youth and the poverty he lived through, Jesus would go on to start a revolution that eventually cost him his life. That may be the case but the question here for the initial readers of Mark in Rome is, would they have even known that Nazareth would produce such a person?

Jewish readers of Mark's gospel would have made the connection, however. Culpepper, citing Joel Marcus, notes that when Jesus takes his

---

23. Crossan and Reed, *Excavating Jesus*, 52.

24. Freund, *Digging*, 137.

25. Aslan, *Zealot*, 24–45, quotes from 26 and 38; likewise, Crossan and Reed, *Excavating Jesus*, ch. 2.

Who Are My Mother and My Brothers?

disciples to the Mount of Olives a connection with the apocalyptic prophecy of Zechariah would have come to mind to Jewish readers. Political ramifications surrounded the hopes of a militaristic Messiah in Jesus' day. Jesus as from Nazareth, right? If Aslan is right about the insurrectionary connections to Nazareth then readers would at least have to ask if Jesus was more a political revolutionary than passive Messiah. Jesus, of course, has different ideas about the Messiah. But, Culpepper points out that Mark's community may have been undergoing persecution and thus were turning away from the church. They, like Peter, may have misunderstood the whole idea of Jesus.[26] Doubts will do this to the faithful.

Along with Jesus' questionable origin and place of birth, Mark presents Jesus' family in an equally strange way. Mark 3:7–35 is a long section that begins with an exorcism where the demons proclaim that Jesus is "the son of god" (I've intentionally kept the lower case to emphasize the point above and help us to see how the text *might* have been read by the first readers). Jesus calls twelve men to be his disciples, a sort of surrogate family, and then an episode at (Peter's?) home in Capernaum presents doubts about Jesus' character (was he teaching divine things or was he of Satan; was he even Beelzebub?) and family.

Jesus enters a house and a large crowd soon gathers to hear and see this itinerant miracle worker. In chapter 3:21 Mark tells us that Jesus' family heard he was there and they came "to take charge of him, for they said, 'He is out of his mind.'" (NIV) Scholars generally point out that this passage is fraught with negative implications. His family wants to "seize" him, a verb with strong negative force. The phrase "beside himself" implies the equivalent of schizophrenia: Jesus is standing outside of himself or is insane. Jesus' mother and siblings "send" for him, a word of negative connotations in the gospel of Mark. Crossan and Reed put the conclusion bluntly: "Jesus' family . . . thought he was insane, not divine."[27]

This is the first mention of Jesus' family in Mark and it reveals a sharp divide in his family that raises important questions. Why did Jesus' family think he was out of his mind? Did they disapprove of his chosen vocation of wandering about, teaching and living off of others? Did some sort of family squabble lead to his departure? Did his somewhat radical philosophies conflict with his family's Jewish traditions? A writer does not normally put

---

26. Culpepper, *Mark*, 497.
27. Crossan and Reed, *Excavating Jesus*, 76.

in information that is as embarrassing as this unless it is so true and important for the story that it cannot be left out.

One clue might be that Jesus' family, at the time of Mark's writing, may have been part of the internal squabbles of the early church. Alan Culpepper points out that "Mark may reflect the conflict in the early church between the Jerusalem church that was dominated by Jesus' family and the disciples (both of whom are portrayed in a negative light in Mark), and the Galilean communities or Gentile communities that grew up independent of the leadership of Peter, the Twelve disciples, James (the brother of Jesus) and the elders."[28] This "family" of Jerusalem was composed of the scribes, Sadducees, and Pharisees who constantly badgered Jesus about his loyalty to the Law of Moses and to Judaism. This scenario also duplicates the situation in Rome: the Gentile Christians were fighting against the Jewish Christians.

As the passage progresses we read, "Then Jesus' mother and brothers arrived." (3:31 NIV) When he was told they were *outside* the house, Jesus surprisingly fires back, "Who are my mother and my brothers?" Pointing to those sitting around him *in the house*, he announces, no doubt much to the embarrassment of his family, that his listeners on the inside of the house are his family. Given Culpepper's observations, the message could not be more clear: for Mark, the real believers are not associated with the Jerusalem church dominated by Jesus' family. Was this a troubling thought for Mark's Jewish readers or a positive point of relief?

How did the initial readers of Mark's gospel understand this cryptic passage? Mark 13, a terrifying apocalyptic passage foretelling the end times, notes that families will be torn apart, brothers will betray brothers, children will rebel against their parents, and fathers will kill their children. Jesus' relationship with his family as portrayed in Mark clearly resembles this prophecy. Was this frightening chapter merely apocalyptic hyperbole? Or was it a sign of difficult times to come as Jews who believed Jesus was indeed the long awaited Messiah separated themselves from their family members who did not? The laws of Judaism feature many regulations about family and support of one's family was paramount. Did Jesus' relationship with his family reveal a break with the norms of Judaism? Might this be a model for today as well? Is Mark suggesting that we need to break with the status quo of our religion?

These two passages do reflect the perilous and trying days of the 60s CE when doubts about Jesus and rifts in the Jewish faith were widespread.

---

28. Culpepper, *Mark*, 119.

Who Are My Mother and My Brothers?

Judaism was splitting into as many as twelve different factions, so the Jews of Mark's day were not united and this surely meant that Jewish families were torn between loyalties to the various Jewish groups.[29] Along with this, Jews who believed Jesus was the Messiah also fought with family members who disagreed with this interpretation of this wandering philosopher. Adding to the fire, some who believed in Jesus' prophecy of an immanent return were now having doubts since his return seemed quite delayed. Was he too another messianic charlatan? Had they been duped again?

The next mention of Jesus' family is in Mark 6:1–4 where we find three troubling statements. First, while at the synagogue in his hometown of Nazareth, those in attendance wonder out loud, "Isn't this the carpenter? Isn't this Mary's son . . . ?" (NIV) In the Jewish world of Jesus' day it was considered an insult to be described as the son of a woman, even if she was a widow. The description of Jesus as the son of a woman validated the rumors of Jesus' illegitimacy circulating in his day and even later.[30] When we read this statement from the perspective of doubt we can see the locals' opinion of Jesus: he was a homeboy from a town with a bad reputation and he was possibly even illegitimate, the son of a mother.

Second, add to this the rather ignominious remark about his profession: a carpenter. It is telling that only Mark mentions the occupation of Jesus. Matthew changes it to read that Joseph, Jesus' father, was a carpenter (Matt 13:55). This term can mean several occupations—a maker of ploughs and yokes, one who works with stone, a simple woodworker—and perhaps they should be placed under the larger category of artisan, builder, or craftsman. Still, this term implied a low station in life, below that of peasants, indeed, one of the lowest classifications of people in the Roman world.[31] The fact that Mark records this scene with no apologies suggests that it was so true or important for his story that it could not be left out of the narrative. Mark's account reveals the very doubts of the Jews but it might also reveal doubts about Jesus' past and occupation in the Christian community. From the perspective of Mark's readers, since Jesus had not returned as he predicted maybe he *was* just an ordinary mechanic instead of the Messiah. If, as Rodney Stark claims, the "early Christians were drawn mainly from the ranks of the privileged," then early readers of Mark's gospel

---

29. Riley, *One Jesus*, 8.
30. Lane, *Mark*, 203.
31. Crossan, *Jesus*, 23–25.

may have looked down their noses upon this humble artisan.³² Interestingly, later manuscripts of Mark apparently followed Matthew's change and thus copyists or more "theologically correct" scribes introduced Jesus as "the son of the carpenter" in Mark 6.³³

This change did not quell many doubts, however, because later church theologians fought against the persistent charges stating that this profession was a demeaning occupation for their exalted Savior. Curiously, Justin Martyr called him the son of a carpenter but also described him as a physically unattractive carpenter who built ploughs and yokes. Ephrem the Syrian, however, in a hymn that brings together several passages from the scriptures, praised the role of carpenters, who, according to the scriptures, built the ark, the temple, and the light yoke of believers (Matt 11:30).³⁴

Third, in this passage Mark introduces Jesus' four brothers: James, Joses (or Joseph), Judas, and Simon. Mark also notes two sisters but does not name them. According to scripture, Jesus' brother James experienced the Lord after Jesus died (1 Cor 15:2). When and where is not known, and this James became a pillar in the early church (Gal 2:9). He participated in what is known today as the Jerusalem Conference as described in Galatians 2 and Acts 15. In this conference he is a stickler for adherence to Jewish law and traditions and, based on James' strict interpretation and enforcement of dietary laws and circumcision, Paul uses the term "pillar" for James in a somewhat derogatory manner. Later Christian writers such as Hegesippus, writing ca. 180 CE, relate that James was martyred by scribes and pharisees just before 70 CE. Nothing is known about Joses or Simon but some scholars believe that Judas wrote the tiny book of Jude based on the introductory verse in the writing.

There are three theories concerning Jesus' siblings and they demonstrate various strands of theological explanations of Jesus family.³⁵ The first states the obvious: Jesus and his siblings were born to Mary and Joseph, possibly after Jesus' birth. Second, apocryphal sources state that Jesus' siblings were foster brothers and sisters, children of Joseph and a previous wife. Many Protestants, Greek Orthodox, and Eastern Orthodox hold to this view. A third theory is that Jesus and James were cousins. This explains Mark 15:40–41 where the author says a Mary was the mother of James the younger and Joses.

32. Stark, *Cities*, 9.
33. Lane, *Mark*, 202.
34. Oden and Hall, *Mark*, 78–79.
35. *New Interpreter's Dictionary of the Bible*, Vol 3, 294–296.

Who Are My Mother and My Brothers?

There were several people named James in the New Testament and Mark may have been alluding to another Mary who had two children whose names were like that of Jesus' siblings. The original readers and listeners only had Mark's gospel, not later sources, thus they would understand that Jesus was the son of Mary and had four brothers and two sisters.

Mark presents potentially troublesome issues for early readers to puzzle over. The snide comments about the residents of Nazareth imply that no authoritative miracle worker could come from there. The issue of the husbandless Mary and her children had to raise eyebrows not only regarding her reputation but of Jesus' credentials as well. The note that he was a carpenter questioned his class status. The fact that his own townspeople questioned him and his family left Mark's readers and listeners in doubt.

Taken altogether, what is Mark saying when he leaves out a birth story, introduces Jesus as a young mechanic from Nazareth, leaves out valuable information about Jesus' relationship, if any, to his father, and only mentions his mother? Does Mark's mention of Jesus as son of Mary imply that he was simply a man, and an illegitimate one at that? Does Mark want the reader to see Jesus as part of a larger family of siblings who did not believe his teachings? If Mark's readers were mostly Jews, whose heritage included a strong sense of family and lineage, might this lack of information be a bit degrading?

That Jesus was the Son of God, a common title of great people in the days of the gospels, was not uncommon. According to existing accounts, other great people of Jesus' day, known as sons of gods, were depicted as born miraculously. Was Mark trying to avoid this confusion by leaving out a birth story? Could a carpenter be a son of a god? Would the mention of a virgin birth have led to further doubts about Jesus? If he was not born miraculously, then was he, from Mark's information (given to him by Peter!), just a man?

To put this in Hollywood terms, was Jesus a tall dark stranger who mysteriously appears on the scene in the first verse of Mark's gospel? Was he a son of a god, or a son of the Jewish/Christian God? Was he human, divine, a hero? Was he proclaimed a son of a god or a son of God by his followers? Mark's readers would have to answer these questions as they read through his story.

What did Jesus say about this matter? In Mark 9:7 Jesus is transfigured on a high mountain into a figure of extreme whiteness. Peter, James, and John witness the bizarre event. Then, in an apparent vision or epiphany these men see Elijah and Moses. A voice from a cloud calls out, "This is my Son, whom I love. Listen to him!" (NIV, note that "son" is capitalized)

Interestingly, Jesus never refers to himself as the son of a god or a son of God in the book of Mark. But Mark does have him *infer* that he is the son of God. In 11:27–33 Jesus is confronted by the leading scholars from Jerusalem. They are asking about his authority. Immediately after this, in 12:1–11, Jesus tells the story of a farmer whose son is rejected. The first readers of Mark would have missed the analogy until they reached the end of the book and even then they would have to decide for themselves if Jesus (the son) was the son of the farmer (God).

In Mark 14 Jesus and his disciples dine in what Christians later would call the Last Supper. After this, Jesus and his disciples go to the Mount of Olives where he prays beginning his supplication with "Abba, Father." What did he mean here?

According to James D.G. Dunn Jesus used the term "abba" in all of his prayers in the New Testament except the prayer in Mark 15:34. The term "abba," as most know, is an Aramaic term for "Daddy, Papa." It is a term of endearment and connotes intimacy. As portrayed in the New Testament, whenever Jesus prayed he thought of God as his Daddy. This is especially interesting when one considers that Jews would never call God "daddy" while praying. The term "Father" was used but not in the sense of intimacy. Jewish prayers in this time were proper and reverent. Jesus was anything but this. When praying, Jesus envisioned God as his personal Dad.[36] The only time Jesus did not use the term "abba" in his prayers was in Mark 15:34, when, as Jesus hung on the cross, he cried out in a very distant plea, "My God, why have you forsaken me?" In Jesus' view, his "abba" had left him to die a lonely death. God and Jesus, in this passage, are two very distinct characters for Mark. Could God be the father of Jesus in this passage?

In Mark 14:61 the reader is confronted once again with the question of Jesus' identity. In the middle of the trial led by the high priest Jesus is asked, "Are you the Christ, the Son of the Blessed?" He answers affirmatively with an appellation that is equated with God: I Am. Most scholars assume that this refers back to Moses in Exodus where Moses asks God's name and God answers "I Am." But this may not be the case. William Lane points out that for Jews in Jesus' time "'son of God' is understood solely in a messianic sense. Jewish hopes were situated in a messianic figure who was a man." Thus, "The question of the high priest cannot have referred to Jesus' deity." Instead, it asked if Jesus was the messianic man expected by the Jews. According to N.T. Wright Jesus did not see himself as the Christian

---

36. Dunn, *Unity and Diversity*, 187.

Messiah but instead as the Jewish man Messiah.[37] Thus, the phrase "I am" cannot mean I Am, as in I am God. Mark's Jewish readers would have read it as Jesus was the manly messiah of Judaism.

The term "Blessed" is called a "circumlocution" by scholars which simply means that it is a substitute for the name "God." The high priest could only use the name of God once a year during the Day of Atonement, a festival celebrated in the fall. According to Leviticus 24:16 anyone who used God's name in vain was guilty of defaming the name of God and, in Jesus' day, would be stoned to death, hung for a day, and then buried out of sight.[38] Even today, devout Jews will not say the name of God or read it out loud. If they encounter it in a book they substitute another word like "Name." "Blessed" would simply be a name for God. When asked if he was the Blessed One, Jesus' answer seems to affirm the question. Yes he is.

This seems to suggest that Mark slowly and quietly built up a case for Jesus as Son of God. However, there is a side of Jesus that has been ignored or glossed over by scholars but Culpepper points it out several times in his commentary: "Mark is the only Gospel that explicitly says Jesus was angry." In this author's estimation some scenes that suggest Jesus' frustration are Mark 1:40–44; 3:5; 7:24–30; and 9:14–29. In essence, Jesus occasionally exhibits a testy, impatient streak. Several times he appears to be affronted by questions and sometimes he snaps back in anger. This seems to suggest that Jesus, as portrayed by Mark, is one who would be a sarcastic itinerant. If, in response to the high priest's question "are you the Christ, the son of the Blessed?" Mark did not mean "I Am" in the divine sense then he probably did not mean to equate Jesus with the Blessed One. The more conservative scholar William Lane confirms this conclusion when he asserts that Jesus is simply responding to the question "Are you . . ." with a proper response, "I am." Lane goes on to note that Jesus affirms that he will be the great judge who judges those who judge him. This would imply divinity but this assertion is from the modern perspective. Would Mark's readers have made this same conclusion? Thus, it is reasonably questionable that Jesus answered that he was the son of God as in God. Interestingly, as Culpepper notes, after this incident Jesus refers to himself as the "son of Man," not "son of God." Might this imply a sarcastic reply from a testy Jesus concerning "I Am"?[39]

---

37. Lane, *Mark*, 535–536; Wright, "The Mission," 47–49.
38. Culpepper, *Mark*, 521–522.
39. Culpepper, *Mark*, 99; Lane, *Mark*, 536–537.

Anderson, while supporting the idea of Jesus as Son of God, raises several doubts within this passage. First, he points out that the high priest would not have used "Blessed" with the title "Christ." Since the Jewish Messiah was only a man, to use a term meant only for God would have been blasphemy. Second, scholars have pointed out what is called the "Messianic Secret" in the Gospel of Mark. This idea is based on the fact that Jesus never identified himself clearly as son of God. This study has assumed the Markan theme of the messianic secret and it should be clear that Mark raises many questions about the titles of Jesus. Thus, Anderson points out that, with the secret intact, why would Mark have Jesus admit that he is the I Am? With this in mind, Anderson thus raises an important doubt for this passage: Is Jesus really guilty of blasphemy? If Anderson is correct, then Mark may have intentionally portrayed Jesus as being sarcastic.[40] The fact that some early manuscripts changed Jesus' answer to "you say that I am" or "these are your words, not mine" suggests that, for some interpreters, Jesus was indeed being sarcastic. There had to be some basis for this change and this suggests that there was a tradition in the Christian communities that Mark indeed wanted to portray Jesus in this light.

Mark does not link Jesus to any particular family. He seems to have no earthly father. He denies any relations to his earthly family and this embarrassing moment perhaps reflects the tensions between his earthly family in Jerusalem and the Christians in the rest of the Roman world. Was Jesus the Son of God? Was he the son of God or the son of god or even the son of a god? There are enough cultural doubts to raise questions about how the initial readers of Mark's gospel would have interpreted this phrase. Did Jesus see himself as the Son of God? Enough doubts can be raised about this appellation as well. Mark's readers would have a difficult time figuring out who Jesus was based on Mark's portrayal of Jesus and his family.

Was Mark portraying Jesus as a testy, blue-collared mechanic from the bad side of town? Was this the typical Jewish story of the hero from the small, obscure village? Did this no-name man rise to the status of hero and thus receive the title of son of God?

In sum, Mark presents a very human Jesus. Maybe we need to leave the old church family that insists on the divinity of Jesus and reconsider this new and very human Jesus.

---

40. Anderson, *Mark*, 331.

4

Jesus as Teacher

He guides the humble in what is right and teaches them his way.
(Ps 25:9 NIV)

JESUS HAS OFTEN BEEN portrayed as a teacher in the Christian community. It is widely accepted among theologians and historians that Jesus was a teacher. In the gospels of Matthew and Luke, for example, Jesus' teachings are a major portion of the gospels' narratives. In the book of John, Jesus teaches the people in an oblique way that he is the great I Am, another name for God. It may be an understatement to say that Jesus was a teacher.

Scholars generally agree that Mark does not emphasize Jesus as a teacher however Jesus clearly teaches in the gospel and in at least one scene acts like a teacher—he sits with his disciples on the Mount of Olives, the classic posture of a Jewish teacher.[1] The very early disciples and believers struggled more with his role as divine or human savior. In Paul's letters, Jesus' role in the salvation of the Jews and eventually Gentiles was the central focus. Twenty years later Matthew and then Luke introduced the idea of Jesus as teacher. In essence, the modern understanding of Jesus as teacher had yet to be established in the early days of Christianity. Mark's reticence may indicate that he was caught in between the two theologies.

Still, Mark's Jesus has disciples and this implies that he was a teacher of some merit. The fact that crowds followed Jesus everywhere—a common

---

1. Culpepper, *Mark*, 447.

motif in Mark—indicates that Mark understood Jesus was an effective teacher. So, how would Mark's readers understand Jesus as a teacher? There are two contexts in which to answer this: the Greco-Roman and the Jewish cultural context.

The Greco-Roman world was filled with itinerant teachers and philosophers. Major philosophies were taught and lived out by students and admirers of traveling itinerants and local gurus. The teachings of the great Greek philosophers Socrates, Plato, and Aristotle were well-known and well-read. Other teachers emerged as well. Epicureanism, Stoicism, and Cynicism were the major branches of numerous schools and philosophies that were studied and practiced. Teachers in the Greco-Roman world generally learned their lessons from a mentor. The best example of this is that of Plato who learned from Socrates. Students attached themselves to teachers or wandering peripatetic educators. They became disciples who eventually left the fold of their teacher and then continued the lessons learned. Some, however, as in the case of Aristotle, criticized the conclusions of his mentor Plato. Roman pagan readers who perused through or heard Mark's story of Jesus for the first time would have easily seen the connection of Jesus as wandering philosopher. One question that might have arisen is, who was Jesus' teacher?

The same scenario is found in the Judaism of Jesus' day. Students gravitated to a rabbi, a teacher of the Law. Several rabbis of excellent repute were known in the first century: Shammai and Gamaliel who was the grandson of another famous rabbi, Hillel. In Acts 5:33–42 we find a story that sheds light on both Gamaliel and the perception of Jesus and his students. The apostles were preaching in the Temple courts when they were arrested by the high priests. The prisoners miraculously escaped from jail that night and continued their preaching the next day. A very puzzled captain and his jailers arrested them again and brought them to the Sanhedrin. Peter preached to the Sanhedrin who became furious about his interpretation of Jesus' resurrection. Gamaliel, a much-respected Pharisee then reminds the council that two other men, Theudas and Judas, also came proclaiming a new teaching. Theudas had four hundred followers who, after he was killed, dispersed and the movement died away. Likewise, Judas led a band of followers who, after he was killed, also disbanded. Ever the wise sage, Gamaliel counseled that the Sanhedrin should refrain from persecuting Peter and the other apostles. " . . . but if it is of God, you will not be able to overthrow it" (v. 39, NRSV). The author of Acts later informs his readers that Paul was trained under Gamaliel (22:3).

While there are some historical problems with this story as presented in Acts[2] this episode still demonstrates that, early in the life of the Christians, when they had not yet separated from Judaism, Jesus could have been dismissed by many Jews as just another upstart revolutionary with a band of followers who ran away after he died. Mark's Jewish readers would have been thoroughly familiar with that scenario. Thus, thirty years after Jesus' death and, with no immanent return of Jesus in sight, the question had to be raised: was he just another Theudas or Judas? Another way to put it is, could Mark's story of Jesus persuade Jewish readers that Jesus was not a failure?

In the opening chapter of Mark Jesus appears out of nowhere and is baptized by John the Baptizer in the Jordan River. This very act could mean only two things to the first-century mind: Jesus was an initiate into a religious cult (thus the reason for the baptism) and/or he was a disciple of John the Baptizer. Thus, other questions arise for the reader. Why John the Baptizer? Why not another teacher, say, a respected rabbi? Why not an itinerant philosopher? Did Jesus adhere to John's teachings or did he change them to his way of thinking? Did Jesus model his teaching and select his disciples based on John's teaching style and requirements for discipleship? What exactly did Jesus teach? How did people respond?

There were numerous opportunities to "study" under a rabbi in Jesus' day. Today many Christians assume that a Jew would study within one basic curriculum, the Torah. What is not so well known is that the Judaism of Jesus' day had many schools of thought that interpreted the Torah in different ways. There were several Jewish philosophies proffered by various rabbis who sought the Jews' attention. It was mentioned in a previous chapter that there may have been at least twelve different sects within Judaism at this time and Reza Aslan points out that, according to the Jewish historian Josephus, there were twenty four "fractious Jewish sects in and around Jerusalem."[3] All fought for the allegiance of the Jews. Some of these are well known to students of the Bible.

Sadducees, aristocratic, land-owning people who adopted and adapted to the Roman culture, were conservative in their thought and wise enough to realize that Jews could either fight against the Roman oppressors

---

2. Chance, *Acts*, 96.
3. Aslan, *Zealot*, 21.

or learn to adapt their religion and culture to the Roman way of life. They chose the latter. They supported extravagant Temple worship and most of the aristocratic chief priests in charge of the sacrifices were Sadducees. The Sadducees believed in the primacy of the Torah, the first five books of the Jewish scriptures, but they did not believe in the resurrection.

The Pharisees were different. They consisted of sincere and devout men of various classes, status and education. They believed that the Law of Moses was passed down through the Torah, as did the Sadducees, but they also believed in an oral tradition of Mosaic laws said to be passed down through the generations. They believed in the afterlife and were generally respected for their adherence to the Laws of Moses, both written and oral. And while they tolerated the Roman occupation, they refused to back down from their religious traditions.

Two of the divisions of Judaism were brigands. Violent political protests occasioned by such groups erupted intermittently in the land of the Jews. A group called the Zealots was more an amalgam of several militaristic defenders of the Jewish way of life. They were willing to fight against the Roman occupiers to regain Jerusalem for God and the Jews. They adopted guerilla warfare tactics somewhat like those witnessed in the Middle East today. They hounded Roman soldiers and preached a dangerous patriotism that threatened the existence of Judaism in the Roman world. A more treacherous group of subversives were the Sicarii, conspiratorial assassinators who moved about in mobs during festivals and murdered innocent people to create panic or who kidnapped citizens and held them for ransom. All of these violent sects were destroyed by the Romans. Interestingly, one of Jesus' disciples, Simon (not Peter) was known as a Zealot and this could mean either he was zealous for the Law or that he was a member of the insurrectionary Zealots. Interestingly, one possible interpretation of Judas' other name of Iscariot means "false one," taken from the word sicarii, which means "assassin."[4]

The Essenes were an ascetic group who lived in the village of Qumran near the Jordan River. They believed in celibacy and ritual washings and looked forward to an apocalyptic day of tribulation where God would redeem the Jews from the oppressive Romans. They felt that the Pharisees were not devout enough and that the Sadducees were corrupt individuals who did not administer the Temple in accordance with the laws of God.

---

4. Culpepper, *Mark*, 111.

There were also various apocalyptic groups of Jews who preached a call to faith, not arms, for a divine war. They believed that God would intervene in a miraculous way to destroy the Romans. Theudas was one such apocalyptic revolutionary. His followers gathered on the Mount of Olives just east of Jerusalem where he proclaimed that God would destroy the walls of Jerusalem. Jesus' prediction of a similar fate for the Temple in Mark 13:1–2 and the following discussion between Jesus and the disciples on the Mount of Olives echoes this prophetic act. This passage, along with the meeting of Jesus with the disciples on the Mount of Olives in chapter 14, both echo the apocalyptic chapters of Zechariah 12–14.[5] Did Jesus see himself and his movement as a fulfillment of Zechariah's prophecy? With this background, Jesus could have been seen as a Jewish, apocalyptic insurrectionary.

Expectations of prophets also permeated the Jewish culture of Jesus' time. Numerous prophetic figures offered their visions of things to come and most proved disappointing to the Jews. Thus there emerged a longing for the prophets of old like the ones in the Jewish scriptures. While the later Church rejected the appellation of prophet to Jesus the very early believers, including the original disciples, debated whether Jesus was a prophet (Mark 8:28).[6]

All of this to say that, during Jesus' life and following his death there was much room for debate and thus doubts concerning Jesus' title. An upstart Jew traveling around preaching and teaching a new way of life was quite common. Jesus' teachings may have been seen as just another rival eschatology that challenged the Roman and Jewish dominance of Jerusalem and called into question the importance of the Temple sacrifices. In one way or another, Jesus, as depicted in the Gospels, fit into many if not all of these categories. For those Romans who lived outside of the Jewish religion, Jesus could easily be seen as a peripatetic teacher or even a dangerous political revolutionary. How do Christians of today view Jesus? Zealot? Messiah? Christ? Great philosopher? Wise sage? The answer might be "yes" to one or more of these appellations depending on one's particular approach and understanding of Jesus.

One upstart Jew was John who baptized followers in the Jordan River. According to New Testament scholar Marcus Borg, John was an

---

5. Wright, "The Mission," 33–43; Wylen, *Jews*, 162–167; Culpepper, *Mark*, 447, 497.
6. Wylen, *Jews*, 167–169.

"anti-establishment figure."[7] He decried the place of the Temple in Jerusalem and his anti-temple rhetoric inflamed the Jewish establishment which emphasized that Jews of all stripes had to make sacrifices in Jerusalem in the temple for forgiveness of their sins. This establishment catered to the lifestyles of the wealthy who could afford the journey to Jerusalem and the often high cost of the sacrificial animals. They ignored the plight of the poor who had to choose which festivals they could attend, if any, based on family economics. In essence, the poor lived a life of spiritual impurity until they could afford another trip to Jerusalem. John the Baptizer's railings against this established aristocratic religion echoed those of the Old Testament prophets who also fought against the influence and opulence of the Temple of Solomon. John also dared to openly criticize Herod Antipas, the ruler of the region in Jesus' time. His actions and rhetoric were exactly like that of the brigand Theudas and a man from Egypt who threatened to make the walls of Jerusalem fall.[8] For this vitriolic he was eventually arrested and killed. In other words, he was seen as a threat to both the Roman and Jewish establishment. His disciples would have been viewed similarly.

The Temple sacrifices were the acceptable rituals for absolution of sins and the performance of them constituted repentance so John's radical baptism for the forgiveness of sins threatened the very core (and economy!) of Judaism. The way Mark introduces John the Baptist immediately raises questions for the Jewish reader (Mark 1:4–8). He is preaching a baptism of repentance for the forgiveness of sins. William Lane asserts that, while baptism might have been part of the Jewish initiation rites or a ritual practiced at the Qumran community and in the Mystery Religions, John's "wholly novel" baptism "appears rather as a unique activity of this prophet."[9] But to Mark's readers such an act was not unique. Jews in the area of Palestine would be familiar with the baptismal rituals of the Essenes. In the Greco-Roman world of the Mediterranean philosophers and religious leaders often used rituals to initiate an adept into the group of followers. Sometimes these rituals involved what might be called a baptism. In Jesus' time some religious groups, called Mystery Cults, incorporated baptisms in their initiatory rituals for new members. The baptism was symbolic of a cleansing from a past life and an emergence into a new life. In Mark the audience

---

7. Borg, *Jesus*, 118 and "Jesus," 59.
8. *Interpreter's Dictionary of the Bible*, Vol. 3, 345.
9. Lane, *Mark*, 49.

Jesus as Teacher

learns that many of John's followers were baptized by this charismatic wild man who lived in the desert.

People from everywhere, probably a hyperbolic note from Mark, came to see and hear and, once convicted of their sins and receptive to his sermons, repent and be baptized by him. Mark's mention of a sizeable crowd implies that John commanded quite a following and that at least some of Mark's readers would have understood that the Romans and the Jews would have looked suspiciously at this movement. According to Josephus, it was feared that John was starting a mass revolt, an insurrection, and this would threaten the rule of Rome. Even Roman soldiers were converting![10] If he was just another desert ascetic Jewish philosopher then he might be ignored. If he indeed was questioning the efficacy of the Temple, then he threatened the aristocratic leadership of Jerusalem that was centered on the importance of the Temple and also accommodated the Roman political, social, and cultural ways of life. This would cause a riot in the Jerusalem community which would bring in the Roman guards to quell the uprising. Would John's mass appeal bring down the wrath of the Romans upon the Jews? To boil it all down, John's preaching was dangerous and his followers were to be watched carefully.

John, like many of the prophets in Jesus' day, predicted that one was coming who was greater than he. Mark provides no more information on this expected person. Thus, Jews would have interpreted John's prophecy as one of many that awaited the return of a great prophet or even a messiah. This person would baptize with a Holy Spirit as opposed to John's baptism in the waters of the Jordan. Presumably Mark interprets this to mean Jesus because he is mentioned in the very next paragraph.

With this in mind, the mid-first century reader of Mark would have made the association that Jesus, along with other believers, became a disciple of John the Baptist. Indeed, Borg, citing Matthew 11:3 and Luke 7:19, asserts that John probably did not immediately recognize Jesus as the One who was coming when he baptized him in the Jordan. In these two passages John sends emissaries to inquire whether Jesus is the one to come. Morna Hooker, in her commentary on Mark, states emphatically "there is no hint that John recognized Jesus as the one whose coming he had proclaimed." Thus, for Mark at this early point in his narrative, Jesus is simply another person who comes to the Jordan River in the wilderness to hear the

10. Aslan, *Zealot*, 82.

incendiary preaching of this prophet. The reader would understand then that Jesus heard the message of John, was convicted of his sins or, as noted by Hooker, desired to be a part of a new and exciting Israel, and therefore submitted to the initiatory baptism centered on repentance. If Jesus was just another man, as Mark often suggests throughout his book, then he needed to be baptized before beginning his own ministry. This baptism would, according to Hugh Anderson, then "be accompanied by a radical transformation of life in which men are opened up to the grace of God that liberated from past sin . . . "[11]

If this is so, then the first readers of Mark faced yet another point to consider. Mark presents John the Baptizer as one who preaches a baptism of repentance for forgiveness of sins. Today this phrase presents a problem. If, according to modern Christian theology, Jesus was the Son of God, as in he *was* God, then he did not need to be baptized. But, this theological worry is based on the knowledge of the other Gospels and later theological arguments. These theological problems were apparently irrelevant for Mark and/or Mark's readers who, unlike current Christian believers, did not have the advantage of centuries of theological debates and denominational dictums.

An astute reader of Mark today can raise a quibble here: Mark 1:1 proclaims Jesus as Son of God, as translations word it today, but, as we have seen, the first readers of Mark could have understood this as just another son of a god. Since men were sometimes proclaimed sons of gods in Roman society, the title was not that revelatory for the reader. As we noted in a previous chapter, there is still some doubt about whether Mark really meant to portray Jesus as *the* Son of God. If this is true, then for Mark, the idea of a sinless Jesus was not necessary for his readers at all. He, like all of the other disciples of John the Baptizer, would be baptized for repentance and forgiveness of their sins. This should be of some comfort and a model for faith for today's believers.

The theological problem was quite embarrassing for later writers. Why would Jesus, the sinless sacrificial lamb, be baptized for repenting of his sins in order to receive forgiveness? Matthew, in chapter 3:13–14 changes Mark's rendering so that Jesus explains to John that the baptism must be administered as an example for others. Luke 3:21–22 downplays the baptism and the gospel of John does not even record the incident. So, why did Mark describe the episode this way? An obvious answer would be,

---

11. Borg, *Jesus*, 120; Hooker, *Mark*, 45; Anderson, *Mark*, 70.

Jesus as Teacher

since Mark received his material from Peter, the disciple closest to Jesus, then that was the way it happened before Christian theologians such as Matthew noticed the "problem" and changed the interpretation.

Since Jesus was baptized as just another convert of John's demanding preaching, what did this signify? Several meanings are important. First, Jesus' baptism of repentance places him firmly within the Pharisaic traditions of the Judaism of his day. The Pharisees strongly emphasized repentance but it was part of a greater theology. Doing God's will consisted of two parts: observance of the law that must be combined with the higher purpose of the law. In other words, what is the intent of the law? As presented in Mark's gospel, Jesus consistently pointed out that the Jewish leaders of his day were preoccupied with observance of the law to the extent that they had forgotten the meaning of the law. Rabbi Stephen M. Wylen puts it very succinctly: "The consistent point of Jesus' message is that the outward observance of the law should be matched by an inner turning to God."[12]

Another meaning is that the baptism indicated discipleship. In Mark 1:7–8 John the Baptizer proclaims that "one is coming after him." "Coming after" is a technical phrase for a student (disciple) of scribes and rabbis.[13] A disciple was a student of a master. The student, out of respect, would not begin teaching until his master died or ended his teaching career. This is the case with Jesus according to Mark who notes that it was only *after* John was arrested that Jesus began preaching repentance and belief in the gospel. Interestingly, Jesus deviated from his mentor's teaching because he did not require baptism for his disciples (1:14–15) and his disciples, according to Mark, did not baptize either. Indeed, baptism in the gospel of Mark, except for the incident with John the Baptizer, seems to be a spiritual idea, not an act performed with water, as seen in Mark 1:8 and 10:38–39. This is a fulfillment of John the Baptizer's declaration of one who was coming who would baptize in the spirit.

According to N.T. Wright, Jesus' preaching of repentance and belief meant to give up one's typical understanding of the coming kingdom of God and instead believe in Jesus' interpretation of the Kingdom. Along with this, repentance and forgiveness were central tenets of Temple faith and ritual. But, when Jesus called for repentance and forgiveness he was calling his followers to forsake the Temple and instead come to him for forgiveness. This call for repentance and baptism was an early hallmark of

---

12. Wylen, *Jews*, 94.
13. Lane, *Mark*, 52.

Christianity. It is a major component of Paul's preaching as Roetzel points out. It was tantamount to calling for all Catholics to forget the Vatican and instead look to a renegade female priest for forgiveness and absolution. Such radical teachings only meant that Jesus was just another leader of just another sect within an already divided Judaism.[14]

By all accounts, Jesus, according to Mark's story, is a disciple of John the Baptist who takes his masters' dangerous teaching and tweaks it into a new philosophy of his own. Since John was a political and religious revolutionary, Jesus, following in his teacher's footsteps, would be considered dangerous too. Since John prophetically preached crisis, judgment, and renewal, then Jesus would supposedly do likewise. And, to go about teaching and proclaiming such propaganda was no different than many other self-proclaimed teachers of the time. Socrates was put to death because he posed a threat for innocent listeners and he might lead people astray from the Greco-Roman ways of life. Other Jewish teachers had seen their teachings quashed and their followers dispersed as well. Indeed, this is exactly what happened to Jesus and his followers at the end of the gospel. For Mark's readers, this introduction of Jesus would not have raised much attention at all. In fact, it might have led some to raise an eyebrow and wonder with a sigh, "Again? Best to stay away from this guy!" But, given this possible (mis?) understanding of Jesus, why did people flock to him?

Jesus the Jewish Teacher/Philosopher sets out to teach his new ideas and, like any teacher, he needed his own disciples (Mark 1:16–20). He sees Simon (later named Peter) and Andrew fishing in the Sea of Galilee and calls out, "come after me." His call to come after him means that he is a master, a rabbi, who has disciples. Along with this, however, Jesus tells them that they will be become "fishers of men." D. E. Nineham points out that this phrase in both Jewish and Greek contexts has a negative meaning. "Catching" men foretold of harmful activities.[15] What did this mean to Mark's readers? Quite possibly it meant that these two men (and the other disciples?) would be subjected to harsh scrutiny and even death. In Mark 3 Jesus calls more men to be disciples yet he does not ask them to follow him. Thus, for Mark and the early church, the first four disciples called were destined for a harmful fate. With this cultural baggage in mind, who

---

14. Wright, "Mission," 39–46; Roetzel, *Paul*, 66.
15. Nineham, *Mark*, 72.

Jesus as Teacher

of Mark's readers and listeners would want to follow in the footsteps of the first disciples?

So, who were these disciples?

The three disciples closest to Jesus are named first in Mark's list in chapter 3 and, significantly, they are given new names as well. Name changes were important in Jewish culture generally indicating some unique purpose. Simon is the first one mentioned. He was a fisherman, most likely one of small means. His name was changed to Peter. According to Matthew, Peter, "the Rock," would eventually be the rock upon which the church was built but Mark does not mention this at all. If anything, in the gospel of Mark Peter seems to be the rock that trips up Jesus and thus impedes his teacher's ministry. When Jesus announced he had to undergo rejection and death by the hands of Jewish religious leaders Peter took him aside and rebuked him (Mark 8:31–33). Jesus returned the rebuke: "Get behind me, Satan." In the Hebrew scriptures Satan was the one who, like a loose paving stone, trips up people (see Job 1–2 and Zech 3:1–2). Despite his bungling Peter is the main disciple in Mark's book yet he is portrayed as one who forsakes Jesus in order to save his own skin. For example, while Jesus is being tried by the Jewish leaders Peter denies knowing him (14:66–72).

The brothers James and John were fisherman as well but, since they used other laborers, they were probably of a higher class than Peter and Andrew. James and John were called the Sons of Thunder. Scholars are divided as to what the title means but it may signify that they would become thundering witnesses of the gospel.[16] As portrayed in the gospel of Mark, the two brothers were ladder climbers, to use the modern phrase, and this may signify a propensity to see themselves in a higher class status. In their eyes the Kingdom of God was a literal kingdom with a palace that would no doubt replace the sprawling palaces of the Roman emperors. Envisioning a palace and a throne they asked Jesus if they could sit on the right and left sides of his throne (10:35–45). To the Romans, this teaching of a new kingdom with a new palace was troubling.

Andrew, Simon's brother, was a fisherman as well. Not much is known about him and his role in the Gospel of Mark is minimal. The other disciples are noted—Philip, Bartholomew, Matthew, Thomas, James son of Alpheus, Thaddaeus, Simon the Zealot, and Judas who would hand over Jesus to the authorities. In Mark 3:13–14 Jesus calls Levi to follow him but he is not named in the following list of disciples. From this list, blue collar,

---

16. Culpepper, *Mark*, 109.

middle class, public worker, and Zealot, as well as traitor and others are all combined into one ragtag group. Again, the reader of Mark would have raised questions about these commoners. None came from a respected class or group of workers.

When Jesus commissioned them to go out and preach (Mark 6) he gave them strict orders about what to wear and take with them. They could take nothing but a staff, sandals, no bread, no bag, no money in their belts, and no second tunic. Mark's readers and audience would have recognized this dress, or lack thereof, because it was similar to that of the Greek philosophical Cynics who were quite prevalent in Jesus' day.[17] Therefore, this type of person was not new to people in Mark's audience. Paul railed against preachers and teachers whose lack of income and dependence upon those who lived in homes and offered food for strangers often duped people into a dangerous acceptance of incorrect doctrines. His vituperations indicate that some teachers were suspect in the first century and one conclusion from this is that Jesus and his followers could have been seen in the same way. So, once again, Mark's readers, familiar with the Cynics or false teachers and probably with Paul's letters or reputation, could easily confuse Jesus and his disciples with yet another band of counter-cultural followers who challenged the political status quo as well as social norms and values.

The twelve disciples listed in Mark's gospel "are portrayed as moving from a lack of understanding to complete failure" according to Culpepper.[18] If Peter taught Mark about Jesus' ministry and the role of the disciples then this characterization of them is puzzling unless Mark is insinuating that Peter, James and John were associated with the Jewish-Christian Temple leaders in Jerusalem and were therefore being condemned by both John the Baptizer and his student, Jesus.

Throughout Mark's gospel Jesus teaches in parables, short earthy stories taken from everyday life. This is rather curious. One would expect a Jew, especially one seen as a rabbi, to cite examples from the Torah or the Prophets or even the Writings (the three divisions of the Jewish scripture). Thus it is interesting that Jesus teaches from the Law of Moses, the Prophets, and the Pharisaic oral traditions mostly when confronted by the Jewish leaders and rabbis. For example, the Pharisees and some teachers of the Law come from Jerusalem and question why Jesus' disciples ignored the oral laws about washing one's hands before eating a meal (7:1–13). The

---

17. Ibid., 194–195.
18. Ibid., 112.

Jewish readers of Mark's gospel would have raised many eyebrows. If Jesus was really associated with Judaism, then why didn't he teach and practice the Law? One logical answer for the Jewish reader was that he was not associated with Judaism proper, thus he was not the long-awaited Messiah. As for Gentiles, why would an itinerant philosopher teach from the Jewish scriptures?

There may be more to this episode, however, but the parallel is a bit of a stretch. John Dominic Crossan and Jonathan L. Reed point out that ritual bathing was one way that Jews could retain their religious identity without selling out to the Roman culture and lifestyle. In other words, it was a form of passive resistance and was a silent statement of Jewish identity. Numerous Jewish houses in the areas beyond Jerusalem contained baths and a new style of stoneware was used by Jews to set themselves apart from the more expensive ware used by Romans and the elite Jews who strove to emulate them. In essence, ritual bathing, including hand washing, was a form of resistance that Jews could perform secretly and quietly to retain their religious identity without drawing a suspicious eye from the Romans.[19] With this in mind, when Jesus and his disciples refused to ritually wash their hands before meals, were they breaking from Jewish solidarity by ignoring such rules? If so, what would readers of Mark's gospel think of such actions? Would they indicate that Jesus' disciples were opposed to a grass roots Jewish protest against Rome? Or, worse, would the disciples be viewed as just secularists who left behind antiquated Jewish superstitions and lived a more Greco-Roman philosophical school approach?

In another episode the disciples miss the point of Jesus' instruction that it is not what goes into a person that is bad but what comes out of him. This meant that the Jewish food laws, as enumerated in the Law of Moses, were now proclaimed null and void by Jesus. The disciples, nearly all devout Jews, do not understand. How can Jesus just ignore the revered food proscriptions in the Law of Moses? As the NIV translates it, Jesus responds to their confusion with an oblique, "Are you so dull?" (7:14–19). What did he mean by this embarrassing accusation?

Again and again Mark depicts the disciples as utterly clueless concerning what Jesus was teaching. After seeing him walk on water at night their hearts are hardened (6:52). They do not understand the import of this stupendous act. After Jesus feeds four thousand people, a feat that only a god could perform, he remarks about the leaven of the Pharisees. The

---

19. Crossan and Reed, *Excavating Jesus*, 207–213.

disciples do not understand and Jesus frustratingly asks why. They have eyes but don't see, ears but don't hear. While others around Jesus see and hear and are healed, the disciples still do not understand who Jesus is. If Jesus' disciples don't understand, then what does this say about them or, for that matter, about their teacher? Did this mean that the Jews would not understand the teachings of Jesus but the Gentiles would? If so, then were Jesus' teachings more understood as those of Greco-Roman philosophers than that of wandering Jewish teachers? For the modern reader of Jesus the miracles may pose a problem but the teachings of Jesus are to be followed. In essence, like the first disciples, one can doubt or completely misunderstand and yet still remain a faithful disciple.

In Mark, preaching was important for Jesus, taking precedence over healing and exorcism. This is apparent in the very first section of healing stories. In Mark 1:21–34 Jesus heals many and his fame spreads quickly. But in the night Jesus steals away to a lonely place. He is weary of the healing and when his disciples find him they exclaim that the people want him, as in they want to see and experience more miracles. Jesus, however, explains that he needs to move on to preach. "That is why I have come" (v. 38 NIV). Teaching, preaching, is the main task for Jesus.

What did Jesus preach? Borg points out that, in general, Jesus preached an alternative wisdom. It was noted in the chapter on Family that the family taught the conventional wisdom of the day. Since Jesus obviously deviated from his family, then it could be expected of him to preach an alternative to his family's Jewish norms. Borg concludes that Jesus preached a subversive and alternative wisdom.[20]

Crossan and Reed offer a similar assessment. Portraying Jesus as a peasant, they assert that he preached an alternative to the Imperial kingdom of Rome and the theocratic kingdom of first-century Judaism. Jesus preached against the urban elites, which included both Romans and Jews, and instead proclaimed the simpler values of the Galilean peasant classes as part of a new kingdom of God. Crossan and Reed argue that Jesus preached a *nonviolent* resistance against the elitist culture and values of Jews and Romans. For the Jewish readers of Mark and the Greco-Roman readers, Jesus as presented in Mark could be easily viewed as a revolutionary disciple of a revolutionary teacher. In other words, given the circumstances

---

20. Borg, "Jesus," 68.

of Mark's readers in the first century, it would be easy to picture Jesus as a troublemaker.[21]

As was customary in those days, a traveling Jewish teacher attended a synagogue on the Sabbath and was offered the opportunity to read from the Torah and then teach or preach about the passage read. According to Mark, Jesus taught as one with authority (Mark 1:22) whereas the teachers of the Law did not. Lane points out that this caused "alarm" among his hearers and this supports Borg's claim above that Jesus' teachings were quite contrary to accepted Jewish teachings, perhaps dangerously so. Culpepper notes that for Mark teaching and preaching are the same and the authority was manifest in his healing of the possessed man. The Jews of Jesus' day were used to hearing recitations that were memorized by students who then passed them on to their students. Just as many people today are tired of memorized and worn theologies and aphorisms, the people of Jesus' day were no doubt bored with the typical Jewish style of preaching as well.[22] This exciting and provocative Jesus was apparently a breath of fresh air. Might it take a new and invigorating perception of Jesus to stir today's believers into action?

A modern-day example will illustrate this. In American religion, nineteenth-century texts of preachers reveal they often used trite and predictable phrases to tackle theological issues of their day. This is especially true when referring to Catholics, who were scorned by preachers even into the twentieth century. When I corrected my generally conservative students' papers or heard their comments in class I repeatedly noticed these same phrases. Their preachers were passing on an oral tradition that began at least a century before them. Those in the pew were not being challenged with new interpretations of contemporary theologies but instead were hearing worn out messages from a time long ago passed down orally through the ages. Likewise, Jesus' authority came not in rehashing the same old scriptures in the same manner that had stifled and stymied the Judaism of his day. And in order to do this Jesus left behind the stale scriptures and lessons of old and taught with refreshing short stories and sayings. In other words, he taught in the vernacular of the people, not the theological babble of the teachers.

Early in Mark's rendition of the story of Jesus a series of troubling teachings are encountered by the reader. In Mark 2–3:6 is a sequence of

21. Crossan and Reed, *Excavating Jesus*, 177–187.
22. Lane, *Mark*, 72; Culpepper, *Mark*, 54–55; Hooker, *Mark*, 63.

episodes where Jesus heals but also antagonizes the religious authorities. For example, while dining with "sinners and tax collectors," he is confronted by the Pharisees (the "teachers of the Law" Mark reminds us) and asked why he eats with such riffraff. Jesus points out that he came to heal the sick—those who, because of Jewish purity laws, were ignored by the Jews—not the healthy. Following along with the analogy, he notes that he came to help the sinners, not the righteous (2:17). At the same time, if Jesus was the long-awaited Messiah, he should be concerned about associating with power people, not underlings. Such teaching subverted the total scope of Pharisaic interpretation.

Likewise, when the Pharisees and John the Baptizer's disciples were fasting, Jesus' followers were not. For Jesus, fasts are part of the old traditions. He cites a proverb that one should not put new wine into old wineskins, that no one should sew a new scrap onto an old garment. In both cases the new will destroy the old. The analogy is simple but also subversively obscure: the new teachings of Jesus cannot be patched onto the old Judaism (2:18–22). Culpepper notes that, for Mark, these sayings denoted the break of Gentile Christianity from the stifling effects of Jewish Christianity and Hooker points out that in these sayings Jesus broke away from John the Baptizer's Jewish prophetic preaching of repentance.[23] The rabbi says the old Jewish traditions are dead and the disciple was now the teacher. And, Jesus' interpretations could not be contained in the old skins and the old garments of Judaism.

Within this section a contradiction arises. Jesus seems to teach that the old Judaism cannot contain his new teaching and therefore must be jettisoned. But, in chapter 1:40–45, he also tells a healed leper to go and offer the proper sacrifices, thus retaining the rituals of Judaism. Which is it? Jesus' teachings were often times very confusing, and his followers and Mark's readers surely caught this conundrum. This can be of help to the readers of Mark today. Many want to retain the old teachings and ethics but want to jettison the old understandings and theologies of Jesus in light of new discoveries about him.

Indeed, the Gentiles of Jesus' day were probably used to it. In the Greek philosophical traditions dogmatic opinions were not part of the curriculum. Socrates tailored his teachings to his varying students and encouraged doubt, not slavish adherence to specific doctrines and facts. As Socrates' philosophies filtered down through Plato to Aristotle the notion

---

23. Culpepper, *Mark*, 89; Hooker, *Mark*, 100.

Jesus as Teacher

of philosophy was not so much facts and knowledge as it was wisdom and a way of life. In the Greek world, dogma was not written in stone but it was changed in accordance with the educational level of the particular audience. These two concepts were still part of the philosophical tradition in Jesus' day. Philosophy, teaching, was about transformation, not theory.[24] There is Jewish precedent for this style of teaching as well. In Ecclesiastes 3:1–8 we see a confusing both/and theology that startlingly states sometimes war is necessary but at other times peace is to be pursued. One can certainly see that Ecclesiastes' assertion that there are times to plant and times to uproot makes sense. Ask any farmer about that one. The note that there are times to love and times to hate might be a bit troublesome but if we love the person and hate the crime then even that teaching makes sense. But war and peace are typically divisive issues. Today, many on the left argue vehemently for peace while a number of those on the right push for war, seemingly ignorant that one book in the Old Testament says both are possible given the right circumstances. It takes wisdom and discernment to determine which is to be pursued.

This notion is quite apparent in the next episode in Mark 2:23–27. When Jesus and his disciples walked through a field and plucked some of the grains, they were considered "working" according to the current beliefs. They were confronted by the ever-present Pharisees: "Why do your students work on the Sabbath?" Jesus was asked. Jesus acknowledged the importance of the Sabbath, but then pointed out that the Pharisees had forgotten the reason for the Sabbath. The Sabbath was made for humans and the Law was to be celebrated on this day. This was lifestyle. Instead, the Pharisees made the law subservient to the Sabbath. The means was more important than the ends. This was theory. Sabbath was made for man but the Pharisees had turned it around. Here Jesus combined the Jewish importance of the Sabbath with his own unique interpretation. The old and the new were compatible when combined correctly. At the same time, however, Jesus had previously said that old wineskins could not be repaired with a new patch of cloth. Which approach did he use?

In Mark 3:1–6 the Sabbath is once more the topic. Jesus is requested to heal someone on the Sabbath, which again constitutes work. The Pharisees await Jesus' decision: will he or won't he heal the man? Jesus asks the Pharisees a loaded question: Which is better to do on the Sabbath, evil or good? The Pharisees, already upset by Jesus, remain dumb and a very angry Jesus

24. Armstrong, *Case*, 58–74.

then heals the man. In the eyes of the Pharisees, Jesus has broken the restrictions concerning the Sabbath. Again, should theory trump praxis? Many people today, liberal and conservative, caught up in endless debates such as homosexuality or the connections of church and state, spend countless hours espousing scripture after scripture to support their particular theologies. Sabbaths are wasted by people in the church who self-righteously point fingers and cite scriptures while people who live in the state await the crumbs of Christians with hopeful, open hands.

The threat of Jesus' teachings is understood in a cryptic note at the end of this episode: the normally incompatible and mutually hostile factions of Pharisees and Herodians joined forces to kill Jesus. This is the most unlikely combination of groups in Jesus' day. The Pharisees were ardently opposed to any conformity to Roman culture and regulations and they despised King Herod. Their joint venture is highly improbable and Mark's readers, Gentile and Jewish, would have shaken their heads at this alliance. Why would these two groups plot to kill Jesus?

One answer comes in a later episode. In Mark 7 the scribes and Pharisees have come down from Jerusalem to spy on Jesus. What they see is troubling: Jesus and his disciples do not wash their hands before eating. As we have seen, this goes against the grains of Jewish ritual purity laws as interpreted by the Pharisees. But there may be more to this.

The answer is in the consequences of the teachings. To overthrow the norms and traditions of Judaism meant unstable times for Jews in Jerusalem. Jesus' questioning of the Law and the significance of the Temple would have undermined further the increasingly unstable Law of Judaism as practiced in Jerusalem. With this, the threat of such stability would have brought King Herod into a very unfavorable light in the eyes of the emperor who would no doubt have intervened if the Jews revolted. The Pharisees wanted to save Judaism and the Jewish Herodians wanted to save their beloved city. If both worked together it was win win. As Hooker explains, "bringing together two such groups to fight a common danger . . . indicates the strength of the hostility to Jesus."[25]

The same twisted connection was seen in the presidential election of 2004. The evangelical Pat Robertson forsook his Christian ideals of keeping the family together and living a responsible life when he backed candidate Rudy Guliani who had been divorced three times and, at the time, was under scrutiny for alleged mafia ties (later disproved). Why would Robertson

---

25. Hooker, *Mark*, 108.

go against his own teachings and do such a thing? It was in order to fight against the "foe" of liberalism. Rather than stand for his values, however, he sold his soul to the very person who exhibited the very opposite of what he believed. Likewise, the 2012 election. conservative Christians who consistently preach and teach that Mormonism is a dangerous cult backed Mormon Mit Romney for the Republican presidential race. In a surprising twist of hypocrisy, Romney was invited to speak at the conservative Liberty University, founded by Rev. Jerry Falwell who was adamantly against those of the Mormon faith. In other words, conservative Christians forsook their "laws" for political gain. Ditto the 2016 election where conservative Christians flocked around Republican candidate Donald Trump whose three marriages, profanity-laced vitriolic and billionaire lifestyle made a mockery of everything Jesus taught.

In Mark 4 the reader finds the major teaching section in the gospel. Teaching at what is probably the Sea of Galilee, Jesus inculcates with parables, short sayings, stories, and pithy witticisms, all of which are earthy and simple. Indeed, one looks hard to find Jesus using the Torah in his curriculum except when confronted by teachers from Jerusalem. Here he talks about a sower who sows seeds, some of which fell on good soil, some on a path, some in the rocks and some in the weeds. After the lesson, when he and the disciples are alone, he is asked about the parable. Jesus replies that he teaches in parables so that people *may not* understand (4:10–12). Imagine a first century reader confronting this verse. Why would Jesus do so? No wonder people of Mark's day were filled with doubts. If, as Mark says, Jesus taught so that people would not understand this might explain why there was so much misunderstanding about Jesus in the mid-first century. "We don't get it because Jesus never explained it." And, if the disciples could not understand the parables, then how could the rest of the believers? Hooker, who holds to the previous interpretation, suggests an interesting point that offers support to the notion of doubt in this time. By the time of Mark's writing the meaning of the parables may have been lost.[26] If the original meaning was lost, then the confusion concerning their interpretation might lead to doubts about their authenticity and their origins. "Why would Jesus teach in parables instead of interpreting the Laws of Moses like the Pharisees do? Maybe he was wrong to do so." Or, maybe he was another philosopher tossing out contradictory koans to make his students think just like that old sarcastic Socrates.

26. Ibid., 126.

When the twelve disciples ask Jesus in private what the story means Jesus replies that the secret of the kingdom of God has been given to those on the inside but those on the outside cannot understand it.

Culpepper points out that in verse 11 Jesus says, "To you has been given the secret of the kingdom of heaven." The word "secret" really means "mystery" and Mark's readers were aware of two groups of believers who used mysteries in their theology: the mystery religions that were abundant in Jesus' time, and the apocalyptic Jewish sects such as those at Qumran. The mystery cults in the time of Jesus emphasized baptism, secret knowledge, and eternal life but only those who were "inside" the pool of believers were taught this. All of these ideas—baptism, knowledge, eternal life—are emphasized in the teaching of Jesus and the early church.[27] Thus, the reader of Mark's gospel could have associated Jesus with a mystery cult leader or follower who taught his disciples in secret. Was this the reason that Jesus said he taught in parables?

The ascetics at the desert commune of Qumran also held somewhat secretive rituals and rules of life. Apocalyptic Jews and those at Qumran cited passages from Daniel where God reveals mysteries. So, was Jesus a teacher of Jewish Christians or, an ascetic Jewish apocalyptic believer, or one of the inductees in a wilderness Jewish sect? Since John the Baptizer was associated with the desert Mark's readers, who have already read that Jesus was a disciple of John, could very easily have come to this conclusion. Thus, Jesus would not have been a Christian leader, as some in the 60s CE would have thought, but instead would have been just another Jewish desert hermit.

When Matthew wrote his version of Jesus' life he changed the story somewhat to read that Jesus taught in parables so that people *would* understand (13:11–17). Since Mark's version was earlier, however, the early believers did not have this story to compare it with. Thus, for them, Jesus might appear as a somewhat cruel, enigmatic and confusing teacher. Did he intentionally mislead his disciples? What kind of teacher would do this? The philosophical traditions in the Greek culture, however, suggested that a very competent teacher would teach like this.

The in and out theme is obvious here but it makes no sense. In Mark, those on the "inside" hear the stories and their interpretations. For example, in the story just before the teaching episode, Jesus' family comes

27. Culpepper, *Mark*, 138–139.

to get him. Jesus is "inside" the house while his family is "outside." They don't understand his mission. Yet in chapter 4 the disciples are "in" but they do not comprehend. In chapter 14, Jesus is inside the house of the high priest answering the question, "Are you the Christ?" Peter is on the outside denying any connection with his beloved teacher. Indeed, as scholars have noted, throughout the gospel the disciples never fully understand Jesus and his teachings. Ironically, people on the outside such as the Syro-Phoenician woman and the father of the epileptic boy understand completely. It was mentioned earlier that the in/out theme may represent the rift between the Jerusalem leaders and the Gentile leaders. This is no doubt so but two forms of doubt enter the picture here.

The parables in chapter 4 teach that from a little comes much, and the common theme here seems to be that from a small sect of Judaism will emerge a great religious congregation. But why, some in Mark's time may ask, do we have so many Jews who have not come around to following Jesus? The answer is in the parables as selected by Mark: Jesus can only be understood by a few because he intentionally taught so that only a few could understand. Thus, doubts are understandable, if uncomfortable, because Jesus taught that way. So, those who doubt the person, message and life of Jesus, as plenty of Christians and Jews did, were actually in good stead. Doubt was exactly what Jesus wanted. The doubters were doing what Jesus taught. Might that be a lesson for some of today's doubters as well? The questions of doubt often lead to the answers of faith.

While scholars interpret this chapter as one of hope, in that the small church would eventually grow, there is another way to read it. In 4:33 Mark notes that Jesus taught in parables "as much as they could understand." And this, too, is the notion of small into great. Those who doubt because they do not understand will only grow as they begin to understand within the community. This echoes the teachings of Paul who noted that some believers young in the faith could only tolerate the milk of simple lessons. Those who were further along needed a real meal. Certainly those disgruntled with the "church lite" fare of today's churches would agree. Some "understand" quite a bit and thus need more than what they are getting on Sundays.

If, as Borg has noted, Jesus taught an alternative wisdom, then a look at brief teachings in the Greco-Roman world might shed light on his method and selection of teachings.[28]

---

28. Borg, "Jesus," 68.

One of the texts used in the schools of Jesus' day was Aesop's Fables. Aesop lived around the fifth century, BC, or possibly earlier. His brief stories featured short pithy sayings that are part of our wisdom today. "Don't count your chickens before they hatch," "honesty is the best policy," and "a wolf in sheep's clothing" are three of the more familiar ones. Aesop was known for his quick, stinging retorts to his detractors and his brief tales are full of wisdom and earthy observations. His stories, like the teachings of Jesus, were passed on orally before eventually being recorded. He was killed eventually by Delphians who deplored his lack of respect to the aristocracy and his irreverence in regards to the temple of Apollo.[29] As can be seen, Aesop's life story has several parallels to the life and teachings of Jesus whose criticism of the rich and the Temple led to his crucifixion. In one sense, the story-telling Jesus of Mark's gospel would have seemed quite familiar, especially if the biography of this character, *Life of Aesop*, was written around the same time as the book of Mark.[30]

After the disciples witness Jesus feed 5000 and then 4000 as well as walk on water and calm a storm, they still do not comprehend who and what Jesus is. In Mark 8 this question is addressed head on. While by themselves near Caesarea Philippi Jesus asks the disciples who people think he is. There is some confusion—might this also reflect the doubts of Mark's day?—that he is Elijah who has returned or John the Baptizer, or one of the prophets. When Jesus asks them who they think he is, Peter steps up and exclaims, "You are the Christ." In Jewish terms, "You are the Messiah."

For the Jews of Jesus' day this would only mean one thing: Jesus was the long-awaited Messiah who would ride a white horse brandishing a sword killing the Roman oppressors. This was a politically charged appellation and it could lead to trouble. Thus, Jesus' later instructions to tell no one about this. On the other hand, for Gentiles, the phrase implied a competitor with the Roman emperor. "Christ" here was the equivalent of Caesar. The phrase "Jesus Christ would have had the same connotations as the phrase Caesar Augustus."[31] Instead, Jesus teaches the disciples that he, the Messiah, would be persecuted, killed, and then rise from the dead after three days. This was the very opposite of what Peter just proclaimed. So Peter rebukes Jesus and his understanding of the Messiah's role. Jesus then rebukes Peter, pointing out that his interpretation gets in the way of Jesus

---

29. *Aesop's Fables*, xii–xvii.
30. Watson, "Life of Aesop," 699–716.
31. Culpepper, *Mark*, 270.

and his role as Messiah as he understands it. Peter needs to get back behind Jesus—recall the invitation to "Follow me"—where he belongs. In other words, the disciples still do not understand who and what Jesus really is.

Does this passage reflect what kinds of doubts existed among Mark's readers? Was Peter, and the other characters for that matter, a substitute for Mark' readers? David Rhoads and Donald Michie answer yes. As noted previously, questions abound in Mark's gospel, questions that are often open-ended that require the audience to provide their own answers.[32] What expectations of a Messiah did Mark's readers have? A list of possibilities is illuminating. Some could have believed that Jesus was indeed the Messiah who died for sins just as Paul had theologized. Others, caught up in the increasing tensions between the Romans and the Jews of Jerusalem, may have been disappointed that he was not the long-awaited warrior Messiah. Some may have believed that Jesus was indeed risen but since his eminent return was late, maybe they now had doubts and thus now thought he was just another Messiah wannabe. Early Christians searched the Jewish scriptures looking for other interpretations of a Messiah eventually settling on passages such as Isaiah 7, 9, and 11 and the Servant Songs in the later portions of Isaiah where the one who was coming would be meek and mild rather than militant. Was this new interpretation correct or just a vain attempt to prove Jesus was the one the prophets predicted long ago?

Jesus taught three times in the book of Mark that the Messiah would be rejected by the Jewish theologians and lawyers (those who studied the Law of Moses), persecuted and then killed only to rise again after three days (8:31; 9:31; 10:33–34). The three episodes produced misunderstanding and disbelief. The disciples simply could not fathom what Jesus their mentor was saying.

Part of the problem was that he did not toe the typical Jewish line of legal interpretation and cultural norms. He questioned the Pharisees who forsook the Law of Moses, which stated that children should take care of their parents, in order to enact their own oral law of Corban, the giving of money to God instead of to parents (7:1–13). Jesus embarrassed the Pharisees when he demonstrated that their oral laws displaced the much-revered written Law of Moses. At the same time, Jesus also nullified the food proscriptions in the Law of Moses when he declared that all foods were clean (7:14–23). So, was Jesus for or against the Laws of Moses? In the

---

32. Rhoads and Michie, *Mark as Story*, 51.

Greek philosophical traditions of his culture the answer was "yes" to both questions. But this again meant doubts concerning the teachings of Jesus.

Jesus, like Socrates long ago, was also sacrificed to save the Roman culture because he did not fit into the Roman world. In the Roman society where ambition supersedes humility, the cross was a sign of shame and defeat and children, especially girls, were tossed out like trash. Thus, Jesus' calls for one to take up a cross and follow him, his denial of James and John's request for a high place in the kingdom, and his insistence that children be respected were ludicrous. In Judaism, to be hung a cross meant one was cursed by God, children were subordinate to parents, and ambition was the hallmark of the Jewish aristocracy and priesthood who liked to dress in fine and costly robes (12:38–40). Again, Jesus' teachings deviated from the acceptable Jewish norm (8:34–38; 9:33–37 and 42; 10:13–16; 10:35–45).

Moses said that divorce was acceptable and in the Roman society it was nearly the norm but Jesus, perhaps inspired by Malachi 2:16, declared it wrong. Riches, a sign of God's blessing in the Jewish scriptures, and the sign of status in the Roman world, were incompatible with the humility required in Jesus' Kingdom of God. Those who forsook their families to follow Jesus deviated from the Jewish teachings where family was a symbol of God's grace and love and the Roman idyll that family was the basis of Roman life (10:1–12, 17–28, 29–31).[33] Was Jesus Jewish or not? Was he supplanting the Law of Moses or reinterpreting it for his time? If so, he was a threat to the Jewish religion and people. Was he a revolutionary who dared to ignore the Roman way of life? If so, he would disrupt the Roman culture and, therefore, must be dealt with accordingly. It is no wonder, then, that the Jewish leaders and the Roman administrators deemed Jesus a threat. Those who initially converted to Christianity now had a choice to make. Was this the kind of person they wanted to give their hearts and lives to? Was their allegiance to Jesus in vain? Might it be safer just to ignore him and go back to living a normal life as a Jew or a Roman? Doubts again.

It did not help that Jesus dumbfounded the Jewish leaders one more time. In Mark 12:1–12 Jesus relates the parable of the vintner and the gist of this story is that previously God had sent various messengers to the Jews only to have them treated shamefully or killed. The chief priests, teachers of the law, and the elders were incensed and wanted to arrest him. When the Pharisees and Herodians return to Jesus they try to trap him. "Should we pay taxes to Caesar or to God?" Jesus points out that a denarius has Caesar's

---

33. Goodman, *Rome and Jerusalem*, 205, 214, 216, 340–344.

Jesus as Teacher

picture on it, therefore the tax should go to Caesar. Likewise, the temple tax should go to the Temple (12:13–17). This answer would have caused the Pharisees and Herodians to fight amongst themselves since the Pharisees did not believe in paying taxes to Caesar and the Herodians would do anything, including paying taxes to Caesar, to support the Roman cause. It is obvious in this case that Jesus is a master teacher. He, like the wandering philosophers, confounds those who believe in absolutes. He confuses those who are hard-bound to their narrow beliefs. He aggravates those who are cock-sure they have all the answers. Many of today's Christians spout off absolutes in a similar cock-sure belief of narrow theologies. Yet some have moved into the realm of doubts concerning these teachings and perhaps they are closer to Jesus' methodology and teachings than most Christians. Doubts knock absolutes right out the door!

When the Sadducees ask a question about levirate marriage and the resurrection Jesus points out to the Sadducees that their scriptural connection between the two is incorrect (12:18–27). When a teacher of the law asks Jesus what the greatest commandment is Jesus answers in true Jewish theological fashion. "Hear, O Israel, the Lord our God, the Lord is one. Love the Lord your God with all your heart and with all your soul and with all your mind and with all your strength. The second is this: Love your neighbor as yourself" (12:29–31 NIV). Rather than citing endless laws in theological debate he instead lives by the succinct summation of the Law. In brief, Jesus does not promote the academic debates of his day. He lives out his teachings. After this sequence in Mark's story, nobody else tries to trap Jesus with trick questions (12:28–34).

The most perplexing teaching of Jesus is found in Mark 13, the passage called the Little Apocalypse. When his disciples fawn over the great Temple Jesus, in words that echo Theudas and the unnamed Egyptian, indicates that it will be torn down. For a religious society centered entirely around the Temple and its ritual sacrifices this was tantamount to treason and insurrection. Would the real Messiah do such a deed? Jesus then reveals that soon deceptive people will claim that they are Jesus. This passage may reveal the growing rift in the Christian community about who exactly Jesus was. As noted previously, there were many Christian churches that taught different views of Jesus. Thus it is easy to see how those who made such claims could be conceived as false Messiahs. Throughout chapter 13 Jesus says that families will be divided and wars and rumors of wars will be rampant. Is this what the Messiah was supposed to do? Doubts would arise here. A Jewish Messiah would lead the Jews against the Romans. Why would Jews fight their own people in a war against Rome? On the other hand, the Christian Messiah was like a reed that bent with the winds of war. Which Jesus was it, bellicose or peaceful? Is Jesus deliberately invoking the confusing opposites of Ecclesiastes?

It is this passage that may reveal when Mark was written and this date would help to understand better Mark's message and the doubts he is addressing (and causing!). Most scholars generally date Mark from 68–72 CE while more conservative scholars place his book in the mid-60s. Two important points help to date Mark but they also cloud up the conclusion. First, Jesus foretells that they (his disciples? his followers?) will be handed over to councils, flogged in synagogues, stand before governors and be arrested. According to Acts Paul arrested the errant group of Christians and shortly after Jesus' resurrection, synagogue leaders, knowing that those who believed in Jesus as the Messiah would cause mass riots among the Jewish faithful, initially hoped to quell the upstart sect. Thus, the Jewish councils no doubt persecuted the Jewish Christians as argued by Marta Sordi.[34] In the time of Nero, Christians were indeed persecuted. But the tribulations mentioned in this chapter also took place in the late 60s and early 70s. The readers of Mark's gospel would have recognized the persecutions noted here and perhaps were also the victims of such atrocities. Given the information above, they would have asked themselves if their beliefs were worth it.

Second, a cryptic phrase hints at a date but it is not that clear. In 13:14 we hear of the "abomination of desolation" standing where it/he does not belong. What is this? There are several interpretations. It may refer to prophetic passages in the book of Daniel (9:27; 11:31; and 12:11) which mention a future time when the altar of Zeus will be set up on the Temple altar. Readers of Mark might wonder if it was in their time. When Caligula reigned a similar event *nearly* took place in 40 CE. Was this what Mark was alluding to? Another interpretation is that a certain high priest of poor reputation named Phanni was inducted into the priesthood in 67–68 CE and maybe this was the "abomination." When Jerusalem was captured and destroyed in 70 CE the conqueror Titus set up his standards in the Temple.[35] So which of these events is Mark referring to? Most scholars think it refers to Titus, thus Mark might have been written after 70 CE.

34. Sordi, *Christians*, 12–13.
35. Hooker, *Mark*, 314; Culpepper, *Mark*, 459–461.

Jesus as Teacher

But, one note must be addressed here. Conservative scholars today argue that Mark was written before 70 CE. Most other scholars, based on the above evidence, suggest right around or just after 70 CE based on the question, How could Mark have known about the destruction of the Temple before it occurred? But, in the Old Testament, Jeremiah correctly predicted the destruction of the Temple. He was no doubt interpreting the very real possibilities of his day. Since the Babylonians were on the verge of capturing Jerusalem and, since the Babylonians destroyed other temples of their victims in the past, then it was only a matter of time before the Temple in Jerusalem would be destroyed. Culpepper reminds us that others had predicted the fall of the Temple and that even the Jewish writer Josephus, writing before the fall of Jerusalem in 70 CE had dreams about the Temple's demise.[36] Thus, to put it in simple terms, with tensions rising astronomically between Romans and Jews in the 60s, the very real possibility was that the Romans would destroy the Temple in a last move to destroy the pesky and ever troublesome Jews.

Whichever scenario, the readers of Mark would be full of doubts as well as fears. In Mark 13:21–23 Jesus predicts that false Christs would be rampant in the end times. But, how would the Christians know which Christ was authentic? Mark 13:26–27 states that Jesus would return after this cataclysmic event, but clearly Mark's readers knew that he had not returned just as he had not returned immediately after his resurrection. With the delayed Parousia, Mark's readers would scratch their heads when reading that Jesus said, "this generation will certainly not pass away until all these things have happened" (v. 30, NIV). Certainly "This generation" meant Peter, James and John who had already been martyred by 70 CE. How long must the believers wait? Was Jesus wrong? More doubts.

In the Greco-Roman world teachers were invited to dine in the homes of the wealthy and here we see the cultural symposium take place. Fine food and learned conversation were the fare for the evening. In Mark 14 Jesus appears to be a bit eccentric and perhaps even wealthy or at least catering to the wealthy. Did he approve of their lifestyle? Here in the home of Simon the Leper the teacher observes the Passover. Rabbi Stephen M. Wylen relates that the Passover celebrations at the time of Jesus were in the style of elaborate Greek banquets or symposiums, which were occasions for learning. The dinner was "formal and elegant and imitative of aristocracy" and

---

36. Culpepper, *Mark*, 447.

featured a "clever speech" by each guest as he reclined. Culpepper notes that there were often outsiders who came to watch the spectacle.[37] It is in this situation that Jesus is anointed by an unknown woman, most likely a spectator, but John 12 notes that she was Mary, sister of Martha and Lazarus. Tradition incorrectly names her as Mary Magdalene but in Mark she is simply unknown.[38] Interestingly, this could be Mary, mother of Mark, who we know was wealthy enough to have a house large enough to hold church gatherings according to Acts. She anoints Jesus on his head with costly perfume: such anointings were common at large feasts. Several issues arise here. First, Jesus is eating in the home of a leper, thus living out the fact that the Jewish rules of ritual impurity are not valid in the kingdom of God. Second, a woman has entered the all men's world of the dinner table. Third, the perfume is *extremely* expensive. The story relates that it cost a year's salary of a common worker—roughly $15,000 if we think of a person on minimum wage at about $7.50 an hour. Either the woman was wealthy, probably not the case since she was not named, or she was poor and giving up one of the few things she owned that was very valuable. Fourth, anointing was usually done to kings but especially to guests.

Those who witnessed the odd event complained that the perfume could have been sold and the money given to the poor and indeed it could. This is a curious lesson because the "poor" are rarely mentioned in Mark and when they are it is less a lesson in benevolence and more a lesson to humble the rich. Recall that in a previous chapter it was noted that the priests in Jerusalem were part of the elite, aristocratic class that was quite visible in Roman society. Important for this discussion here is that in the Roman culture the poor were seen as spendthrifts and debtors and were held in contempt because of their lack of money. In other words, they were people who could do better for themselves if they tried. Slaves were better off in every respect than the poor. In Mark 10 an obviously aristocratic Jewish man who has followed the Law is told to sell his wealth and give the proceeds to the poor *so that* he can gain access to heaven, not so that the poor may benefit. In Roman culture the rich were seen as virtuous and the poor as cheaters and liars. In giving away his money to the poor, a wealthy man would have been seen as one supporting the irreligious, who lost his social status and, in a society that felt the poor were supposed to do more to help

---

37. Wylen, *Jews*, 101–102; Culpepper, *Mark*, 484.

38. It is tempting to note a parallel here to the Greek symposia, where an exotic female dancer would entertain the guests.

Jesus as Teacher

themselves, he would be deemed as one who was wasting his money. The whole episode demonstrates that Jesus' teaching caused doubts among his readers because he turned the whole Greco-Roman, Jewish world upside down. Why should I worship one who would do such a dangerous thing?[39]

In Mark 12 the example of a widow giving a seemingly useless coin is an example for those of wealth to give more. Here the Roman idea of patronage is important. A patron was expected to give of his wealth (for those who have, more is expected, as the New Testament relates it) to families, businesses, and building projects. What would it say about a wealthy patron who let a poor widow out give him? From these two examples we can see that helping the poor in the Roman society of Jesus' time was not a high priority. In Rome itself, the place for whom Mark was probably written, there were no state sources or resources for the widows, orphans, disabled, and the sick, which are the very people that Jesus helped in Mark. The poor did piecemeal work to survive and were given bread and circus tickets and this was deemed enough.

With this background in mind, Mark 14 is an interesting lesson for the first century readers. Here is the passage on which Christians base their observance of the Lord's Supper. There is ample evidence that this supper took place in the home of a wealthy family because there is a large upstairs room where the banquet dinner was served. Only the homes of wealthy persons could have such rooms. In this time period there was an increase in ostentatious houses with elaborate and baths and statuary. This cultural trend was criticized but many Romans built such houses. Jerusalem was no stranger to such buildings however they were not of the scale as the houses of the Roman elites.[40]

There is another aspect of this domestic setting that deserves a segue. The supper indirectly resembles the ritual celebration of the god Pan. Such celebrations which featured the preparation and consumption of food were initially held outside in pastoral shrines or caves but Crossan and Reed note that by the time of Jesus these now watered down rituals were being taken indoors into large halls of elite homes. These rooms were decorated with bucolic themes and featured windows with panoramic views. Such rooms

---

39. The information about the poor comes from Jeffers, *Greco-Roman*, throughout. The conclusions are mine.

40. Goodman, *Rome and Jerusalem*, 300; Crossan and Reed, *Excavating Jesus*, 150–151.

were imitated by Jewish elites as well.[41] Some will balk at such a comparison but the Corinthians' celebration of the supper reveals the similarities with Roman lavish dinners and religious, even Bacchanalian/Dionysian rituals. Paul makes the connection with pagan festivals and the fact that the Corinthians were getting drunk while celebrating the Lord's Supper not to mention that the Corinthians were being invited to homes where meat, most likely sacrificed to idols, was being served. Only the wealthy could afford meat (1 Cor 10:14–22; 11:17–22).

Oddly enough, however, Jews in the Roman world styled their Passover dinner after Roman dinners. Jewish suppers and sumptuous feasts appear to have been attempts to emulate the Roman elite. Drinking wine was encouraged and Passover celebrations began with four glasses of wine. Diners reclined to their left, both women and men. "Jews believed that wine brought joy" and that those who took a vow of abstention went far beyond the necessities of religious devotion.[42] Recall that Jewish leaders often flaunted their status, thus copying the Roman culture. Thus, in Mark 14 Jesus may very well be reclining at such a banquet in a home that can seat more than just a poor family. This setting is important. Lane, commenting on Mark 2:15, where Jesus was reclining at table with sinners and outcasts, suggests that Jesus was the host at this banquet.[43] This is curious because Jesus and his disciples are said to have given up all for their ministry. How could a poor Jesus afford such a feast? Jeffers notes the poor often combined their resources to host a banquet but he also goes on to note that the rich often stayed with rich hosts while traveling.[44]

In sum, this scene in Mark 14 could have been interpreted initially by Mark's first readers, Jewish and pagan, as just another lavish banquet attended by Jesus and his disciples (or followers, the text is unclear) for public display.

The disciples are offended that the woman wastes the ointment on Jesus when it could have been sold and the money given to the poor. The celebration of Passover was not only a time of remembrance of the exodus but also a time when money was given to the poor. Jesus' retort to the ones who protest the woman's waste of oil is simply that the poor will always be with the citizens, but that sometimes one has to waste some extravagance

---

41. Crossan and Reed, *Excavating Jesus*, 136–142.
42. Goodman, *Rome and Jerusalem*, 293; Jeffers, *Greco-Roman*, 40.
43. Lane, *Mark*, 106.
44. Jeffers, *Greco-Roman*, 36, 40.

for God. This resembles the very notion of a patron who *could* give to the poor but instead gives to a greater cause. Scholars are quick to defend an obvious question: did Jesus not care about the poor? Their answers are not encouraging, however. Spontaneous favors for the poor are better than planned giving; Jesus was the epitome of the poor man thus the lavish anointing was justified; religious observance was less important than one's reaction to Jesus, thus the woman's anointing was far better than giving of alms to the poor. These theological defenses of the woman's action just don't add up. If anything, the act might be saying that the *rich* people are preparing Jesus for burial by anointing him early. Jesus does not favor the poor at all in this passage and this, for first century Roman readers, would make him seem like any other wealthy Roman citizen who has no regard for the poor.[45]

For those who read Paul's letters this behavior would seem very suspect. These are not lessons to take care of the poor; they are instead lessons to the rich who, in the book of Mark, have turned away from Jesus' message. It is no wonder that Matthew and especially Luke suggest that the poor are actually blessed (which made no sense to Romans) and that they should be taken care of. Those of Christian beliefs, and those of Jewish faith who were taught to take care of the poor, orphans, widows, and children, would shake their heads. Was this the Messiah?

This Markan depiction of Jesus as a snobby patron may seem contrary to what is believed today. Christians portray Jesus as one who gives to the poor, reaches out to others, eats dinner with sinners and outcasts, and is generally inclusive. It is helpful to remember that Paul, frustrated with the refusal of Jews to believe in Jesus, reached out to the Gentiles while Peter, James and John insisted that Christians adhere to the Jewish tenets of the Laws of Moses. Thus, there is some precedent for a bit of a Jewish elitism in the early church. Also, recall that Rodney Stark, rowing against the tide of normal assumptions of New Testament scholars, argues that the early Christian message was preached to the wealthy, not the poor. Last, remember that Mark does not have the advantage of other Christian texts and theologies, thus his portrayal of Jesus, as has been noted throughout this study, has been very rough around the edges. And this may explain a peculiar story in Mark where a non-Jewish woman teaches Jesus, the teacher, something about inclusivity.

---

45. Lane, *Mark*, 493–494; Culpepper, *Mark*, 486; Hooker, *Mark*, 329.

Help My Unbelief!

In Mark 7:24–30 Jesus is in a house in Tyre looking for respite and quiet from the ever present crowds. Tyre is outside the region of Judea and Galilee thus Jesus is on "foreign" soil. Important for this story is that a house in Mark is a place of private teaching between Jesus and his disciples. A Syro-Phoenician Gentile woman breaks into this Jewish enclave and requests, indeed, demands, that Jesus heal her daughter who is lying on her bed back home. Jesus is miffed. "First let the children eat all they want," he says because "it is not right for the children's bread to be tossed to the dogs." The persistent woman retorts, "Yes, Lord, but even the dogs under the table eat the children's crumbs" (vv. 27–28 NIV). Humbled, Jesus heals her daughter from afar.

This passage has troubled scholars because it portrays Jesus in a very bad light. Did Jesus really say such a thing? Anderson says the words are "of doubtful authenticity as a word of Jesus" and thus were probably added by Mark. If so, what does this say about Mark's feelings towards the Gentiles? Hooker, basing her comments on the fact that scholars today often question the historicity of some gospel stories as inventions by the later church, says that it is so embarrassing that it has to be true, that is, Jesus said it and it cannot be left out just because it is embarrassing. She goes on to say that the story presents Jesus as almost "churlish." Today Christians assume that Jesus included Gentiles in his ministry but up until this point Mark does not and this may reflect a teaching in Matthew where Jesus says he was sent only to save the lost sheep of Israel (Matthew 15:24). Indeed, this is the only time when Mark says specifically that Jesus healed a Gentile.[46]

Culpepper provides a little background that is revealing. Tyre was a prosperous island and the residents bought their bread from Galilee. In times of famine, they had the money to buy bread while the Jews could not afford to. Thus, there was Jewish resentment toward the Gentile "dogs" who literally kept bread from the Jews. When in Mark Jesus says it is not right to take the children's bread and toss it to the dogs there is a strong hint of ethnic tensions. Most scholars agree that he is not calling the woman a dog. He was saying that God wanted to feed the children of Israel (the Jews) first. Let the rich people of Tyre feed you bread! The feisty woman fires back, in essence saying "Lord, even the little dogs under the table eat the little crumbs from the little children." This stinging indictment causes Jesus to heal her child. Culpepper notes that "the experience may have been a turning point for Jesus' ministry" because in the next scene in Mark Jesus heals

---

46. Anderson, *Mark*, 190; Hooker, *Mark*, 182.

the demoniac in the area of the Decapolis and then feeds 4000 across the Jordan River.[47] Jesus, a Jewish teacher who was not above treating others condescendingly, had learned an important lesson from a foreign woman who came from a wealthy land: Feed the people from a foreign land.

Jesus the teacher taught his disciples many things. They could break Jewish laws, the poor would be rich and the rich would be poor, the new can't be patched on the old. Much of his teaching could be interpreted as subversive, either to Jewish culture and religion or to Roman rule. He appeared to be a roaming philosopher who had no home and no belongings and who taught in often contradictory ways. At the same time, Jesus attends lavish feasts with hosts who are wealthy and, if Lane is right, he may have been the host of such a party. Thus, while critical of the Jewish religious elite who excluded the sinners and foreigners, he was no stranger to the exclusion of Gentiles where, in at least one setting, his propensity to condescension was brashly confronted by a Gentile woman.

These qualities of Jesus go against the common threads of unified theologies of our day. Some Christians are willing to embrace such a rogue teacher. Mark's first readers, knowledgeable of both Roman and Jewish cultures and biases, would have to make a decision about Jesus. Today's Christians likewise have to decide for themselves as well.

---

47. Culpepper, *Mark*, 238–242, quotes from 242.

5

Miracle Worker or Demon Possessed?

You faithless generation.
(MARK 9:19 NRSV)

MY WIFE IS A certified healing touch practitioner and her healing art is part of an emerging movement of what is called complementary medicine. This includes healing touch, Reiki, chiropractic, herbal medicine, homeopathy, acupuncture, and massage. Hospitals such as the much-respected Wake Forest University Baptist Medical Center in Winston-Salem, North Carolina, are beginning to incorporate this form of medicine into a holistic approach to health care. Not all doctors approve of such therapies, calling them hocus pocus, superstition, folk medicine, or simply bogus. Indeed, libertarian news journalist John Stossel has taken these therapies and their practitioners to task as outright snake oil.[1] Some pastors think it is of the devil, never mind the fact that, when the disciples told Jesus that others were casting out demons in his name Jesus said, "Whoever is not against us is for us" (Mark 9:38–41 NIV).

    I can attest to the power and efficacy of healing touch. Several years ago I fell off of a ladder, smashed my face and broke my arm. For some reason the emergency room did not set the break in my arm. (Later I found out that there were almost no bones to attach to each other) They sent me home with some pain medicine but the pain was so bad the medication

---

1. Stossel, *Myths*, 213–215.

could not catch up with it. I can tolerate pain fairly well but this pain was so intense that I writhed on the couch all night. Another trip to the emergency room for the pain resulted in a very satisfying explanation of "just take the medicine and it will be all right."

It was not all right. I was writhing, nearly screaming in discomfort. So I asked my wife to try healing touch. She went through the movements (which, frankly, look silly) and it felt like a steel screw was being pulled out of my arm, making the pain much worse. Suddenly, though, the pain was nearly gone. I was able to tolerate what pain that remained for the next few days until the operation. But there is more to this story. The doctor told me that I would be out of commission for several weeks, from November into February. The break was very severe and even a new type of titanium plate could barely connect the bone fragments. Had the plate not been available, a halo would have been attached to my arm to foster the healing process. My wife continued to perform healing touch on me and I healed up faster than expected. On the first of January I played Christmas music for a Lutheran church on guitar and dulcimer. I was four weeks ahead of schedule.

I can tell of similar stories. These therapies work but they are not new. They have been around forever. Shamans, medicine women and men, folk healers, and even ministers and their parishioners have performed healing exercises on people with miraculous results. Certainly some of these cases are fake but this should not overshadow the numerous instances when healing took place. In the late 1800s Mary Baker Eddy fell and broke her leg and was not expected to live. Through her reading of the gospel of Matthew she became convinced that she could heal herself. She did, thus defying the doctor's prognosis of death. She went on to found the Christian Science Church. Since that time Americans have seen a tremendous surge of complementary medicines emerge in our culture, especially with the New Age movement of the past few decades.[2]

In our scientific age, dominated by trial and error research, ruled by reason and logic, structured against lawsuits, it is understandable that some see this movement as bogus. In the health care "industry" as it is called now, there has been an academic debate over whether prayer really works or not. Scientific studies have been performed and statistics compiled. The quantitative and qualitative methods have been analyzed and scrutinized and still the jury is out although the conclusions lean toward prayer being a legitimate part of the healing process. Harold Koenig, a professor of Psychiatry

2. Albanese, *Republic of Mind*, 283–285.

and Behavioral Science as well as Medicine at Duke University, argues that prayer, indeed religion, is good for one's heath.[3] As one who endures the ill effects of bipolar disorder, I know the calming effects of religion and spirituality, especially prayer/meditation. Sometimes relying on medicine only just doesn't work completely. Used regularly religion and/or spirituality can calm the manic side and has pulled me through two suicidal episodes. And this is why every book I have read on this illness recommends it.[4]

Is it real? Is it just based on mind over matter? Does it really matter as long as healing takes place? For some it does indeed matter. It has to be of the devil! That is what some said in Jesus' day (Mark 3:22). From Jesus' response it represents another way that God can heal broken bones and broken souls. Questions abound, just as they did in Jesus' day. For Mark's readers, the miracles performed by Jesus sometimes raised questions and other times were seen as just part of the culture of his day. Thus, doubts about the source of power plagued Jesus' healing ministry. Along with this, and this is something Christians of today generally do not consider, is the fact that Jesus' ability to perform miracles led to doubts among some about his own ministry.

Christians today inaccurately tend to see Jesus as the only miracle worker in the first century Roman Empire, indeed the only miracle worker period. One example is noted Pastor Timothy Keller who relates that Jesus' miracles led to awe, wonder, indeed, worship. The implication here is that only Jesus produced awe-inducing miracles that resulted in wonder and worship. I have heard the same from other well-intended but naïve ministers.[5]

This assertion is certainly true but Keller's affirmation of this major tenet of the Christian faith ignores several important biblical points. In the Gospel of Mark, Jesus' miracles led to confusion and fear which brought about more doubts. The first half of the gospel is dominated by miracles. Initially the people are amazed and excited (1:27–28). But, when Jesus heals a paralytic by forgiving his sins, the Jewish authorities raise questions. Can a man forgive sins? Only God can forgive sins (2:1–12). From this point on Jesus' miracles in the book of Mark either raise the ire of the authorities

---

3. Koenig, *Religion*, throughout.

4. Hunter and Hunter, *What Your Doctor*; Jamison, *Unquiet Mind*; Bloch, *Everything*.

5. Keller, *Reason for God*, 99.

Miracle Worker or Demon Possessed?

or Jesus requests that the news of these miracles be kept silent. Why the silence?

Along with this, many today claim that only Jesus the Christ can really heal and everybody else who claims healing powers, and those who claim to be healed by them, are charlatans or dupes of charlatans, perhaps even of the devil or tricked by the devil. However, this also ignores strong biblical evidence. First, in the Old Testament Elisha the prophet heals two people, a Shunammite woman's dead son and Naaman, the leprous commander of the army (2 Kgs 4–5). In the Gospel of Mark, the disciples were sent out by Jesus to preach but they also exorcised demons and healed the sick (6:12–13; 8:6–1). Later Christian traditions affirm Mark's recollection of these stories. Peter healed several people, Philip cast out demons and healed the sick, and Paul could inflict afflictions on people as well as heal them. Such powers among mere mortal men produced proclamations of deity. After Paul healed a crippled man the people of Lystra proclaimed him and Barnabas gods (Acts 3:1–10; 8:4–8; 9:32–43; 14:8–10). James encourages his readers to heal each other by confessing their sins to each other and praying for each other (James 5:13–16). Mark also reminds early Christian readers that others healed in the name of Jesus. When asked if he approved of such actions Jesus shot back, "whoever is not against us is for us" (9:8–41). Thus, as the Bible clearly points out, Jesus was not the only one who had healing powers in his day. In Mark's gospel, healing is healing no matter who does it or in whose name it is done. So, Mark's readers would not have viewed a miracle-working Jesus as over and above other miracle workers of their day. In their minds, it would be a miracle if a great and charismatic person could not perform miracles.

Second, Jesus himself was no stranger to the accusation that his healing was of the devil. Jesus was accused of being allied with Beelzebul, the prince of demons, and Jesus, responding to this accusation, equated Beelzebul with Satan (3:20–30). Then, as now, people can heal but healing other than that associated specifically with the Church and Jesus is often equated with evil.

The name Beelzebul deserves some mention. In the NIV and the KJV the name is Beelzebub which comes from the Latin Vulgate edition of the Bible. In all of the available Greek manuscripts the name is Beelzebul. The name comes from the Hebrew nickname of the Philistine God and means "the God of the Flies" but there are other meanings as well: lord/master of the house; lord of the dung; the adversary; and Baal of the flame. Through the centuries the name came to mean "Lord of the House," perhaps as in a Heavenly Temple. By New Testament times the name was a pejorative Jewish term for the chief demon, known as Satan or Belial.[6]

There is more, as C. Clifton Black demonstrates. In this section of Mark, Jesus goes "home." To whose home did he go? In this story his family goes to him so he is not at his boyhood home. "Home" may mean back to Galilee, the "home" of Jesus' ministry. Black reminds us that the home is the very center of Jewish life and society. Meals, relationships, teaching, divisions, unclean and clean houses and more occur in the home.[7] But there may be more here. Recall that Mark has an "in home/out of home" theme in which those who understand Jesus are considered "in" and those who don't are deemed outside of the home. Mark's readers and listeners would have picked up the home theme and, if they were aware of the name Beelzebul and its connotations, then they would have a made a quick connection between Jesus and his followers. The fact that Jewish leaders labeled Jesus Beelzebul demonstrates that, in their eyes, he was misleading his "house." If Jewish and Christian listeners of Mark's gospel were in doubts about Jesus' identity and his teachings and motives, then this appellation would have raised serious questions. Might this be why Jesus redirects the meaning of the name Beelzebul to Satan and prince of demons?

Third, along with this, Mark's Jesus was never comfortable with the title of miracle worker. Indeed, after a string of miracles in chapter 1 Jesus goes off to pray early in the morning. The disciples track him down and point out that the people are looking for him, ostensibly for more healing since the previous passages are only about healing. Jesus replies, however, that he came to preach (1:38–39). Mark then writes that Jesus left and went out to preach and cast out demons. It is very telling that he did not say anything about healing people or performing miracles. In other words, it seems that healing is more of a distraction in the book of Mark than a significant part of Jesus' ministry.

In the first century miracle workers were part of the everyday culture. For Mark's readers, stories of a wandering healer were not new. L. Michael White asserts that, "Everyone in the ancient world knew of the many miracle workers and their wondrous feats . . . "[8] One specific example is illuminating. Bart Ehrman relates the story of Appolonius of Tyana, who lived

6. Boring, *Mark*, 105; Black, *Mark*, 110.
7. Black, *Mark*, 109.
8. White, *Jesus*, 54.

in the first century. Appolonius' biography reads like an exact duplicate of Jesus' life. According to contemporary writers, Appolonius was born miraculously, taught disciples, and worked miracles and, according to his followers, he, too, rose from the dead. Because of this, he was proclaimed a son of God.[9] Since the news ran rampant about Jesus' healings and miracles we can safely assume that such acclaim also followed and preceded Appolonius of Tyana as well as other healers of the day. Thus, the reputation of this healer and miracle worker was common knowledge in Jesus' day. When the followers of Jesus taught about his miracles and teachings and claimed that he was born of a virgin and lived after he died, those familiar with Appolonius could very easily identify with this person. Some questions would arise for Mark's readers. If Jesus and Appolonius do the same things, then why should I give up my faith in Appolonius for this upstart newcomer named Jesus? Or, is Jesus better than Appolonius? To confuse matters even more, in the Greco-Roman culture, Asclepius, the founder of the medical profession, was noted for his healing miracles. Gregory Riley points out that "Asclepius was the most formidable alternative to the claims of Christians for Jesus as a miracle worker and source of divine healing."[10]

The matter is complicated even further when examined from the perspective of Mark's Jewish readers because some charismatic Jewish rabbis were also miracle workers in Jesus' day. The Jews knew of such stories from their scriptures. Moses performed several feats of "magic" throughout his life, especially when faced with a feisty pharaoh. Joshua brought down the walls of Jericho with seven days of marching and trumpets tooting. When faced with an unproductive and filthy well, Elisha tosses salt in it to cure the water and make it flow forever. Hearing that a widow could not pay her bills, he miraculously made one pot of oil fill all the pots in the village, providing her enough money to pay her debts. He cured a pot of stew that potentially was deadly and then fed a hundred people. When a prophet lost his axhead in the Jordan River Elisha tosses a stick into the Jordan River to retrieve it (Exod 7–17; Josh 6; 2 Kgs 4–6:7). Jewish history made miracles seem commonplace.

In Jesus' day, one rabbi named Honi was revered for his miracles associated with rain. While some Jews saw him in a negative light, others such as the Jewish historian Josephus portrayed him positively. A certain Hanina ben Dosa worked miracles in the region of Galilee during the first

---

9. Ehrman, *New Testament*, 17.
10. Riley, *One Jesus*. 41.

century, which is where Jesus lived and ministered as well. According to the Jewish lore, Ben Dosa was immune to snake bites and could perform healings from a distance. The disciple Matthew included a similar distance-healing in his gospel. A centurion came to Jesus and requested healing for his son. When Jesus offers to go to the centurion's house the Roman soldier says he believes Jesus can heal him from a distance. For this show of faith Jesus does just that (8:5–13). Ben Dosa, like Jesus, also had power over demons. To add more fuel to the fire of confusion, these and other miracle workers were also given the title "son of God." Since these Jewish rabbis did the same miracles as Jesus and were considered sons of God, then Mark's Jewish readers would have seen little difference between rabbi Jesus and the other rabbinic healers. To portray Jesus as a miracle worker would have made him no different than other miracle workers of his time.[11]

Along with this, Roman readers and listeners of Mark's gospel would have seen Jesus' miracles in the light of the contemporary magical worldview. The "miracle worker, or magician, was the one who knew how to harness the supernatural powers, usually by means of special knowledge of incantations, spells and rituals." Such skills were commonplace in Jesus' day and even prayer was one of the tools of these magical miracle workers. Coupled with this is the fact that writers in the Greco-Roman world "scripted" their miracle stories in the same way. This pattern was followed exactly by the gospel writers. Mark's audience understood the miracle stories in the same way they had encountered them in their everyday reading.[12] Again, in Mark's day, healers were simply part of the everyday life and literature of Rome's citizens.

So, for Mark's readers, presenting Jesus as a miracle worker naturally led them to compare Jesus with other miracle workers, both Jewish and pagan, of his day. Mark's task was to answer the question from his reader: So what? What made Jesus, the itinerant Jewish teacher and healer, different from the numerous Appolonius's and ben Dosas's of the first century? One answer from his Greco-Roman readers would be that Jesus was not different at all. This means that other qualities of Jesus led many to follow him.

Wendy J. Cotter has thoroughly addressed the miracles in the New Testament, focusing mostly on the Gospel of Mark. She demonstrates *why* Mark employed these stories in his narrative about Jesus and her

---

11. Culpepper, *Mark*, 67, who cites Gerd Thiessen and Annette Merz, *The Historical Jesus: A Comprehensive Guide*, 307–308.

12. White, *Scripting*, 165.

conclusions confirm what is being suggested in this work. Mark was comparing Jesus to contemporary heroes in his day.[13] This raises an important question: why was Mark comparing Jesus to other miracle-working heroes? Was Jesus losing out in the battle for prominence? Did early Christians and potential converts need a better reason to choose Jesus over another hero? What was special about Jesus that other heroes did not have?

As Cotter explains, the miracle story in the ancient world is really an original tale that is composed by the author. The miracle is the climax to the story and its context. However, the miracle was not the point: instead it was the message. The miracle was presented against the backdrop of the miracles of the writer's day and Jewish and non-Jewish readers of Mark would have understood these messages and stories since they were not different than the ones they regularly heard about.

The focus for the New Testament readers, according to Cotter, is the encounter between Jesus and the petitioner who is viewed by those in the Greco-Roman world as a "rough and ready character." In essence, Jesus moves from the side of the typical Roman citizen who views these characters with disdain and takes the side of the petitioner, an act that is considered outlandish. Why do such a thing and why would Mark portray Jesus as such a person? Cotter's answer is simple: Because Mark wanted to persuade his readers that Jesus was a man of virtue.

A virtuous man in that day was a hero whose example was to be admired and imitated, the very qualities expected of the emperors of his day. Along with this, he was a man of "loving concern of others" who exhibited restraint when confronted and when offended by rough and ready petitioners who have slighted someone with an arrogant request. The hero's regard and concern concerning "others" who were ignored by the regular citizens was one of a gentle, restrained and compassionate response to a brusque, nearly intimidating demand.[14] All of this is to say that, as far as miracles go, Jesus was just another miracle man among many. But, Mark's intent in presenting Jesus as a miracle worker was to display him as a man of virtue, one to be emulated by his readers, Christian, Jewish and Roman.

This is born out with New Testament evidence. According to James D.G. Dunn, the earliest traditions of Jesus passed down in the early church were teachings. Some time afterwards, though, there arose a collection of miracle stories adopted by many of the churches. Both Mark and John may

---

13. Cotter, *Christ*.
14. Ibid., "Introduction."

have employed such a miracles source for their writings however not all of these stories were accepted as authentic or even valuable. This explains why the apostle Paul fought against many believers who "falsely" portrayed Jesus as a miracle worker and thus, by his example, employed enthusiastic actions to demonstrate their faith. According to these elitist Christians, most of whom were in the Corinthian church, Jesus was a divine miracle worker and a mighty man. Recall that in the Gospel of Mark, Jesus is baptized by John the Baptizer. This is not a new thing. In the Old Testament Elijah the prophet likewise passed the mantle to his protégé Elisha, who continued the traditions of his mentor. Also, for Mark's readers, the baptism of Jesus would have been interpreted as the endowment of the power to heal according to the religious understandings of the Hellenistic culture. Dunn notes that this would have been the case for the church at Corinth where Hellenistic, not Jewish, influences dominated the congregation.[15]

We have noted above that Mark may have been influenced by Paul and if so, then Mark, like Paul, may have been trying to move his readers away from the notion of Jesus as miracle worker. This certainly seems to be the point in chapter 1 of Mark's gospel where, after Jesus performs three astounding miracles, he ignores the pleas of the sick and instead moves on to the next town to *preach*, not perform miracles. The first half of Mark is all about healing and miracles but as Mark moves his story of Jesus toward Jerusalem and the cross, there is a shift to teachings and prophecy. If Paul was questioning the antics and teachings of those who claimed Jesus was a great miracle worker then there were doubts among the believers. Was Paul right or were other teachers correct? Obviously the miracle tradition persisted creating problems for the early believers. Mark, according to Dunn, was trying to quell these doubts by tying the mighty man to the suffering Savior, not miracle worker.[16]

There is another angle to consider as well. There is a tradition in sources outside of the New Testament that Jesus was a magician. Celsus, writing around 175 CE, attacked Christian beliefs and accused Jesus of, among other things, being a sorcerer and a magician. Celsus based his conclusions on New Testament writings and Jewish criticisms of the early church and Jesus. Jewish rabbinical writings from around the second century CE and beyond present Jesus as a magician who learned his craft while in Egypt. Many of the criticisms, stemming from the battles between Judaism and the

---

15. Dunn, *Unity and Diversity*, 179–180; 279.
16. Ibid., 70–71, 77, 157, 220, 179–180, 196.

Miracle Worker or Demon Possessed?

growing group of Christians are dubious but some are considered as worth further scrutiny. Jesus' "magic" might have been alluding to his miracles and some note that his disciples continued his healing ministry.[17]

Years ago Morton Smith startled and rankled the Christian world by asserting that, based on New Testament evidence compared to ancient Greco-Roman sources, Jesus was a magician. The evidence is compelling and thus disconcerting. Many scholars disagreed but others listened. One was E.P. Sanders who examines Smith's assertions and basically agrees. Sanders does not conclude that Jesus was a magician, but he does emphasize that, in the eyes of many, Jesus was very much a magician.[18]

There are only two episodes in Mark's gospel that hint of Jesus as a magician. In Mark 7:31–37 a deaf man is brought to Jesus for healing. Rather than heal him in public Jesus instead goes away to a private place where he inserts his fingers into the man's ears and then spits before touching the man's tongue, looks up to heaven, sighs and says "Ephphatha!" The second story occurs in Mark 8:22–26. In Bethsaida people bring a blind man to Jesus for healing. Again, rather than remain in town in public Jesus takes the blind man out of the village where he then spits on the man's eyes and lays his hands on him. This initial attempt was not entirely successful: the man could see but all was blurry. Again Jesus lays his hands on the man and this time full vision is the result.

Interestingly, today most preachers will spend hours in study and in the pulpit to defend the historicity of these miracles. But, there are two other ways to look at this type of healing. Mark Twain wrote a hilarious spoof on Christian "pilgrims" entitled *The Innocents Abroad*. He points out that many blind people came to his group while they toured the holy land. For most, their eyes were encrusted with what looked like dried mucus. A simple cleansing removed the materials and suddenly the blind could see. Miracle or common sense? On the other hand, not all interpreted this episode in Mark as literal fact. Early Christian theologian Jerome urged moving from the literal to the spiritual interpretation in these stories. In his comments on Mark 8:22–26 he writes: "after the film of sin is removed, he might clearly behold the state of his soul with the eye of a clean heart."[19] So, the "miracle" may not have been the miracle that today's preachers claim it is. Recall the above note that miracle stories were told to illustrate a point,

---

17. Van Voorst, *Jesus*, 64–66, and ch. 3.
18. Sanders, *Jesus*, 164–173.
19. Oden and Hall, *Mark*, 109.

not prove that one could actually do miracles. Jerome leads us to see the point here: if one is having problems seeing "correctly" one may be spiritually blinded by the crusts of sin. Or, maybe Jesus just knew that a good cleansing with saliva would clear out the ocular gunk.

When these two stories are compared it is evident that the "plot" is the same. As Eugene Boring points out, each story takes place in Gentile territory, an unknown group brings the afflicted person to Jesus, requests are made for Jesus to lay his hands on the sick person, Jesus takes the person away from the crowd, touches him and uses saliva on him, and demands that the healed person not tell anyone. Boring goes on to note that these two episodes are exactly like contemporary healing stories Mark's listeners and readers would have been familiar with. Indeed, a contemporary could have claimed that Jesus learned these techniques from the healers in Epidaurus. Even the Roman emperor Vespasian was noted for healing a blind man with saliva. Thus, Jesus would have been understood as a typical "divine man" in the Greco-Roman world. Interestingly, neither Matthew nor Luke use these stories in their gospels.[20]

Boring goes on to note that physical touches, saliva, sighs/groans and "magical" sounding words (as in "Ephphatha) "are for Mark no longer merely the healing techniques of Hellenistic magic." This demonstrates that Mark was fully aware that his audience knew such rituals were performed by magicians. If this was a negative, potentially embarrassing issue for Mark he could have left these stories out of his account of Jesus, as Matthew and Luke did. Instead he deliberately uses them in the middle of his story where Jesus' true identity is now introduced. This indicates that for him these two magical stories were quite important. Those who were not familiar with the Jewish stories of old which have some affinities with these two stories, would have appreciated the Jesus as presented by Mark.[21]

Apollonius of Tyana, noted above, was a magician and Greek magical sayings are well-preserved from the time of Jesus. Magicians were often deemed sons of a god. Indeed, if Jesus was believed to be a magician then this would explain why crowds followed him everywhere. Sanders concludes that we cannot say for certain that Jesus was a magician but, those outside of the faith could certainly regard Jesus as a charlatan and a magician.[22] But, this could also mean that those within the faith who were disap-

20. Boring, *Mark*, 215–216, 233.
21. Ibid., 217.
22. Sanders, *Jesus*, 173.

pointed with Jesus and his belated return may have begun interpreting him simply as a magician.

Surprisingly, there were later Christians who believed that Jesus was a magician and their beliefs were manifest in magical ways that were difficult to distinguish from their pagan Roman neighbors. Groups of Christians that today are deemed heretics practiced "sorcery and magic, and made use of foreign names and various magical formulas." A Roman critic of Christianity recalled that early Christian "presbyters" owned books that contained names of demons and abominations. Walter Bauer sums up this information: "Obviously the accusation of sorcery by the pagan civil authorities against the new religion [Christianity] also renders feasible or even encourages the idea that Christianity actually presented such an image when considered from *one* point of view."[23]

In Jesus' day hunger was everywhere. The poor wandered the streets of the major Roman cities and in order to prevent the homeless and destitute from rioting and looting they were given free bread and tickets to the local circuses to keep them fed and off the streets. In the Jewish communities poverty was rampant as well. The apostle Paul regularly took up an offering for the poor of Jerusalem. In short, many people needed bread throughout the Roman Empire. Any person who could feed people in this time was one worthy of more consideration.

Mark records two episodes where Jesus miraculously fed thousands of people. The first episode begins a series of stories that focuses on food with one exception:

- Feeding the five thousand

- Jesus walking on the water in the storm (where the disciples were afraid but, as noted, they did not understand the significance of the event because they did not understand the previous miraculous feeding)

- The ritual washing of the hands before a meal with the lesson that it is not what goes into a person's mouth that makes him unclean; instead it is what comes out

- A Syrophoenician woman's demand for the "crumbs" of the teachings of Jesus

---

23. Bauer, *Orthodoxy*, 237, n. 13.

- (A brief interruption of the sequence with the healing of a deaf mute man: is anybody listening to these stories?)
- The feeding of four thousand
- Then a conclusion where Jesus teaches about the yeast of the Pharisees. In this last food episode the disciples don't understand (because they are not *hearing* Jesus correctly?) that Jesus is talking about the misleading teachings of the leaders of Jerusalem. They instead think Jesus is talking about the fact that they have no bread to eat

The only indication of amazement, a major emotional theme in the Gospel of Mark, in this whole string of feeding stories comes in the interruption of the sequence with the healing of the deaf mute. This may be because, as Morna Hooker notes, this section is about understanding the divinity of Jesus, not feeding multitudes. Indeed, the specific details of each of these stories, especially the feeding stories, are to remind the disciples "of the magnitude of the miracles." It is not the details; instead it is that Jesus has met the needs of the people. Only God can meet the needs of this many people. The conclusion? Jesus is God.[24]

The first feeding in Mark 6 is the most familiar. Somewhere in the vicinity of the Sea of Galilee, Jesus' disciples arrived after a brief missionary episode that most probably included healings and exorcisms. The disciples were hungry and tired so Jesus leads them to a quiet place across the sea. After rowing some distance away it becomes obvious that the crowds, hungry for more lessons from this itinerant teacher, are following the boat along the shore. After landing, Jesus proceeds to teach but the daylight is ebbing away. The disciples point out that the people are hungry. Jesus rather curtly tells them to feed the crowd. The disciples balk: there is only enough food for one person. Undaunted, Jesus asks for the simple meal, blesses it, and then multiplies it so that one meal feeds five thousand *men*. This in itself is a tremendous feat but scholars have long noted that, when wives and children are accounted for, the number could easily have been near twenty thousand. After the meal the reader is told that twelve baskets of scraps are then collected (6:30–44).

A similar episode follows two chapters later where the scenario is nearly the same. A crowd has listened to Jesus for three days when their food runs out. Ever compassionate, Jesus points out that they should leave but then concludes that, because of their lack of sustenance, they might

24. Hooker, *Mark*, 169, quote from 196.

faint on the journey home. The disciples, apparently having forgotten the first miraculous feeding (how exactly could one forget that?), ask Jesus where the people can stop and stock up on food. Finding out that seven loaves are available Jesus once again blesses and distributes the bread to the crowd and then seven baskets of leftovers are collected. Afterwards, the crowd of four thousand men, now well fed, left for home (8:1–10).

In the history of the Jews miraculous feedings were well-attested as New Testament scholars have always pointed out. Three Old Testament stories of miraculous feedings are compared with these two in Mark's gospel. Jesus is equated with God who fed the Israelites as they wandered in the wilderness for forty years with manna from heaven (Exodus 16). Next is the prophet Elijah. Meeting a poor widow he asked if she had food to feed him. She replied that she only had enough flour and oil to feed herself one meal. Elijah responds by asking her to prepare a meal for him and that, if she did so, she would still have enough flour and oil to make a meal for herself. Indeed, she had enough ingredients to fix meals for the duration of the years' long drought (1 Kgs 17).

The third, as noted above, Elisha, the protégé of Elijah, performs many miracles that echo those of Jesus. Elisha, like Jesus, rises to the fore after his mentor is taken to heaven. He turned deadly water into fresh, provided a miraculous amount of oil to a godly woman whose credit had suddenly failed, revived a dead boy, and also fed a hundred people with only twenty loaves of bread (2 Kgs 1–4). When Elisha's life is set next to that of Jesus as described in the Gospels the comparison, for many, is too close to ignore.

So, for the Jewish readers and listeners of Mark, several questions arise: is Jesus indeed God since he can feed large groups of people? Is he Elijah returned from heaven (Elijah never died; he was instead taken to heaven)? Some people believed so because in Mark 8 the disciples tell Jesus that many think he is indeed Elijah who has returned to earth. Could he be *Elisha* resurrected?

The astounding numbers of people in these stories have produced much speculative ink by scholars trying to explain how this many could be fed with so little. I was taught in seminary that, if we include wives and children, then the five thousand may have been more like fifteen or even twenty thousand. This sounds a bit dubious since the total population of nearby Caesarea was only about 2000–3000. In the other episode, were there more than four thousand? Could it reasonably be expected that local villagers could scrape up enough food to feed them? Along with this, there has been much speculation about the significance of the number of baskets of leftovers. Could the twelve baskets recall the twelve tribes of Israel? How about the twelve disciples? Could the seven baskets anticipate the first seven deacons in the fledgling church? No wonder that some scholars question the veracity of these two episodes.[25]

There is one side note about the numerology in these two stories. While the numbers twelve and seven can be interpreted from the Jewish and Christian perspective as significant, Roman pagans might see them through different lenses. The number twelve is the number of the constellations in the zodiac. Seven would recall the number of visible planets or the seven days of the week. Can such a meaning be found in a pastoral setting? Jerome Carcopino points out that Romans who attended the games, which were held in honor of the deities, were so fascinated with astrology that they looked for patterns in such odd places as the dirt in the arena and the moats that surrounded it. The twelve stalls that the chariots emerged from represented the twelve constellations of the Zodiac and the seven tracks made by the chariots recalled both the major stars in the heavens and the days of the week.[26]

While these suggestions might appear to be a stretch there is evidence that Christians and Jews retained many pagan symbols in their arts up through the Middle Ages. Recall that the Apostle Paul always went to the local synagogue to spread the good news of Christ. When he was run off then he took the message to the *pagans*, the Gentiles. These people were quite familiar with pagan beliefs, behaviors, and rituals. Paul, frustrated and worried at how the people of the fledgling churches in Galatia have so quickly reverted back to their pagan ways, calls them to task concerning their celebrations of "special days and months and seasons and years!" (Gal 4:10 NIV). Christian commentators and theologians point out that this refers to Jewish holy days but, as Calvin Roetzel reminds us, there were issues from "local folk religion" that also plagued the early Christians. Donald Guthrie asserts that these ways were so similar to pagan sacred days that the Galatians could have also interpreted Paul's vitriolic as against paganism as well.[27]

Paul, following the customs of the Corinthians, was quite comfortable eating with pagans and the meals would have included meats butchered

---

25. Boring, *Mark*, 184.
26. Carcopino, *Daily Life*, 209.
27. Roetzel, *Letters of Paul*, 97. Guthrie, *Galatians*, 116–117.

Miracle Worker or Demon Possessed?

with the blessings of pagan deities. Indeed, most of Paul's listeners and converts were Gentile pagans who were quite familiar with the worship of Isis, Serapis, Dionysus, and Cabirus as well as local and city gods and goddesses.[28] As noted before, the cult of Dionysus was very similar to aspects of emerging Christianity. Even into the fourth century, during the reign of Constantine who declared Christianity a legal religion (but did not convert until on his deathbed), Christians and Jews employed the sun god Sol Invictus in their calendrical arts.[29] Thus, it certainly seems possible that Mark's pagan audience could have associated these numbers in the feeding stories with beliefs other than those from Judaism. Was Jesus demonstrating some miracle made possible by the gods in the heavens? In honor of the heavenly deities? Roman pagans, hearing the story of Mark, would have asked such questions. How did the early Christians answer?

But, there is also the Greco-Roman side of this story to consider as well. Mark uses terms that were sometimes interpreted as having militaristic overtones. The stories of the miraculous feedings in Mark 6 and 8 could have been interpreted as the formation of a nationalistic army. When Jesus asked the thousands to sit in companies of 100s and 50s (Mark 6) he may have wanted them to sit in rows. Culpepper points out that the Jewish ascetics at Qumran organized themselves into companies and, more dangerously, the political revolutionaries known as the Zealots organized themselves likewise. Hooker, aware of the potential militaristic overtones of this seating arrangement, notes that, "it is conceivable that there is in this description a hint that the crowd could easily become an army prepared to march behind Jesus." If any of the Roman authorities witnessed the event, or, heard about it later, they could have interpreted it as the commencement of a revolt against Rome.[30] Since Jesus preached about a new kingdom, it could be assumed by the Romans that Jesus was indeed forming a militant group to secede from Roman rule. (This would imply that the crowds of 5000 were only men) Interestingly, when Pilate asks Jesus if he is King of the Jews it is telling that Jesus does not deny the accusation (Mark 15:2). No wonder the Romans were afraid of an insurrection begun by Jesus' followers! Five thousand men is a large contingent of potential soldiers.

With this in mind there is mention of a certain "Chrestus" who was either the inspiration behind or an actual motivator in a disturbance by the

---

28. Roetzel, *Paul*, 14, 37, 65.
29. Goodman, *Rome and Jerusalem*, 545.
30. Culpepper, *Mark*, 211; Hooker, Mark, 167.

Jews of Rome perhaps around 49 CE. The historian Seutonius relates the quick actions of then emperor Claudius who expelled the Jews from Rome for their constant agitations. There is much debate about how to take this reference, running from the incident is about a man named Chrestus and not Jesus Christ to the assertion that this is about certain Jews who, claiming Jesus as their Messiah, were causing problems among the less-convinced Jews of Rome. "Chrestus" was either a misspelling of Christ or was an alternate spelling of the title. Still, Robert Van Voorst concludes that there is ample evidence to suggest that the report is indeed about early believers in Jesus the Christ.[31] We have seen that the actions of Jesus, indeed even the reputations of some of his disciples, could have led to the fear of rabble rousers. Thus, the notion that the seating of the people at the miraculous feedings could be seen as an insurrection in the making is not that absurd.

More important might be the total lack of amazement at such a feat in Mark's presentation of these two feedings. This is odd because there is a consistent theme of amazement and fear throughout the book of Mark. After Jesus' first exorcism the people are amazed (1:21–28). After healing a paralytic man and a brief lesson in compassion delivered to the legalistic Pharisees who witnessed the event, the people are once again amazed (2:1–12). After Jesus calms a storm the disciples are frightened (4:35–41). Following the healing of a man possessed of many demons the people of the Decapolis are amazed (5:1–20). When Jesus brought a dead young girl back to life those around him, including the family and some disciples who were with him, were astonished (5:21–43). When Jesus cannot heal the sick in his hometown *he* is amazed (6:1–6). The one consistent theme in these stories is that, in some way or another, they all involve "firsts." First exorcism; first healing with a scathing attack on Pharisaic teachings; first meteorological miracle; first miracle outside of the Galilee; first dead person healed; first time Jesus cannot heal. All of these stories end in some form of amazement or fear, major themes in Mark.

So, why is there no mention of fear or amazement after the first miraculous feeding? The story ends with the disciples collecting the scraps and a bland "The number of the men was five thousand." Shouldn't there be an incredulous "Wow!" here?

There is one more way to view these stories as well. Rather than insisting on the literal interpretation of these episodes, as many do today, the early church theologians looked at them as analogies or types or models or

---

31. Van Voorst, *Jesus*, 29–39.

stories of inspiration. The breaking of the bread symbolized God opening the minds of the people. The bread of life is most cherished in the deserts of life where God is still present. Jesus, who hungered during his forty days of temptation, knows what hunger is. Sitting on the grass was a humbling gesture. The numbers—hundreds, fifties, 1000, five—hold symbolic interpretations. In the midst of hunger Jesus paused to give thanks. The breaking of bread was an act of creation like that seen in Genesis. The giving of the food is indicative of God giving gifts to God's church.[32] It is interesting that nowhere in these comments of the early church theologians was there a question of whether Jesus fed real food or that he fed such large crowds with the equivalent of a Happy Meal, or even that only he could perform such a feat. Instead, the point for these early church teachers was the spiritual significance of the event, not the historical facts. Indeed, either these church fathers stayed away from the actual feeding itself or it was simply not understood in their day as a big deal.

So, questions for Mark's readers are abundant here. Did Jesus actually feed these thousands? If so that would make him as one of the gods. Was he one of the ancient Jewish prophets? If so, he has been resurrected or brought down from heaven. Was he a pagan whose miracles included astrological numerology? Possibly. Was he organizing a revolutionary army in the wilderness? Dangerous! Might he have been all of these?

Exorcisms are still practiced today by the Catholic Church and many church people, lay and professional, have laid on hands and anointed the sick with oil and then witnessed the miracle of healing and new life. James 5:14 advises the elders of the church to pray over the sick and anoint them with oil. In order to be beatified by the Catholic Church it must be demonstrated that the candidate for sainthood must have produced a miracle. The appearance of a long-deceased saint to a suffering soul has often been associated with miracles. This is not to diminish the work of Jesus but instead shows that Jesus' healing ministry has been carried on throughout the centuries.

The first miracle of Jesus that Mark presents is the exorcism of a demon. If we recall that Mark received his information from Peter but that it was not in historical, chronological form, then we have to ask why this miracle is presented first. The episode begins with Jesus teaching with authority and, given Dunn's comments about the miracle and mighty man

32. Oden and Hall, *Mark*, 89–93, 105–106.

tradition within Christian churches, Mark may have been making a point that miracles must be interpreted along with teaching, not in and of themselves. In the synagogue a demon-possessed man cries out: the demon knows who Jesus is. In essence, the first healing episode presents a major motif for Christians: the battle between God and the demons of the world, the Kingdom of God versus Satan's Dominion. The story ends with the proclamation by the witnesses that Jesus has authority. They are astounded, amazed—themes that are important for Mark—at what they have seen. Also, the secret is out: this miracle-worker is proclaimed the "Holy One of God," at which Jesus commands the spirit "Be quiet!" (1:24–25 NIV).

After a generic statement that many demon-possessed people were brought to Jesus (1:32), the next mention of exorcisms is in 3:11 where the crowds, fresh with the message that Jesus is a miracle-worker, swarm him. The demons, once exorcised, fall prostrate before Jesus and cry out, "You are the Son of God" (NRSV). Lane points out that this scene recalls similar crowds that followed the healing itinerant Appolonius of Tyana whose life, we have seen, echoed that of Jesus. Boring notes the "international gathering" of peoples from nearly all points of the compass. He suggests that this reference is not literal—King Herod would surely have taken notice of such a large crowd as a sign of possible insurrection—but that it indicates Mark's audience at the time of writing. Thus, Mark's diverse audience could have made the association that Jesus was just another traveling healer and teacher. But, how would people from such diverse lands who came from disparate cultures and thus worshiped many deities have understood this Jesus as presented by Mark? Just as in the first exorcism, the ousted demons recognize Jesus as "Holy One of God" (NRSV; NIV: Son of God). Boring points out that Isaiah uses this phrase thirty times and thus Jews would have caught the significance. But, Boring also suggests that Mark has a Gentile audience. Would they have made the same connection? Whose god was Jesus son of? The Gentile god or the Jewish god? Lane also notes that this region around the Sea of Galilee was notorious as a hotbed of demonic activity. Again the demons are told to desist with this proclamation. Despite the acclamation, in 3:20–30, Jesus' exorcisms result in two "charges."[33]

First, his family believes he is "out of his mind" (NIV). Culpepper notes that the word here is the same for amazement or astonishment but that it carries a more charged meaning. Thus, it could be taken as, "Jesus was so amazed by his power that he was beyond himself." The NRSV seems

---

33. Lane, *Mark*, 128; Boring, *Mark*, 64, 97.

Miracle Worker or Demon Possessed?

to capture this meaning by translating "He has gone out of his mind." Lane describes Jesus' state as "psychic derangement." Culpepper also points out that his family was afraid that the throngs of people were coming to get him as part of an insurrection. Did they want him as a leader? The second charge was brought by the scribes ("teachers of the law" according to the NIV): Jesus himself is possessed by demons. Here Jesus points out the illogic of the accusation: why would Satan fight against Satan? Following this, in chapter 4 Mark relates Jesus' parable of the sower and several other parables. Then he tells the story of Jesus calming the storm.[34]

With awe-full and extraordinary implications and questions produced by this miracle fresh on the minds of Mark's readers he introduces a long story about Jesus' exorcism of a legion of demons from an afflicted man (ch. 5). The use of the term legion is interesting and it would remind the audience of the Roman military and their legions. Indeed, Culpepper points out that the way the demoniac approached Jesus—running up to him and bowing to him—was exactly the actions of one welcoming a conqueror. Culpepper then draws a connection between the demons that inhabited the man and the Roman army that occupied the region. The scene "may also signal a political commentary" where a parallel between the demon spirits and the Roman army that occupied the land is suggested.[35] Again we see possible connections of Jesus to a military operation. If Jesus was able to conquer a legion of demons might he be able to defeat a legion of Romans as well?

The people of the region were both afraid and amazed at this frightening miracle. Indeed, some asked Jesus to leave! But there is something to this story that commentators seem to miss. They remind us that this is a Gentile region and the demoniac is likewise a Gentile. When the demons are exorcised they describe Jesus as "Son of the Most High God" (NIV). Commentators note that this is Mark's affirmation of Jesus as God's Son but given our discussion in a previous chapter would the Greco-Roman readers of Mark have made this connection instantly? Might a Gentile audience have thought that Jesus was the son of the Gentile Most High God?

In Mark 7:24–30 Jesus exorcises a demon from a little girl from a distance. The girl's mother is described by Mark as a Greek Syrian-Phoenician from Tyre. For the Jewish audience of Mark these descriptors would raise eyebrows if not hackles. From the Jewish perspective, no one could have

---

34. Culpepper, *Mark*, 114; Lane, *Mark*, 139.
35. Culpepper, *Mark*, 166, 168.

been more outside the Jewish ethnic faith than this woman. She is the ultimate outsider. Indeed, even Jesus exhibits some of this cultural and social prejudice when he tells the woman that his food is for the Jews. Best to feed them than waste good food on the dogs of the non-Jewish world. The woman fires back quickly that even dogs get the children's crumbs. Jesus, apparently awakened to his insensitivities, then heals her daughter from a distance.

Liberal Christians have a difficult time with this story because it goes against modern social and cultural correctness. Conservative Christians have a difficult time defending a passage that makes Jesus appear as an insensitive louse. Scholars often reflect these reactions when treating this pericope.

Boring points out that this "feeding story" comes right in between the feeding of Jews and the feeding of Gentiles. He then notes that this story is more about the tensions between Greek Christians and Jewish Christians than a miracle story. Pointing out that the woman represents the rich Greeks who took advantage of poor Jews, the story immediately raises the ire of Jewish readers while at the same time appeasing the Gentile Christians who have entered the fold of the Church. The exorcism is not important for the overall import of the story. Lane focuses more on the exorcism than Boring and he suggests that "Jesus' apparent refusal to help in a situation of clear need conveys an impression of harshness and insensitivity." He further explains that Jesus' reluctance to heal the woman's daughter might stem from the fact that he was aware of other miracle workers in the Hellenistic region and wished to avoid the hoopla that a healing would inevitably bring. Jesus thus pushes the woman to see how much faith she has by asking her a question. The woman's pluck "delights" Jesus thus indicating her daughter deserved a miraculous exorcism.[36]

Anderson says that the woman's wit has nothing to do with the resultant healing. Instead, it is the Gentile woman's humility and deference to the Jewish Jesus that commends her to healing. "It is rather the account of a miracle of healing at a distance, by which *the wall of partition between Jew and Gentile is broken down*" (his emphasis). Hooker disagrees and argues that this incident is actually a distraction from the mission of Jesus which was to Jews only. Instead she interprets this episode as a lesson in what is clean and unclean. Hooker then gets to the grit of the story: the "presentation of Jesus as almost churlish in his reluctance to help the Gentile woman,

---

36. Boring, *Mark*, 209–210; Lane, *Mark*, 262–263.

erratic in the way in which he then changed his mind." She notes that, while many see this story as an aberration from the usual depiction of Jesus as sympathetic to all people, because of its crudeness it has to be genuine.[37]

To me, while scholars quibble over what exactly is meant by the word "dogs" and do their best to make Jesus into a respectable savior there is something more at stake here: the humanity of Jesus. He obviously exhibits the prejudice of contemporary Jews in this episode; he is exclusivistic in his insistence that the kingdom is only for Jews; he places the persistent woman in the category of dogs, a derogatory term that Jews used in regards to Gentiles; and he is forced to change his beliefs when countered by this "outsider." In essence, Jesus the man takes another step toward becoming Jesus, a son of God. And, if a prejudiced human can become a child of God, so can other humans as well. Might that be the underlying message of this embarrassing story?

Lest Mark's readers think that only Jesus can call demons out of people Mark tells us that he gave this power to his disciples as well (6:7). Still, the power, however, was limited. In chapter 9 Jesus, accompanied by Peter, James and John (who had just witnessed the magnificent, mysterious and no doubt troubling transfiguration of Jesus), encounter a crowd consisting of the other disciples and townspeople. It seems that these disciples cannot heal a demon-possessed boy. Jesus is visibly disappointed with the disciples' failure to rid the child of his demons. The father of the child asks, "if you can do anything, take pity on us and help us." Jesus, rather indignantly, shoots back, "If I can?" He then commands the evil spirit to come out of the boy. The child convulses and apparently passes out only to be revived. When asked by the disciples why they could not exorcise the demon, Jesus, in a rare mention of prayer in the Gospel of Mark, tells them that this kind of demon can only be exorcised by prayer. After this dramatic story, Mark does not mention any more exorcisms.

Jesus' power to exorcise demons, while instilling awe both then and now, presents a dilemma for Mark's audience. His power over demons is linked to his authoritative preaching and teaching yet as the stories build the power is more troublesome than positive. Crowds smother Jesus so that he must leave to continue preaching. Accusations of demon-possession dog the itinerant teacher. This conclusion damaged the reputation of Jesus for centuries as critics claimed Jesus was a magician and Christian apologists

---

37. Anderson, *Mark*, 191; Hooker, *Mark*, 182.

worked to remove the derogatory appellation. Last, crowds might want this man of power to lead them in an uprising.

Still, there is one point that emerges which is not readily apparent in these stories: demon-possession means the person is unclean, thus unable to attend the Temple and carry out the sacrifices necessary for spiritual cleansing.[38] Those who were kept outside of the religious rituals necessary for inclusion among the forgiven are now free to join the cleansed. Thus, Jesus is clearing the way for the marginal sinners to go to the Temple and be declared sinless.

In Mark 4:35–41 the reader finds Jesus asleep in a boat while the disciples rowed along with other boats across the Sea of Galilee. This body of water is known for its storms that can arise with no warnings at all. Suddenly a powerful storm full of threatening winds arises and the disciples are understandably afraid. As fishermen they understood very well the danger of such a storm. While they fret and frantically try to keep the boat from capsizing Jesus is still fast asleep. The disciples cry out to him, "Don't you care about us perishing?" One can imagine that they would like him to at least grab a bucket and toss water over the gunwales. Jesus gets up and says *to the wind* "Peace! Be still!" A better translation would be along the lines of, "I said shut up!" The wind ceases to blow and the sea turns calm. We can imagine the emotions of the disciples, who at this point in Mark still are confused about Jesus' identity. And they have every right to be confused, indeed, even afraid, because in their religious culture only the gods can calm the seas.

From the Jewish perspective it was understood that God was associated with the winds and storms. In Genesis 1 we read that God tamed the mighty Deep, the "waters" as some translators note it. In the ancient Near Eastern mythology (as recalled by Isa 51:9–10) this Deep always threatened to overtake the world and destroy it. This is seen in Genesis 7 where God opens up the windows of Heaven where the rain waters were stored and then sets free the Deep from its underwater cages (Job 38:8–11) and then destroys the world with the Deeps. In Exodus 15:8 and 10, in the song that describes the defeat of Pharaoh's army, God blows a wind from his nostrils and the Deeps rise forth and consume the charioteers.

In Job 38 God appears to the frustrated and angry not in scripture or commandments or historical stories but in a whirlwind. In Psalm 18:1–19

---

38. Culpepper, *Mark*, 104.

the singer relates how he was caught in the cords of death which he describes as the waters. God appears in a mighty thunderstorm that shook the creation like an earthquake. Once again a blast from God's nostrils blows the seas back and the psalmist is saved. In Psalm 69:1–4, 13–18 the Deep waters have surrounded the singer and threaten him with certain drowning. The psalmist cries out for deliverance by God from these rising waters. Other psalms such as 60; 68; 77; 107; and 135 also describe God in tempestuous words. The book of Jonah is probably the most famous description of God who casts a mighty wind on the sea that stirred up a huge tempest. The sailors, as per their beliefs, think that someone has caused the gods to be angry. Jonah, like Jesus in Mark 4, is asleep as the storm threatens the boat and crew. He is awakened by the frantic crew: "Don't you care that we might sink and perish?" Lots are cast to see who has made the gods angry and Jonah's lot reveals him as the culprit. At his request he is thrown overboard. Tossed about in the sea, Jonah prays that God will save him *from the flood and from the Deep*, not the storm.

Jews would have been familiar with these associations of storms with God. So, when Jesus calms the storm the connection between him and God was easy to make. And this is no doubt why the disciples in the boat were so afraid. They utter what can be understood as a rhetorical question: "Who is this that seas and winds obey him?" The obvious answer is that Jesus is God. Imagine if God was in the boat with you. What would you do and how would you respond?

But, what of Greco-Roman readers of Mark's gospel? How would they interpret such a story? In the Roman pantheon of gods several were associated with storms or winds. Zeus/Jupiter was known as a storm and weather god. In the Roman literature Jupiter, mad at the creation, imprisoned the North wind in Aeolus' caves and held back other winds that might prevent a storm and then he sent the South winds to create a flood. On top of this, Jupiter then called upon Neptune, god of the sea, to let loose the rivers as well. Thus, just like the biblical flood, Jupiter destroyed the world but, reminiscent of Noah and his family, only Deucalion and Pyrrha survived. Jupiter then called an end to the storm and floods. Neptune soothed the waves and Triton blew on the conch shell to signal that the seas were to retreat to their original shores.[39] The similarity between this Roman myth and the biblical story of the flood would have been obvious to Hellenistic Jews and Christians of Mark's time.

39. Leeming, *Myth*, 56.

There were other gods associated with storms in the Roman pantheon. Taranis, the thunder and storm god of the Celts, was equated by Julius Caesar with Jupiter. Poseidon/Neptune threatened mariners with violent seas. In Ovid's *The Metamorphoses*, written in 8 CE, the god Boreas claims he can drive dark clouds and shake up the sea, send forth thunder and lightning, and then, after this boast, he bellows out a blast that "ruffled the ocean." Scylla, notorious for threatening sailors, bays in the seas and Charybdis, associated with whirlpools, "sucks in and again spews forth the waves." Medea, often with the help of other gods, stirred up seas, winds and clouds. These and other weather/storm deities were well-known by the Romans of Jesus' day and were feared for roiling up violent seas and horrible weather at the drop of a hat.[40]

In 29 BCE Octavian commissioned the poet Virgil to write an epic poem along the lines of the Greek epics *Iliad* and *Odyssey*. Octavian understood the necessity of having a national story to demonstrate the divine and heroic origins of Rome. The book was well-known by Romans and taught in schools. Thus, one story from this new book has important relevance for Mark 4. In one episode of the *Aeneid*, the hero Aeneas sets sail from Carthage. Suddenly an unexplained storm arises: "When overhead there stood a dark gray cloud/ Fraught with night and tempest. The Waves grew rough/Amid the gloom." The helmsman Palinurus calls out "Why have such clouds filled up the skies?/O Father Neptune, what do you have in store?" He commands the sailors to row faster and with more strength against the heaving waves and winds. Indeed, the winds change and "from the black west blowing. Roar athwart/Our course. The air is thickened into mist;/ Nor can we strive against it, nor proceed." Palinurus believes that even Jupiter himself cannot offset the tempest. The similarities with Jesus and the disciples rowing on the sea in the black of night are intriguing—indeed striking—and any Greco-Roman person knowledgeable of the *Aeneid* could have made the connection between the two stories.[41]

But there is another connection that Greco-Roman readers could make between Jesus and weather deities: weather gods such as Zeus and Poseidon were also associated with fertility deities. In the Roman world fertility cults were everywhere. The basic fertility myth is that a god is killed or dies (introducing winter, the time of death), a significant event in the underworld occurs (deal made; battle won), and then the deity reemerges

---

40. Ovid, *Metamorphosis*, 120, 123, 127.
41. Virgil, *Aeneid*, 114.

from death (the grave) and life begins anew.⁴² These fertility cults were everywhere in Jesus' time thus the story of Jesus' death and resurrection was no different than many other stories of gods or even great people.

So, for Mark's Greco-Roman readers who went on to finish the *Aenied*, a connection between Jesus, who has the power to verbally calm the winds just as a deity has the power to invoke the winds, and the fertility cults, could easily be made. Once again, for Mark's readers, confusion and then doubt could arise after reading or hearing the story of Jesus and the calming of the storm. Was he Zeus/Jupiter? Son of Zeus or Jupiter? Was he connected with new life after death? If so, is he Zeus incarnate? Or, Yahweh, god of the Jews? Or. . . . ? Who is this man?

There is a curious note in Mark 6:14–29. The identity of Jesus is being bandied about the region as Jesus' reputation increases. Some claimed he was John the Baptist who King Herod had beheaded, as Mark describes in the following verses. Mark rather blandly relates that these people said John the Baptist was raised from the dead in the form of Jesus and this explains how Jesus could do miracles. Others, however, claimed that Jesus was Elijah, who, according to Jewish belief, was expected to return to herald the coming of the long-awaited Messiah. Still, others believed Jesus was just another prophet like ones of the old days.

All of these responses reveal that, in the eyes of Jesus' contemporaries, any one of these manifestations was expected and thus considered normal. That is, there was nothing that set Jesus apart from other healers and miracle men of this time. Others had done the same thing. For Mark's readers, the issue once again was what set Jesus apart from other healers and miracle workers of his day. Why follow him when other miracle men were just as noteworthy?

For Christians today, we have the hindsight of our religious heritage of theology and apology (defense of Christian beliefs). I have heard many a sermon preached and many a disciple proclaim that Jesus is set apart from, say the Buddha or Muhammad, because Jesus died and was resurrected from the dead. But in Jesus' day this was not an unusual occurrence. And Mark gives us a hint of this in his rather laconic line about the resurrection of John.

Scholars today dodge the issue. Culpepper notes that from Mark's perspective, the connection between John and Jesus is incorrect. John the

---

42. Leeming, *World Mythology*, 318, 410.

Baptist, Culpepper points out, never did miracles. Thus, Jesus' miraculous powers did not come because he was John resurrected.[43] The implication, therefore, is that Jesus' powers are from his divine status. The problem with this argument from silence is, in the story Mark has not established this fact yet. Thus, the first time reader or listener may not have made a decision about Jesus' divinity.

Lane is more on the mark here. He points out that the three explanations of Jesus' identity are some "of the earliest attempts to explain the enigma of his person and work." Lane notes that Jesus was indeed a disciple of John and that people who only knew that Jesus suddenly appeared on the scene (recall the introduction to Mark), explained this appearance believing Jesus was John resurrected. But then Lane argues that these people did not know Jesus directly and had not seen him perform any miracles and thus could not connect him with John at all.[44] But this seems a stretch given that Mark's account has them making this connection. Sure, they may have been making this claim based on hearsay but *somebody* saw the deeds and related *something* to others. There is no evidence in Mark in this particular episode that they had or had not witnessed these deeds. The issue is not whether the crowd knew Jesus personally or not or that they had witnessed Jesus' miracles. The point for Mark and his audience is that Jesus, in the eyes of some, is a resurrected person from the past. And, Mark presents this fact as if there was nothing special about it all. Why would he do so? Maybe because it was not as special as we have been led to believe.

The notion of resurrection was a divisive topic in the days of Jesus and the emerging church. In the Greco-Roman world there were mixed conclusions as to the status of the deceased. While Moyer Hubbard's observations are centered around the city of Corinth they illustrate the problem for Mark's audience. Stoics and Epicureans were not convinced that the dead would be resurrected. Opinions of the populace ran from one side—you are a fool if you believe in this—to the other—various depictions of the new life on funeral stones. Some thought the spirit of the dead lived on in the tomb. The deceased were sometimes clothed for the afterlife and the tombs might even be decorated. The Greeks, inspired by the works of Homer, believed in the underworld of Hades, simply a place where the deceased continued to live after death. Mystery religions offered the lure of everlasting life after death. Given these disparate ideas about the afterlife, Hubbard concludes

---

43. Culpepper, *Mark*, 210.
44. Lane, *Mark*, 212.

that all held one thing in common: all agreed that there was no resurrection after death.⁴⁵

For the Jews, the idea of resurrection came from the agricultural calendar according to Stephen Wylen. Nourishing rains arrive in the Fall and continue into Spring, the time of grain farming, and then the region turns dry as fruits and vegetables grow. The desert becomes a lush green in the winter and turns to brown in the summer. "The seeds of next winter's grasses and flowers hide in the desert soil." This agricultural cycle of wet and dry, growth and dormancy, led to the doctrine of resurrection.⁴⁶

The Jewish doctrine of resurrection began in the 160s BCE and was later adopted and taught by the Pharisees who believed that, "sometime in the future everyone who ever lived will return to bodily life on earth." God then judges each person by their earthly life and actions. Those who fail are doomed to die again while those who pass muster will be given another thousand years to live and then they will move to a "World to Come." The important point here is that Jews believed in a physical resurrection of the dead, not a spiritual resurrection as the Greeks came to believe. Daniel 12:1–2 is the first biblical mention of an idea of a bodily resurrection. This doctrine was a marked step from the ancient Jewish belief that the dead just went to Sheol, a place of "shades" or "shadows" where they continued their existence. In this early notion of death there was no judgment, just an after life very similar to the Greek belief in Hades, the place of the dead. This was the belief of the Sadducees.⁴⁷

Based on Mark 12:18–27 Jesus clearly believed in a physical resurrection. What is curious, however, is that in the original ending of Mark (16:1–8) there is no indication of what form of resurrection Jesus exhibited. He clearly was not in the empty tomb. Did he resurrect physically or spiritually? Does Mark assume that his readers, having already heard of Jesus' teaching on a physical resurrection, will just make the connection that Jesus was physically resurrected and thus on his way to Galilee, as he predicted? Possibly, but some confusion may have resulted in the adoption by the Jews of Jesus' day, and thus the early Christians, of the Greek belief in the separation of the soul/spirit from the physical body at death. Wylen notes that this may have occurred around the time of Jesus. Was Mark torn between both views and thus not able to decide? Was he insisting that his

---

45. Hubbard, *Christianity*, 98–99.
46. Wylen, *Jews*, 17.
47. Ibid., 59.

audience decide for themselves? If so, he was not the only gospel writer. Luke leans toward the physical in his gospel (Luke 24:13–49) yet relates a spiritually resurrected Jesus in the Book of Acts (9:3–9). We have already noted that Paul only saw a spiritually resurrected Jesus. Yet, as Charles Talbert notes, Paul preached the Jewish doctrine of resurrection whereby Jesus' resurrection was initiating the resurrection of Jews who were dead (1 Cor 15:20, 23).[48]

But Paul has moved on from this initial Jewish belief. He says that Christ is resurrected and that, when he returns, the general resurrection of believers will take place and then comes a final judgment. Paul's use of the agricultural term "first fuits" in regards to the resurrection of Christ recalls the Jewish connections of resurrection to the agricultural cycle we noted earlier. In essence, Paul believes in the Jewish doctrine of the bodily resurrection that takes place in the end of days. In this case, Jesus' resurrection meant that the end times were upon the people, not an event in the far distant future as many Christians insist today. Wylen points out that Jews were very divided on this issue and it was a matter of heated debate. It looks like the early Christians were equally torn between the two beliefs. Still, there is no real distinction between the resurrection of Jesus and the believers except that Jesus was the first to be resurrected. Or was he?[49]

Interestingly, there is a curious passage in Matthew about resurrection. While other references to resurrection in the New Testament are often unclear as to what type of resurrection occurred, Matthew notes that, after Jesus died, tombs broke open and the bodies of "many holy people who had died were raised to life" (27:52 NIV). We are told that, after Jesus' resurrection the bodies of these holy people went into Jerusalem and were seen by many. This two-fold resurrection is not mentioned by any other writer in the New Testament. How have scholars interpreted this passage?

Ben Witherington dodges the issue by noting that Jesus was resurrected in an immortal body while these Jewish saints were (apparently) only in earthly bodies. But Matthew, often touted as the most Jewish of the Gospel writers, does not make this distinction. There are hints of Jesus going to an eternal life in heaven in the Gospel of Matthew (26:64), however, the book ends with the disciples worshiping Jesus on the mountain. Based just on Matthew's account, it seems that Jesus will remain on earth with his disciples until the predicted end times arrive which should be soon. John

---

48. Wylen, *Jews*, 61; Talbert, *Romans*, 164.
49. Hubbard, *Christianity*, 99–100; Wylen, *Jews*, 61; Nash, *1 Corinthians*, 404.

Fenton barely addresses the issue and concludes that this "legend" is "an extrapolation of Christian faith in the form of a story." Worse still, W. F. Albright and C. S. Mann do not even comment on verse 52! Leon Morris takes some time to explain this incident but concludes that, "Matthew is making the point that the resurrection of Jesus brought about the resurrection *of his people.*" Morris does not elaborate on this comment but it implies the resurrection of the Jews. Early church theologians seem to shift the emphasis to the *Christian* saints where Jesus' death defeated the power of death, thus unleashing the buried saints and his consequent resurrection led the way to the eventual resurrection of believers in the end days. Still, it is interesting that Matthew mentions that, while facing the risen Jesus on the mountain, some doubted Jesus (Matt 28:16–20). It would seem that, for Matthew, Jesus was resurrected in a bodily form as predicted and believed by Jews.[50]

Thus, scholars do not seem to know what to make of this cryptic episode. But one obvious conclusion is that ten or more years after Mark penned his gospel this Matthean passage in itself indicates that the resurrection of Jesus is not as singular as has been presented by Church theologians. Indeed, the Jews were expecting it. Thus, Jesus' resurrection was the harbinger of the final days where the resurrection was to take place. The Pharisees were correct! And, it is no wonder that the women at Jesus' empty tomb were afraid. The end was near! Still, it is informative that in the early church tradition, other people in Jesus' day were resurrected and, if we take the verses literally as presented by Matthew, they were initially resurrected *before* Jesus was! There was a resurrection before Jesus' resurrection. And this fits within the Jewish understanding of resurrection as taught in Jesus' day. Resurrection, any resurrection, implies that death has no hold over us. And this may have been Mark's intention. The resurrection of Jesus was the first of a whole host of resurrections to follow. There is hope for all believers.

So, was the resurrection of Jesus as presented initially by Mark, and even a few years later by Matthew, as singular and magnificent as later church theologians have made it? One answer would be "no."

It would seem then that these miracles of Jesus were not quite as miraculous as Christians have been led to believe. In Jesus' day, according to Mark, there were other miracle workers. In Jesus' day, according to

---

50. Witherington, *Matthew,* 522; Fenton, *St. Matthew,* 444; Albright and Mann, *Matthew,* 352; Morris, *Matthew,* 725, emphasis mine; Simonetti, *Matthew,* 297, where he cites Hilary of Poitiers and Apollinaris.

Matthew, people were resurrected. This raises the question, is Mark trying to make Jesus into an ordinary miracle man who competed with other similar miracle workers? If so, why? Why not present Jesus as more than just an everyday miracle worker? Again, given the context of Mark's era, it is just not clear what Mark is trying to make of Jesus.

So, today, if believers seem indifferent to the miraculous Jesus they should take heart in Mark's gospel. But this raises a larger question: Why believe in Jesus at all?

6

The Cloud of Unknowing

Then Solomon said, "The Lord has said that he would dwell in a dark cloud."

(1 Kgs 8:12 NIV)

A QUICK LOOK AT images for and of God in the Bible leads one to consider clouds. The pillar of cloud by day, God riding on the clouds, the cloud in the Exodus tent and eventually in the Temple in Jerusalem. The prophet Nahum describes God's way as "in the whirlwind and the storm, and clouds are the dust of his feet" (Nah 1:3 NIV).

But to keep the spiritual sense of the cloud, clouds are literally and metaphorically difficult to grasp. A cloud can be the shade that provides rest from a hot sun or a destructive, torrential storm. Clouds are hard to predict. They ride on the unseen winds. They are light and then dark. Puffy or whispy. When times are rough many would say that God is like the clouds, unpredictable.

In what seems a well-intended move, King Solomon builds a temple for the ephemeral cloud of God to reside in Jerusalem, a mighty and imposing structure constructed for the glory of God yet it also was a symbol of Solomon's power and wealth to those who visited the Holy City. Now a multitude of priests and singers and keepers will implement worship, sacrifices and a myriad of other services for the believers who need their sins cleansed and their hearts made whole. Pilgrims migrated there several times a year for the major festivals, bringing with them penitent hearts and sacrificial animals as well as money that filled the locals with an economic boost.

King Solomon meant well but the biblical record suggests that not all were impressed with this edifice. Indeed, it seems that once the Temple was built and the priesthood put into place, the faith of Israel deteriorated. In the account in 1 Kings beginning at chapter 9, no sooner than the Temple was finished and God appeared to Solomon and implored the king to keep the commands of God, we read that Solomon began breaking all of these commands. Then adversaries arose and soon the Kingdom of Israel split apart. Now there are two nations, the sinful Israel to the north and her sister Judah, home of Jerusalem and the Temple, to the south.

Still, the Temple continued to dominate the religion of God's people. Yet as the centuries continued it was apparent that the dwelling place for the cloud of God did not lead to a spiritual and faithful people. Isaiah railed against the sacrifices of the faithful—"I have no pleasure in the blood of bulls and lambs and goats . . . Stop bringing meaningless offerings!" (Isa 1:11, 13 NIV) Jeremiah, like Isaiah, saw that Temple worship was not changing the behavior of the people. The deeds of the faithful who attended the religious festivals and offered numerous sacrifices did not reflect the love of God. The fatherless were neglected, the foreigner ignored, the widow shunned. Justice was gone and the people of God revered other deities as well. Indeed, according to Jeremiah 7:9 half of the Ten Commandments were regularly broken by God's people who, in an insult to their God, fled to the temple to hide behind the mantra, "This is the Temple of the Lord." Jeremiah asks a question that implies a fierce condemnation of the people and their Temple: "Has this house, which bears my Name, become a den of robbers?" (Jer 7:11 NIV) A few years later God led the Babylonians to Jerusalem and they destroyed the idolized Temple.

The Temple was eventually rebuilt, the sacrificial system reinstituted and strict adherence to the law was required to avoid a similar attack and destruction of the new Temple. And this was the system that stymied Jesus' ministry, led to numerous squabbles with the Jewish teachers and priests, and impeded the construction of the Kingdom of God. Jesus condemned what can be called Temple Judaism and its priests and servants for its neglect of the poor. He questioned the heavy Temple tax that was required of all to worship there and maintain the thousands of Temple employees, priests and singers. Frustrated with the sales of blemished, over-priced sacrificial animals, Jesus answered the question that Jeremiah prophetically asked centuries before: the Temple indeed had been turned into a den of robbers. Again.

Christians today are too busy forcing the Cloud to live within the Temple of creeds, faith statements and fundamentals of the faith. One of the major criticisms I hear from non-Christians and those who have fled the hypocritical Church is, why do you make such a big deal out of going to church on Sunday when you don't live the teachings of Christ the rest of the week? We have become the very Temple of the Lord that Jeremiah condemned and Jesus abhorred. Too many Christians go to church and intone, "This is the temple of the Lord!" and then neglect to fulfill the mission of God. Maybe it is time to set loose the Cloud of God. Clouds need to be free to roam the skies, rain upon whom they will, stir up tempests and provide cooling breezes while teaching us to listen to the wisdom of the winds.

Karen Armstrong, in her book *The Case for God*, puts forth a strong thesis that Christians today spend too much time splitting theological hairs to the point that we have forgotten how our ancient ancestors maintained their faith. She cites evidence from various religions but centers specifically on Christianity. All of these religions focused on actions to demonstrate faith. In Christianity, from the beginnings up through the Middle Ages, people came to know God by actions: liturgy, prayers, initiations, living out the acts of Jesus. Based on solid evidence she argues that we must live in the mystery of the faith, not try to explain it. *Mythos*, the stories of the Bible, not *logos*, the reasoned logic of theology, creeds, faith statements and proofs, is the realm where true knowledge of God comes about. Middle Ages mystics described the process well. One must push out all the facts and theologies and proofs of the faith in order to encounter God. Citing the unknown author of *The Cloud of Unknowing*, Armstrong writes, "If we want to know God, all thoughts about the Trinity, the Virgin Mary, the life of Christ, and the stories of the saints—which are perfectly good in themselves—must be cast under a thick 'cloud of forgetting.'"[1]

I would add the resurrection as well. One "Temple of the Lord" that Christians hide in is the resurrection of Jesus. Part of the litmus test of a true Christian is whether you believe in the literal, physical resurrection of Jesus. Interestingly, in the original story Mark has no resurrection appearance of Jesus. That Jesus was resurrected is quite clear in the Gospel of

---

1. Armstrong, *Case*, 156.

Mark. *How* he was resurrected is never addressed. Unlike Matthew, Luke and John, Mark left it as a mystery. And perhaps that is as it should be.

According to the original ending of Mark, two mornings after Jesus was crucified and buried, Mary Magdalene and Mary the mother of James and Joses arrived at the tomb to apply spices to the body of Jesus in order to assuage the stench of the decaying body. They worried about the large stone that covered the entrance—who would move it?—but this did not keep them from their self-appointed task. They were suddenly frightened by the open tomb and when they looked inside a young man dressed in white addressed their fears and told them to rush to Galilee where a risen Jesus would meet the disciples and Peter, just as he had told them before his death. The terrified yet astonished two women fled the tomb and, in a reminder of a constant theme in the Gospel of Mark, told no one because they were afraid. This is how the oldest and most reliable manuscripts of Mark's gospel end. There is no description of a resurrected Jesus. This raises a most important yet curious question: what, if anything, did Mark know about the resurrected Jesus?

Scholars sometimes suggest that Matthew, Luke, and John added more additional material to their resurrection stories to make up for this rather embarrassing account that lacked any mention or description of the resurrected Jesus. Thus, these evangelists added to and even changed Mark's account somewhat. Matthew adds that an angel of the Lord came and caused an earthquake that shook the stone loose from the tomb, scaring the guards posted there by the Roman ruler Pilate at the request of the Jewish leaders. As in the book of Mark, the angel tells them to go and tell the disciples that Jesus will meet them in Galilee. As the women rush away Jesus meets them and they bow down, hold his feet and worship him. In Galilee the eleven disciples, *some of whom doubted him* (Matt 28:17), gathered on "the mountain" and listened as Jesus commissioned them to go, teach and baptize the whole world. It is curious that we never hear in Easter Morning sermons that some of these disciples doubted Jesus.

Questions arise about this curiosity and scholars dance around the issue. Leon Morris prefers the word "hesitated" to "doubted." He goes on to argue that surely none of the eleven disciples would doubt Jesus. "It can scarcely mean that the hesitators were included among the worshipers ... It is difficult to think that the hesitation was coming from the eleven, considering all that had happened to them during the recent past." To defend this assertion Morris then suggests that there were more than the eleven there on the mountain and it was among these extra worshipers that the hesitation occurred.[2] But the text is quite clear: the eleven went to the mountain, they worshiped and some doubted. There is no indication that there were more than the eleven.

William F. Albright and C. S. Mann translate "some were doubtful" here. They suggest that Matthew was aware of Luke's resurrection stories in Luke 24. But then they dismiss the doubts altogether: "Apart from such awareness of other traditions, it is not possible to find any good reason for this assertion, especially in light of [Matt] 28:8." John Fenton comes closer to the problem when he writes "It is not at all clear why Matthew says this, though we may compare the resurrection stories in Luke and John, which in each case contain references to doubt and unbelief."[3] If Luke records episodes where doubt could be one conclusion and John records episodes of doubting, including that of Thomas, then clearly there was a tradition of doubt that was not embarrassing enough for the very early Church to leave out of the resurrection narrative. This begs the question for believers today: Why are we dodging this issue?

Based on Matthew's text, then, it would seem that doubt is acceptable among those who worship Jesus. This is what early Christian theologian Chrysostom suggests: " . . . admire the Evangelists' truthfulness. Even up to the last day, they were determined not to conceal even their own shortcomings. Nevertheless even these are assured by what they see."[4] Why did they doubt him when he ostensibly stood right there in front of them? Were they questioning whether Jesus had actually died? Did they actually question his appearance, as if he was a ghost? Did they question the fact that he could not be the long-awaited Messiah because he was killed? This went against the grain of expectations that the Messiah was to be a great warrior who conquered the persecutors of the Jews and restored them to their once glorious days of a mighty kingdom. The Romans would die, not the Messiah.

Otto Michel points out that, for Matthew, seeing is not the issue here. Belief and obedience are key to the early Church's preaching and teaching. Michel points out that Matthew and John clearly have sources that indicate doubt among the disciples. He goes on to suggest that, immediately after Matthew notes that some doubted, Jesus then says, "All authority in heaven

---

2. Morris, *Matthew*, 745.
3. Albright and Mann, *Matthew*, 361–362; Fenton, *Matthew*, 453.
4. Simonetti, *Matthew*, 312–313.

and on earth has been given to me. Therefore go and make disciples of all nations, baptizing them in the name of the Father and of the Son and of the Holy Spirit, and teaching them to obey . . . And surely I am with you . . . " The verbs are clear: go, make disciples, baptize, teach. These will be the things that remind you that I am with you.[5]

In Luke 24 the Evangelist changes the account even more. As the story begins, "the women," as Luke calls them, arrive with their spices to anoint the body. A few verses later he provides their names: Mary Magdalene, Joanna, and Mary the mother of James, along with the "other women" who went to the tomb where they find the stone rolled away. There is no mention of who or what rolled it away but perhaps it was the "two men" in dazzling apparel who suddenly stood by the now frightened women. They leave the tomb, run back to Jerusalem, and tell the disciples—some of whom thought the story was a tale told by the women—and others who were present what they found. Peter runs back to the tomb to see firsthand what the women report, perhaps to verify their story.

On that same day two men, one named Cleopas, were traveling on the road to Emmaus. Here a stranger catches up with them and the three join in conversation. The two men relate the news of the day of Jesus who had risen from the grave (word traveled fast that day!). In this story they note that the women had seen a vision of angels. The two men do not recognize that their companion is Jesus until they invite him to dinner where, as Jesus blessed the bread, broke it and gave it to them, the ritual awoke them to the identity of their guest. Upon this revelation, Jesus vanishes. The two incredulous men rush to Jerusalem and report their story to the eleven disciples.

During this report Jesus suddenly appears to the disciples, who, hearing Jesus, think that he is a spirit. After inviting them to touch him (a spirit does not have bones and flesh, he reminds them) they still disbelieved though, Luke says, it was with joy. Jesus then eats bread and fish while his disbelievers watch. After Jesus' brief reminder of how he had predicted his persecution, death, burial and resurrection so that scriptures might be fulfilled, the eyes of the disbelievers were opened and they now understood everything. With Jesus at the lead, they go to Bethany where Jesus blesses them and then ascends to heaven. The disciples worship briefly and then return to Jerusalem where they blessed God in the temple.

Notice that nobody in this story goes to Galilee. It is apparent that Luke deviates from Mark's script. Matthew follows Mark's story and interestingly

5. Michel, "Conclusion," 30–41.

has no resurrection appearances other than what occurred on the mountain in Galilee. Luke has two significant resurrection appearances where Jesus seems to be physical yet also ghostly. In Luke 24 we are told that Peter has also seen Jesus but we have no direct report of the resurrection appearance.

Norval Geldenhuys strains to prove that the Jesus in Luke's story is "clothed in a glorified, celestial body that was not bound by limitation of an ordinary earthly body." But he stumbles when he gets to the scene where the disciples are asked to touch the body of Christ. "He makes them realize that it is not merely His spirit that has appeared before them but that it is He Himself—in spirit and in body. (His body of course, to this extent different from an ordinary body in that it was now a glorified, celestial body . . .)" To back up this qualification he refers the reader to Paul's description of the resurrected body in 1 Corinthians 15:35–58.[6] But as we will see below, this description in Corinthians does not really support a physical resurrection of Jesus at all. What, then, did these disciples see when Jesus appeared to them after the resurrection? If it was as ghostly as Luke presents it, then there would have been some confusion and perhaps some doubts as well concerning the resurrected form of Jesus. Yet, their doubts are apparently assuaged when Jesus eats before them and then takes them out to Bethany where he ascends into the heavens.

Joseph Fitzmyer examines these scenes in Luke 24 and notes that the disciples "are terrified, startled, full of doubt, incredulous, overjoyed yet wondering" but he goes on to note that this pericope as presented by Luke "is intended also to stress the identity and the physical reality of the risen Christ." Even Jesus recognizes their doubts as verse 38 reveals. That Jesus ate with his disciples is noted again in Acts 1:4 and 10:41. Jesus instructs the disciples to touch him and see but interestingly there is no record of them doing so. At the risk of speculation, if Luke's goal was to prove that Jesus had a physical body, wouldn't he have reported that disciples touched Jesus if they had indeed done so? This lack of response on the part of the disciples and Luke suggests what Fitzmyer alludes to: there was a doubting problem in the early Church. Apparently both Luke and John are possibly using the same "common material" presenting episodes of Jesus eating with the disciples. Curiously, Fitzmyer does remind the reader that even angels can eat food, based on the text from Genesis 18:8 where heavenly visitors are fed

---

6. Geldenhuys, *Luke*, 640.

by Abraham. Is Fitzmeyer suggesting that Jesus may indeed be "physical" yet in an angelic sense?[7]

Once again we meet with disciples, perhaps all of them since Luke is not clear on this matter, who at least initially disbelieved Jesus even though he stood in their midst and ate food with them. It seems that disbelief, a major theme in Mark's gospel, still permeated the stories of the resurrection of Jesus years after Mark's gospel was heard in synagogues and churches throughout the Mediterranean.

John's account varies even more. On the morning of the resurrection only Mary Magdalene goes to the tomb (what happened to the other women?), this time in the dark, where she finds the stone has been rolled away. She runs to tell Simon Peter and another disciple—John just cryptically says that he was the disciple who Jesus loved—about her discovery. In an echo of Matthew's story where guards were posted to thwart someone from stealing Jesus' body in order to prevent anyone from saying that Jesus had resurrected, Mary exclaims "they" have taken Jesus out of the tomb and laid him somewhere else. The disciple who Jesus loved, along with Peter, race to the tomb where Peter then finds the burial cloths and the face cloth which is folded and laid in a separate place.

Mary remained outside the tomb where she wept over the whole episode. She then looks into the tomb and sees two angels in white. She turns around and immediately sees Jesus but does not recognize him because she thinks he is the gardener who removed Jesus' body. Why can't she recognize this person who had such an impact on her life? Jesus calls out "Mary" and then she recognizes him. She goes to embrace him but Jesus warns that she cannot because he has not ascended to heaven (how can she embrace him when he is in heaven?). She is then told to go to Jesus' brothers (the disciples) and announce that he is ascending to heaven to meet their God and Father. This odd warning and description should raise an eyebrow. Was Jesus not yet a fleshly body? What does this mean? What *did* he look like? This seems to contradict Matthew's and Luke's stories of a physical Jesus who can be touched and who can consume a meal.

On the evening of the same day, in a locked room, Jesus suddenly appears to the ten disciples (Thomas is not with them) and, after showing them his wounds, blesses them. Eight days later Jesus again suddenly appears in a locked room where he invites the infamous doubting Thomas to put his fingers on the wounds. (Has Jesus now ascended to heaven so

---

7. Fitzmyer, *Luke*, 1574–1577.

that people are allowed to touch him? How is he in heaven and on earth?) Interestingly, like Luke, the account does not say that Thomas did so. Thomas exclaims "My Lord and my God" to which Jesus responds that, while Thomas believed because he witnessed the scars on Jesus' body, others who had never seen them were even more blessed. Once again we see the theme of disbelief.

In an episode that some scholars believe may have been added to the Gospel of John, Jesus appears to the disciples while they are fishing. The reason for scholarly dispute is that the same story appears in the Gospel of Luke but it is near the near the beginning of Jesus' ministry, not after the resurrection. This oddity recalls the fact that it was common knowledge in the second century that Mark knew the stories about Jesus that Peter taught him but deliberately did not arrange them in historical order. At the end of this story in John's account Jesus tells Peter "Follow me."

There is one more account to consider. In the opening chapter of the Book of Acts Luke relates that Jesus proved himself to be alive in various ways. These are not listed thus we can only assume that he is talking about the events he mentioned in his gospel. Jesus stayed on the earth forty days and he ordered his believers not to depart from Jerusalem until the gift of the Holy Spirit came upon them, which takes place in Acts 2 in the story of Pentecost. At the end of the forty-day period, when asked by the disciples when the day will come when Israel will be restored, Jesus tells them that this is something they are not to know. Instead they should be witnesses for Jesus throughout the world. With this commissioning Jesus then ascends to heaven.

So, we see that five different versions of the resurrection of Jesus are in the New Testament. What really happened on that morning when the women arrived at the tomb only to find it empty? Mark leaves the reader dangling answers. Did Jesus rise up from the dead? Was he really waiting in Galilee? Or, did he remain in Jerusalem, as Luke says? In the original ending Mark does not answer these questions. He simply leaves the answer to the reader. And, as we have seen, there is room for much doubting in Mark's story and the other gospel accounts. Was Jesus a ghost, a spirit, a physical human? From the view of the disciples, any one of these answers could be correct, and therein rests the problem. The account of John where Mary is told explicitly that she cannot touch Jesus until he has ascended to heaven is quite important for this discussion because John never tells us if Jesus ascended to heaven or not. Would that mean that Jesus was indeed not in a physical form when he appeared to the disciples, the "other women" and the "other" people in these various accounts? Adding to the frustration, the account in Acts seems to contradict this assumption.

Since Mark did not witness the resurrected Jesus, what did he know about the resurrection? We recall that, according to Acts 13:5 and 15:36–41, Mark, also known as John, was an early traveling companion with the apostle Paul. Although the relationship did not last long, surely Mark would have heard Paul talk about his amazing conversion experience as they journeyed from Antioch to Seleucia and then to Cyprus and eventually Pamphylia. Surely Paul described in detail the vision of Jesus he saw as he traveled to Damascus. Most certainly he would have discussed his emotions, his change in theology, his new view of Judaism and his strong conviction that Jesus was the long-awaited Messiah. If we imagine Mark and Paul sitting around at dinner, conversing during the long travels over Roman roads and Mediterranean seas, or, having intimate talks deep into the night at inns and the homes of Christian converts, then we can say with some conviction that Mark knew well Paul's vision of the resurrection of Jesus.

So, what did Paul see?

Before we explore Paul's understanding of resurrection we need to understand the Greco-Roman and rabbinical attitudes toward death and life after death. In Jesus' day "Postmortem existence was not itself a major preoccupation of the Romans," noted scholar Martin Goodman writes. Epicurean philosophers and adherents did not espouse any idea of life after death. However, occasionally an exceptional person such as Julius Caesar, who was deified in 42 BCE after his death, existed happily after death in the heavens. Otherwise, the dead were generally cremated and placed in urns which were then set into cemeteries outside of town. The dead joined the other spirits of the dead and this belief may coincide with the Roman belief in ghosts. The Greeks were appalled by the notion of a resurrected body but their belief in the immortality of the soul was part of the Roman culture and it also permeated the rabbinical teachings on death. There was a clear distinction between the fleshly body and the post-death spirit or soul. The Pharisees taught about the resurrection although it was not clear what they meant. Was it the immortality of the soul, thus it survived death, or was it the reincarnation of the soul? The rabbis taught that the resurrection was bodily but this referred to the dead body which was to be interred properly, not to a fleshly body that appeared on earth. Thus, for Jews, the

Roman practice of cremation was not allowed.[8] All of this to say that, in Jesus' day, the preoccupation with a physical, earthly resurrection was not part of the everyday discussions and worries. Once the body was buried it was believed that the soul existed forever, either in a place of shades for the ordinary folks or a home of heavenly bliss for the chosen few. Paul in Ephesians 1:20 follows the latter when he describes the resurrected Jesus as one who resides in the heavenly realms. Interestingly, this is exactly how Julius Caesar was described after he died.

While Paul is acknowledged by scholars for arriving at the doctrine of the sacrifice of Jesus for the sins of the world, it was not until Matthew, Luke, John and the Book of Acts were penned, between roughly 80–90 CE, that stories of a *physical* resurrection of Jesus emerge in the preaching of the early church. If we remove these three gospels and the Book of Acts from our reconstruction of the resurrection of Jesus, what the Middle Ages anonymous author called the "cloud of forgetting," then we can see better what Mark had received from Paul and Peter. The overarching issue for believers both then and now is, was Jesus resurrected in a visionary, spiritual form as opposed to a physical bodily resurrection.

The sticking point for early believers was Jesus' promise to return soon. The first biblical instance where this prophecy was questioned is in Paul's letters to the Thessalonians. The converts in Thessalonica were concerned that their brothers and sisters who had already died would not participate in the resurrection. Thus Paul had to address this issue head on in the first of his many letters to the churches in the Mediterranean area. In the Thessalonian correspondence, written around 51 CE, Paul tackles the problem.

There is only one specific passage in these two letters where Paul mentions the resurrection of Jesus. In 1 Thessalonians 4:14 Paul notes that he and the converts at Thessalonica believe that Jesus died and rose again. Without the help of the later gospels and Acts the interpretation of this phrase is open to suggestion. Given the cultural mindset of the time, Paul's converts would have understood the phrase as meaning that Jesus was still alive in a spiritual form. Surely Paul, understanding this cultural belief, would have taken pains to describe the physical, earthly resurrected body of Jesus to convince his readers that the resurrection of their Lord was unique. Beside this, there were enough stories of other teachers and

---

8. Goodman, *Rome and Jerusalem*, 239–248.

healers resurrecting that the story of Jesus' resurrection would not have raised many eyebrows.

Scholars point out that this passage is a difficult one to interpret. First, Greeks understood that resurrection into a wonderful afterlife was only for special people. The rest simply were buried to live a forlorn eternal existence and this did not bring any sense of hope neither to those who had died nor to their surviving kin. Christianity, however, offered a ray of hope in the resurrection of Jesus. The dead would be raised with Christ. But when would this take place? In the Parousia (the return of Jesus), or by Jesus' death? If the latter, then how could they be certain? The issue here is, what exactly did Paul mean by "through Jesus, God will bring with him those who have fallen asleep." What does "through Jesus" mean? The verse puzzles scholars and no clear and sustained interpretation of it has been offered.[9] On the other hand, if the former, well, Jesus had not returned as promised in their lifetimes. Either way, they no doubt were filled with despair, forced to confront death with no hope at all, the very belief that they joined Christianity to leave behind. In an encouraging word, Paul tells them to await the impending coming of Christ, heralded by the sound of a trumpet, when the dead in Christ will rise first. But the Thessalonians had heard this before and Jesus had not returned yet. Why should they believe it again when it might let them down once more?

Around 53–56 CE Paul wrote his next series of letters, what is known as the Corinthian correspondence. Some of the Corinthians doubted that Jesus resurrected from the grave. Paul confronts this erroneous notion by addressing the issue of resurrection. In 1 Corinthians 15 Paul defends his apostolic credentials against the claims of some that he was not of the caliber as Jesus' original twelve followers. Paul says that, after the resurrection, Jesus first appeared to Cephas (Peter), then to the twelve, then to five hundred people (not mentioned in the Gospels or Acts) who witnessed Jesus all at one time. Paul goes on to note that Jesus then appeared to his brother James (again not attested in the New Testament) and the other apostles. The key word here is "appeared" as used in verse 5.

The fact that some scholars do not address the word suggests that, for them, it means what Matthew, Luke and John point out in their defense of the uniqueness of Jesus compared to other holy men. C.K Barret does not address the word at all nor do William F. Orr and James Arthur Walther. Conservative scholar W. Harold Mare, however, opens the door

---

9. Morris, *Thessalonians*, 137–140; Marshall, *Thessalonians*, 122–125.

The Cloud of Unknowing

to speculation when he notes that the word means appeared rather than "was seen." This is interesting because the understanding of this particular translation of the Greek word *horao* means to "become visible, appear" *in a supernatural form* [my emphasis]. It can also mean "experience" or "witness," "notice," "recognize" or "understand." All of these definitions fit well within the Greco-Roman and rabbinical understandings of resurrection of a spiritual body or soul.[10]

There is no doubt that Paul was convinced that Jesus was alive, having conquered death to arise from the grave. 1 Corinthians 15 is Paul's lengthy defense of this theology. This may have been because of Paul's understanding of the term "resurrection." In 1 Corinthians 15 Paul describes the resurrected body. He notes a difference in the physical body, the one we have when we are alive on this earth, and the spiritual body, the one we will have in heaven. The physical body is earthly; the resurrected body is a spiritual body. For Paul there is a very clear distinction between the earthly and spiritual bodies. He goes on to affirm this when he describes the final resurrection: all would be changed from the physical to the heavenly body. For Paul, this whole crucifixion episode of life, death, burial, and resurrection was a symbol of the last sacrifice to expiate the sins of all humankind. It was a familiar theme in the Greco-Roman religious culture—many of the mystery cults and myths believed likewise—but Paul interprets it through the lens of Jewish sacrificial theology. His consistent theology of resurrection is confirmed again in 2 Corinthians 5:1–10 where he points out that we would rather be away from the earthly body and at home with Jesus in the heavenly, spiritual world. For Paul, in the Corinthian correspondence, there is no clear evidence of a physical resurrection either of Jesus nor of believers.

In Romans 4:24 Paul testifies that those who believe in the God who raised Jesus from the dead will be saved through righteousness. Again, Paul certainly believed that Jesus arose from the dead. The question for us and, consequently for Paul's pupil, Mark, is, *in what form* did Jesus arise? This can be answered by raising another question: in what form did Paul actually see Jesus? In 2 Corinthians 12 Paul describes his Damascus road conversion as if it were some sort of mystical experience. Indeed, the event was so odd that he could not put it into words. As Paul describes it, he was caught up into the third heaven, or he was physically taken to paradise, or was he

---

10. Barrett, *First Corinthians*, 334–346; Orr and Walther, *First Corinthians*, 316–323; Mare, *1 Corinthians*, 284; Bauer, Arndt and Gingrich, *Lexicon*, "horao."

spiritually taken? He cannot say for sure. In Galatians 1:1–17 he notes his persecution of those who proclaimed Jesus as the Messiah and then his vision (he calls it a revelation) of Jesus, but this time there is no mention of the Damascus road. In this account he states clearly that God revealed Jesus to him. Thus, there is still no mention of a physical vision or experience of Jesus. The writer of Acts echoes these Pauline accounts when he notes that Paul saw a light from heaven and then heard the voice of Jesus (9:4; 22:6–8; 26:13–14). In each of these accounts Paul's experience of Jesus was clearly a spiritual one. He never mentions a physical resurrection of Jesus.

Two other epistles from "Paul" provide more light on this dark subject. Colossians and Ephesians are considered by many scholars to be pseudonymous writings. That is, they were written later than Paul by some who believed in Paul's theology and thus wrote as if they were the apostle. This was a common practice in the Greco-Roman world.

In Ephesians Paul's theology of resurrection reflects the Greco-Roman and Jewish culture of his day. In Ephesians 2:5 Paul writes that those who were once sinners but are now saved by grace are raised up with Jesus and seated in the heavenly places in Christ. This same theology is confirmed in Ephesians 4:8 where the author cites Psalm 68:16, a passage revealing that when Jesus ascended to heaven he led a host of captives with him. Are the saved resurrected physically? In the same way as Jesus was raised by God and taken to heaven so also are the saved. Again, given the Jewish and Greco-Roman culture of death this does not seem to substantiate a physical resurrection of Jesus nor of his believers. It does, however, remain consistent with the Greco-Roman and Jewish beliefs about resurrection except that Paul includes the saved among the notables who are resurrected to heaven and not left to live in the shades of the afterlife. This was the hope that Christianity brought to the Mediterranean world! A heavenly afterlife was no longer just for the elites. Now all could enjoy eternal life!

A more narrow clarification of Paul's (or the early Church's) understanding of resurrection is found in Colossians 2. Here the writer connects the resurrection of Jesus with the earthly life of the saved. As Jesus was raised from the dead to conquer death so also the saved are raised up to continue their new life of salvation while still on earth. Paul continues by stating that those who once were dead in their trespasses are now made alive through God's forgiveness. He then implies that their Christian life is a heavenly realm on earth, a realm where the old Jewish and Greco-Roman values are no longer relevant for the new believers. With this chapter from

Colossians in mind, there is no clear notion of a physical resurrection of Jesus. Indeed, the resurrection is a symbol for a new life on earth, not of eternal life in heaven.

It is curious that Peter, who instructed Mark in the life and teachings of Jesus and who was the main disciple of the original twelve and who travelled with Jesus and was privy to the most spiritual and confusing events in his life, never mentions the physical resurrection of Jesus at all in his two letters. He comes close when he refers to Jesus but he always calls it the revelation of Jesus, not the resurrection. Jesus was raised in glory, according to Peter, but again there is no direct mention of a physical resurrection.

Thus, the best evidence that we have, although incomplete, is that Mark may have been aware of Paul's theology of the resurrected body of Jesus and his believers. But, did he know of other accounts that suggested Jesus was indeed physically resurrected? If so, was he as confused, as unbelieving as these disciples and others we have mentioned above? In essence, was Mark like the man whose child was possessed by demons? Did he believe yet also not believe?

Mark's ending does not present the conclusion in either or terms: either Jesus was just another Greco-Roman-Egyptian deity or Jewish Messiah has been, or, he was a unique Son of a God. While the centurion guarding the cross exclaims that Jesus was the son of God, the women who found an empty tomb were not so sure. They were told to go to Galilee. Somewhere in between the cross and Galilee the Christian must make a decision. I believe; help my unbelief.

Norman Perrin proposes an interpretation that might help our unbelief. First, he points out what I have illustrated above: "Mark has an understanding of the resurrection of Jesus radically different from that represented by the Apostle Paul . . . or by the other evangelists." Second, Perrin asserts that, "Mark is not concerned with the resurrection in and of itself; he is concerned with it as the essential prelude to something else." What is this "something else"? The return of Christ. But, in between the resurrection of Jesus and the immanent return of Christ lies the last important point: Galilee. The women who experienced the empty tomb were reminded that Jesus would meet the disciples in Galilee, as he had foretold. Why Galilee? Why not Jerusalem, the home of Judaism and the Temple (which is where Luke has the resurrection appearances of Jesus)? Because Galilee is symbolic: it represents the Gentile mission of Jesus and also the early Church.[11] It is as if Mark is saying in coded language, leave the established and cold religion of Judaism and its holy city and its idolized Temple behind and instead focus on the "other" people.

Another way to put this is, because the disciples all throughout the Gospel of Mark never fully understand who and what Jesus is and they never fully grasp the meaning of his teachings, then go back to Galilee and do the gospel of Jesus until it sinks in who and what Jesus is. As Perrin suggests, why would Mark waste time with resurrection appearances when the disciples never understood the physical Jesus?[12]

What does the now absent and apparently resurrected Jesus and the region of Galilee represent in the Gospel of Mark? Eugene Boring has an answer.

Mark's note concerning the resurrection of Jesus as "he is not here" is, according to Boring, the actual reality of the early believers and the early Church. Jesus was literally not there as the Church continued in its ministry. Jesus would not be there for the Lord's Supper, he would not be there as the disciples preached, taught, healed and ministered. "The absence of Jesus is an aspect of the community's experience . . . " Along with this, Galilee has significant symbolic meaning. "Mark is opposing the apocalyptic interest that centered on Jerusalem in the final phases of the war and the destruction of the city and its temple." Instead, Mark's community, which Boring suggests might have been in Galilee, "is to look beyond Jerusalem to its Gentle mission represented by Galilee." What took place in Galilee in the Gospel of Mark? Very simply, the work of Jesus. Healing, teaching, preaching, ministry.[13]

Rather than storing Jesus in the box of the Temple, or keeping him confined in the Church, or restrained in the creeds, the spirited cloud of Jesus must be loosed to go to the people who are not associated with the established religion of the day. Leave behind the authoritative Temple and head to the mission fields. If Mark is writing for today's Christians, this is a stinging indictment of the current state of affairs.

Christians today might reconsider what Mark was trying to accomplish in writing the first biography of Jesus in the late 60s–70 CE. Amid frustration about the delayed Parousia, competing claims of Jesus' Jewishness,

---

11. Perrin, *Resurrection*, 19, 23, 26.
12. Ibid., 30–31.
13. Boring, *Mark*, 446–447.

diverse expectations of the Messiah, feuds between Gentile Christians and Jewish Christians, and developing theologies among the various churches, Mark writes a book about this enigmatic man called Jesus. Jesus is son of God, healer, exorcist, teacher, one who is involved with demons, persecuted and, resurrected in some mysterious way. Choose one of the above, all of the above, or mix and match? No matter which you choose, go to Galilee and do what Jesus did.

Do we really need resurrection appearances to continue the work of Christ? Mark did not think so. People will see the resurrected Jesus when we minister to them.

7

Who Do You Say That I Am?

The secret of the kingdom of God has been given to you.
(MARK 4:11 NIV)

I WAS INTRIGUED THE other day when I received an email from one of the Christian bookstores in my area. There was a book out by Judah Smith entitled *Jesus Is* _____.[1] I was curious so I purchased a copy. The idea for *Jesus Is* _____ came from an ad campaign by Judah's church in Seattle, Washington. They wanted to get this otherwise religion-less city to consider what Jesus was to them. Billboards, Facebook, a website and other media were employed to get the city talking about Jesus. Seventy five thousand people responded, some with meaningful answers, others with sarcasm and downright crude remarks. Still, the campaign worked. A chalkboard was set up in the church where members and guests could fill in the blank themselves. A mission was born from a simple marketing campaign. Now people can make Jesus into literally whatever they believe he is.

So I began reading this *New York Times* bestseller. Much like Jefferson Bethke's *Jesus Is > Religion* the banter is hip, relating to the millennials. Many of Smith's ideas are quite worth the read and there are some preachable nuggets to consider for Sundays. But, discerning Christians will raise a flag or two as they ponder what Smith has to say.

1. Smith, *Jesus*.

Who Do You Say That I Am?

The problem with the book is, the theology is sometimes suspect. Smith makes some leaps in interpretation that reveal weak Bible backgrounds. Did you know that tax collectors in Jesus' day were also pimps? According to Smith Zacchaeus was both a gangster and a pimp. Such declarations may make the story more amenable to the young in faith but, seriously? Then, like Bethke, he makes assumptions about women that are a bit tenuous: the woman caught in adultery in John 8 was probably a prostitute. Really? Smith makes a huge leap into the incredulous when he asserts all people are righteous. He eventually cites Proverbs (no specific verse given but 24:16 is the verse) where the righteous man falls seven times but rises again. From this and his own reasoning he believes that all people are righteous. In a fit of proof-texting he declares, "The man is righteous because God said he's righteous." But this ignores the context of Proverbs where one becomes righteous by learning from Lady Wisdom and resisting Woman Folly (chapters 1–9). One becomes righteous by following the Way, not from just being alive. One has to do something in order to be considered righteous in Proverbs. A quick look back at the character of Job confirms this. Job was righteous because he did what was right before God. But, in today's church where all want to be affirmed (and get the trophy even if they failed?) we don't have to do anything to become righteous.[2]

Last, among other theological snafus, Smith, reading Ecclesiastes, concludes correctly that life is not about being happy. But then he missteps when he states that life is about God. "Focusing on God brings about meaning to our lives." But, not all scholars of Ecclesiastes will agree. Some point out that Ecclesiastes is at least agnostic if not worst. In fact, the very ideals of God are rejected because they have not led to the blessings promised. Maybe life is not about God after all. That is the real lesson of Ecclesiastes. The book dares to question the very basis of the Old Testament law: do good and God will bless; do bad and God will curse.[3]

Besides that, just six pages later Smith fills in the blank by saying that Jesus Is Happy. Smith arrives at this conclusion because he is frustrated with the artistic depictions of Jesus as "a zombie" who "never smiles." Smith knows Jesus was happy because children hung around with him and, he concludes, kids "don't like creepy people. They don't like grumpy people."

---

2. Ibid., 5, 23, 101.

3. Smith, *Jesus*, 109; Horne, *Proverbs-Ecclesiastes*, 376, where he concludes that "God cannot be known" because the created order does not reveal God. Instead, "God is responsible, as creator, for that which is twisted and perverted in human existence." Other scholars are not as pessimistic as Horne.

What Smith fails to realize is that Jesus did not have children around him unless they were invited. Children would not be allowed around Jesus: that is why the disciples held them back from the Master. The children only came to Jesus because he invited them. Then they gathered around him.[4]

Besides, maybe Jesus was depicted as "grumpy" by artists because he had the weight of the whole world on his shoulders? Just sayin'. Smith concludes that Jesus "was the happiest guy around. He told jokes. He poked fun at people. He laughed."[5]

Jesus did not laugh. He did not joke. I checked my NIV concordance and found that people laughed *at* Jesus. Jesus also said those who morn will one day laugh and those who laugh would one day morn (maybe that is why he did not laugh? See Luke 6). The word joke does not appear in any story about Jesus. Clearly Smith and others are guilty of creating a Jesus that never did exist.

If we want to get to the real Jesus we need to take a hard look once again at the biblical Jesus so we can fill in the blank with an adjective or adverb of substance, not imagination and wishful thinking.

This study began with a look at how doubt permeates a rising sector of Christians today. From evangelicals to noted authors to highly respected religious leaders and secular historians it seems that the old, traditional Christian beliefs are being questioned for three reasons. First, there is ample evidence from historians (not necessarily theologians) that, within the early Christian churches, there was a historical, theological progression from the human Jesus to the Savior Christ to the creed that Jesus was divine and finally the doctrine that he was God in the flesh. We see this progression in book titles. Tom Harpur's *The Pagan Christ*, Paula Fredriksen's *From Jesus to Christ*, Gregory Riley's *One Jesus, Many Christs*, and Richard Rubenstein's *When Jesus Became God* all reveal how early Christian believers slowly worked through a theological progression of Jesus' divinity. One seemingly obvious yet often ignored conclusion from these studies is that, in the very earliest days of Christianity, Jesus was more human than divine.[6]

This is not an ancient phenomenon. Throughout history Christians have continued to examine Jesus and assert various claims about him. American religious history demonstrates the same progression. "Jesus"

---

4. Smith, *Jesus*, 115, 123.
5. Ibid., 123.
6. Harpur, *Pagan*; Fredriksen, *Jesus*; Riley, *One Jesus*; Rubenstein, *Jesus*.

has assumed many forms throughout American history as a few examples demonstrate. The natives in South, Middle, and North America, when they were confronted by the European missionaries in the 1400s and 1500s, understood Jesus as a miracle worker and healer. Catholic missionaries themselves interpreted Jesus from the point of self-sacrifice and good works while Protestant Puritan believers focused on assuaging guilt before good works, a model also based on Jesus. Eighteenth-century revivalists in America turned Jesus into a catchall term meaning piety as achieved through atonement. Within African American circles Jesus was viewed as a liberator. In the late eighteenth-century Unitarians ditched Jesus' divinity to portray him as a philosopher and teacher while Shakers emphasized a more feminized Jesus. In the mid-1800s Jesus was schizophrenic: he was both for and against slavery. By the late 1800s Jesus was a friend of the business tycoons such as J.P. Morgan and Andrew Carnegie. Jesus justified their cruelty and indifference towards the poor and indigent and their personal greed by saying that hard working people deserved their rewards and that the poor were poor because they were lazy. On the other hand, Jesus was the model for a social gospel that took care of the victims of the greedy. These are just a few of the ways Americans have interpreted Jesus through just three centuries.[7]

Nothing has changed. Today I hear the same uses of Jesus' name to justify about anything. He is a muscle man role model for males, he is pro-gays and lesbians, a Republican, the exemplar of business management, a coach. He is both for and against abortion. It seems that we make Jesus into whatever we think he is based on how we perceive our spiritual needs. And, within spiritual reason, I am not so sure this is bad. But, if we deviate from the scriptures then, as we saw in the previous chapter, we enter dangerous roads. What if my answers are not like yours? Does this imply a new relativity to the person and idea of Jesus? The fact that Mark asks so many questions about Jesus suggests that his readers likewise were trying to fill in a blank space in regards to who Jesus is.

Richard Wightman Fox argues that faith is ultimately a cultural phenomenon. Anticipating criticism of this assertion, he notes "Recognizing that knowledge of Jesus is culturally shaped does not compromise his divinity. Suppose there is a God who wishes to make contact with individuals through their religious experiences. That God would have no choice but to work with the cultural norms that people can recognize as religious

---

7. Fox, *Jesus*, throughout.

experiences." Some may reply in a strong statement of faith that God can transcend any cultural barrier that impedes salvation. Indeed, this is the case but ask any missionary about Fox's point and she will provide example after example that proves his assertion.[8] In fact, if one studies the history of Catholic missions one will find that the idea of Jesus is very malleable: it can conform to about any cultural perception of a deity. Perhaps that is what divinity is.

In Hinduism there are 330,000,000 million gods. I often joke to my students that I wonder who counted them all. If one studies Hinduism he or she will find out that there are many personal deities that fulfill the diverse spiritual needs of Hindus. This is polytheism at its best but many spiritual leaders within Hinduism point out that the One in Hinduism is composed of the many. It takes all of these various aspects and attributes of the Many to make up the One. The number 330,000,000 gods is simply a way to suggest that the One has many ways to reach out to the many. Isn't that how a deity works? Given the examples above, that is certainly how Christianity is working today, no matter how many times we insist that our orthodox version is the only one that is valid. Since this religious phenomenon has been practiced from the beginning of Christianity and, despite the attempts of first the Catholic Church and then the Protestants through the centuries to quell this diversity, maybe we should acknowledge that this is the way it should be. We would certainly cease condemning and killing each other if we did so.

Here is an excellent example of how Jesus can meet the needs of a specific person in a specific cultural context. Noted author Kent Nerburn followed the Lakota elder "Dan" for weeks to listen to his wisdom. Dan tried his best to teach Nerburn, as he called him, to listen to the winds, to watch the birds, to learn from the dirt and nature in general. Eventually Nerburn began to see and hear. "How does one learn of forgiveness?" Dan asked Nerburn one day. The answer was simple. Look at the mountains, Dan pointed out in one of his many lessons. "If the mountain can forgive the scarring and the mining, and can cover over her gashes with the fresh grasses of summer, should I not, too, be able to cover over the gashes [of the white man's abuses of the Indians] with the fresh grasses of kindness and understanding?"[9] This lesson sounds just like Jesus' teaching about looking at the flowers and the birds to see the wisdom of their simplicity.

---

8. Ibid., 18.

9. Nerburn, *Neither Wolf*, 24.

Who Do You Say That I Am?

Lest one be quick to dismiss Dan's Native American wisdom as less than Christian he goes on to affirm his belief in Jesus. Indeed, he associates Jesus with the spirit of the Lakota Ghost Dance. He looks forward to the day when Jesus returns. For him, this is an affirmation of the elders' predictions of a savior coming to save the Indians from the oppressions of the white man. Isn't this the same theology that Christians believe in? But, and here is the major point, Dan does not insist that all must conform to his interpretation of Jesus. It simply works best for his faith, his spirit.

Along with this, Ewert Cousins, who envisions a new, mystical, cosmic interpretation of Christ in the 21st century, pointedly states that, "we must not isolate from culture." One example of such a cultural interpretation is found in R.S. Sugirtharajah's edited work that presents many Asian understandings of Jesus. Defying the long-standing Jesus of Catholic missionaries who visited Asia centuries ago, modern Asians are now interpreting Jesus from their particular contextual needs. Jesus is compared to the Hindu Krishna as well as the Buddha and Jesus is interpreted anew by Asian women.[10]

A second reason Christians need to rethink their traditions is that, as we have seen, the narrowly focused theology that emerged as the official dogma of the Church 1500 years ago came as result of deadly theological and political wars among Christians in the fourth and fifth centuries of this era. I was not taught this when I was in seminary in the 1980s and one can see why. I scanned through my church history book to make sure and these actions were glossed over as simply theological debates. The reason for this is that the historical documents describing these vicious theological scraps were ignored or deemed irrelevant by past scholars who were descendants of the European Christian academic tradition.

Along with this, revered early church theologians and apologists such as Irenaeus made some claims about Jesus that today would strike us as heresy. Irenaeus believed that Jesus did not die but instead lived to an old age. In the early second century Papias, the one who told us that Mark did not follow the chronological life of Jesus but instead wrote the story of Jesus to fit a particular theology, believed that Jesus died in bed. St. Augustine, early church historian Eusebius, and theologian Justin Martyr all claimed that the Christian faith was nothing new but instead existed centuries before in other cultures and simply came to light in the life of Jesus. In a seemingly prescient interpretation of Jesus that would ring an ecumenical tone

10. Cousins, *Christ*; Sugirtharajah, *Asian*.

today, Origen, a student of St. Clement of Alexandria, taught reincarnation, emphasized karma and even preached universal salvation. He also opposed the literal interpretation of the Bible.[11]

From such defamatory revelations, assertions and accusations it is now clear that many early Christian communities had very different theologies based on their own interpretations of Jesus as presented in their own gospels and literature. Respected historian Philip Jenkins counts twenty-two different early interpretations of Jesus the Christ and these theologies originated from various parts of the Roman Empire. Seven different church councils were held from 325 CE to 787 CE to determine which interpretation of Jesus would be the proper one for the church. Another historian, Charles Freeman, has demonstrated that there was a major effort by bishops and Roman emperors in the fourth and fifth centuries to suppress these disparate doctrines and force the numerous theologically diverse churches into a theologically united Church. The war was fought with words as well as violent, even deadly force. Smear campaigns were initiated, monks walked about the streets with thugs to bludgeon those who disagreed with their interpretation of Jesus, and politics and ambition were the causes of these ugly actions. To their credit, the Roman culture of that time interpreted everyday events as the actions of the gods. Please the gods and life would go well; disobey the gods by, say, believing in heresy, and the gods will retaliate. Since the barbarians were conquering Roman lands and people the emperors and their Christian allies believed that it was the errant beliefs of some Christians who were causing such wrath from God. The answer to whether Jesus was God or God in the flesh had to be solved so that the Roman Empire would survive. Thus, the theological battles took on national importance. It was literally a matter of life and death. The victors were the ancestors of the current "correct" Christian faith.[12]

In the light of this evidence, the old notion that God, through the Holy Spirit, led the bishops to select the correct books for the New Testament and the proper theology for the believers seems rather innocent and even naive. Again, this is what I learned in seminary. However, the mounting scholarly evidence reveals unscrupulous church leaders and desperate Roman emperors working in collusion to cement a fragmented Roman Empire with the glue of a "creedaly-united" Church. Suddenly the fruits of the labors of the past Church leaders seem tainted if not rotten. Doubts about the

---

11. Harpur, *Pagan*, 27–28; 64;161–162.
12. Jenkins, *Jesus Wars*, 35–37 69–73; Freeman, *A.D. 381*.

faith arise as more Christians ask, "Is this how God does things?" But these Christians do not want to turn loose of their scriptures as a means for finding God's will. What should they do? Where can they go for spiritual advice and nurture? If we look at Christianity before these wars where the divinity of Jesus was declared by forced votes we see a Christianity that utilized and tolerated a multifarious Jesus. In other words, until Christianity became enmeshed with the state and power, Christians who interpreted Jesus in different ways agreed to disagree over their interpretations. Might this be an example for us today? If I correctly hear and understand the growing voices of the disgruntled among Christians today this is exactly what they want. They want to see Jesus for who they think he is. They want a Jesus who meets their individual needs, not the needs of a cold and conformist denomination, let alone a national, evangelical faith.

Third, there are simply more ways to envision salvation today. Since the 1960s America has seen a rise in non-Christian religions. These different faiths bring with them new ways to live in peace and contentment. Traditional Christian paths to salvation are being replaced with new avenues of nirvana. Churches are combining yoga and meditation into their religious devotions and rituals. It is very easy to be both Buddhist and Christian and authors such as Thich Nhat Hanh are demonstrating that the Buddha and the Christ are very similar. Many Native Americans still retain their indigenous beliefs and practices while adhering to the basic Christian tenets. And, as we saw in the Introduction, such religious choices are found not only in liberal circles but increasingly in evangelical believers as well. This diversity brings with it comparisons with the salvation stories and theologies of these faiths. Suddenly, it seems that what Jesus taught and what the Buddha preached are the same thing. The Ten Commandments and the ethics of Islam are the same. The Golden Rule, most likely originating with Confucius, has been handed down through the ages up to today. Might this mean that all religions are the same in general beliefs but differ only in particulars? If so, then might Jesus be just one of many saviors in the world? An increasing number of Christians are willing to answer yes.[13]

If we recall several works used throughout this book then we remember that many critics of religion and especially Christianity argue that it is the insistence upon the exclusivity of Jesus as savior of the world that is causing much of the religious tensions among world religions and within the family of Christians. If we release our claim of salvific exclusivity and

---

13. Hanh, *Living Buddha*; Armstrong, *Transformation*.

acknowledge that Jesus is one of several avenues for salvation, then these tensions will be alleviated. This would lead to people finding their own savior figure while agreeing to let others find their savior figures. But this means that Christians will have to bypass centuries of persistent indoctrinations and beliefs. Traditions will have to be repudiated in order to move back to this primitive Christian type of faith.

Which brings me to the last point. Today many people feel free to question authority and even buck the traditional Christian status quo altogether. Liberals have been the vanguard of such approaches and women today, filled with the righteous indignation of feminist spirituality, have raised serious questions that the Church either ignores or refuses to even tolerate. But, as we have seen in this study, even today many within the ranks of the more conservative churches are asking questions and walking against the grain of the denominational and evangelical dogmas. Some are taking new paths to find the answers they seek.

None of these Christians wishes to leave the fold altogether. Tired of the selfish individualism and buffet style of spirituality of the Seekers, they want to find some respite in the comfortable pews of the old faith. Wary of New Age spirituality that adopts some of anything to fill a hunger they cannot even identify, frustrated Christians sincerely believe that there is still a delicacy on the communion table for them to partake of. But the traditional Church does not wish to serve them at all.

So, where do we go from here?

It seems that, for many Christians today who are disgruntled with the continuously digressing and devolving antics of the Church, there is a way to retain one's faith in Christ amid the ruins and rubble of today's Christian indifference, stubborn insistence and even political and theological warfare. While the Church implodes, a victim of its very theological intransigence, and while church billboards such as "My Religion Sucks" (yes, seen on Highway 70 in North Carolina; see churchrelevant.com for a chummy, trendy version of the faith) repulse many, both in and out of the faith, some Christians quietly wish to simply move on to a new start. Like the Jews of old who returned from Babylon to their Jerusalem home after 538 BCE they want to rebuild the Temple of old, but, unlike the Jews of old, they understand that they cannot and should not replicate the way things used to be. The new Temple will not resemble the elegance of the old and the rituals and their supporting myths will not be performed and recited as they were long ago. Just as Isaiah warned the Israelites in the seventh century BCE, that, while they would reenact the exodus of Moses' generation they would not be chained to the past, so God will do a new thing through a new Exodus to a new Jerusalem and in a new Temple.

It is time to recognize and admit that throughout its 2100 year history the Church has always reevaluated Jesus and God through the centuries, either officially or through the believing populace. This is seen first in the Gospels themselves. Never mind the plethora of non-canonical gospels that describe Jesus in myriad odd (although regionally appreciated) ways. One read through the four "official" gospels reveals a multifarious Jesus. To simplify the matter, Mark's Jesus seems very human, sometimes testy, and he performs miracles while trying to stick to his calling of preaching the good news. Matthew's Jesus seems very Jewish and divine and Matthew appears to be defending a Jewish interpretation of the Messiah. Matthew's Jesus, like the Moses of old, has a miraculous early life and goes on to teach a new set of commands from a mountain. Luke, on the other hand, features a miraculously born Jesus who is compassionate to all people, even reaching out to the marginalized Gentiles. He befriends women and outcasts and the role of the Holy Spirit is ever present in the gospel. John's gospel deviates from these Synoptic Gospels by presenting a Jesus who does various signs indicating his divine status yet he also would be very much at home amongst a circle of philosophers. John, it seems, has Jesus criticizing the stubborn Jews who refused to deviate from their traditions, thus dividing their own religious community. Some scholars have called John's gospel anti-semitic, a claim that has credence if qualified with the notion that very conservative Jews and very liberal Jews could not agree on who Jesus was.

We should also add that, as we have seen, these individual gospels often disagree on various aspects of Jesus. Did Jesus use parables to so that people would not understand him (so Mark 4) or did Jesus use parables so that people would understand him (as in Matt 13)? As discerning readers have pointed out, the details of Jesus' birth differ markedly in Matthew and Luke no matter how much scholars try to harmonize them. When was the Last Supper? John has a totally different date than Mathew, Luke and Mark. Yet, these four different views were put together in one New Testament. Shouldn't that very fact tell us that, in the very earliest days of the Church, the people did not view these stories as historical facts and instead looked at the stories within? At the very least it should tell us that the earliest believers were just fine with theological discrepancies. Shouldn't we be the same?

Just from this evidence alone, two ideas emerge. First, each region in the Mediterranean Christian world had its own special interpretation of Jesus. However, by the fifth and sixth centuries the various interpretations of Jesus as believed in the Middle Eastern, Eastern and African churches had been deemed incorrect and blasphemous. There is simply no getting around this conclusion. Before the gospels were combined into one New Testament that circulated about the Christian world, Christians read them separately before reading them together. If one wants to get to the root of early Christianity, then one has to understand that, in the very early church, different evaluations of Jesus were the acceptable norm. Why should we deviate from this today? Using this model, Christians today can use this study of Mark as one (of many) ways to reinterpret Jesus.

Second, Christians today should take heart that the early church fathers, no matter what their political/religious reasons, included four testimonies about Jesus that in many ways refute each other. Surely these theologians were intelligent enough to know that these gospels, while agreeing in principle about Jesus, were sometimes contradictory about him as well. Were the compilers of the New Testament trying to suggest a composite Jesus? Or, were they aware that various regions held distinct views of Jesus that, in their judgment, were acceptable, indeed, necessary for the faith? If so, then were they trying to appease each region?

So, if the early churches held different beliefs and interpretations of Jesus, what does that mean for Christians today? Perhaps Christians should look at the evidence (all of it, not what the Church or pastor or denomination or culture or politician deems "official" or acceptable) and make an informed spiritual decision as to what depiction of Jesus best fits their religious needs. In other words, we need our own personal myth of who Jesus is.

Noted therapist Rollo May, in 1991, described the same symptoms of disjunctive faith as have been pointed out above. While his book diagnoses people of all religious allegiances, I want to place his conclusions in the Christian context. In the late 1900s people in general began to question authority and the insistence upon facts as opposed to story. Turned away from their religious communities for asking such questions, they became lonely people in search of a new home. Frustrated with the cold reasoning of doctrine and tired of the bulwarks of religion that impede personal explorations of faith, they gave up on the ways of the Church but this led to debilitating personal issues. May noticed that, in their descriptions of their troubles, they often referred to archetypes of mythical plots and even characters. But, May notes, the reliance upon myth that is so essential for a healthy faith was replaced by the religion of reason during the Enlightenment and this has wreaked havoc upon the religious faithful ever since. The Church did not offer the myths that keep people psychologically healthy. It served up rational doctrines and statements and creeds and denominational guidelines, the very opposite of stories and myths. May concludes that our society today suffers from "mythoclasm," the destruction of our myths.[14]

May argues that myth "is a drama which begins as a historical event and takes on its special character as a way of orienting people to reality."[15] In essence, history becomes mythologized. This was especially true in Jesus' time: ancient stories had been turned into myths and these were read as national literature and religious story. The ancient battle of Troy was, until recently, thought to be just myth, fiction. But recent archeological findings reveal that there was indeed a battle at Troy. Thus, a historical event was transformed into a myth that justified the rise of Greece. When Greece needed to justify its emerging navy in the fifth century BCE it took the stories of the hero Theseus and created a new myth. The Roman version of this story, *The Aeneid*, followed the same pattern. Likewise, the historical annals of great Roman emperors and military leaders were later mythologized into stories that were used to teach Roman values and morals. The same pattern is found in the gospels, especially Mark. Recall that, according to very early church traditions, Mark took Peter's stories of Jesus and rearranged them to fit his own timetable, his own spiritual needs, most likely for his own religious community. History was intentionally transformed into myth. May recommends going back to the notion of myth, not fact, story instead of history, if we are to overcome this serious demise of faith and spirituality. This type of reconstruction is necessary if we are to revive a healthy spiritual life.

At this point we need to stop and dispel a myth about myth. Myth is not about falsehood. It is not a lie. It is not untrue. Myth is Truth. Myth explains what cannot be explained in any other way. Myth is a powerful way to relate experiences that cannot be described in everyday language. Here is an example.

I once had an elderly student in an Old Testament class who was not buying my interpretation of some biblical stories as myth. She simply refused to budge no matter how I explained that myth retained a historical nugget

---

14. May, *Myth*, 25.
15. Ibid., 26.

but went on to tell a greater truth. Then it hit me. I asked the predominately evangelical and very conservative class if they had been born again, washed in the blood of Jesus. Most raised their hands, as did my elderly student in a proud display of faith. So I asked her to describe this experience. She said that Jesus shed his blood for us and that his blood washed her sins away. Then I asked if she was baptized in the blood of Jesus and she replied yes. So I asked her if she went home that day and washed her clothes. She looked puzzled and pointed out that when she was baptized there was no blood. But then I countered that she said she was baptized in the blood of Jesus, to which she said yes. So I asked if her clothes were ruined with the blood. She looked puzzled again. Finally, after repeating this question a few more times it clicked that she had not been baptized in the literal blood of Jesus but that she had indeed been baptized in the blood of Jesus *mythically*. And, despite the mythical implications, the experience was just as real as if it really happened because *it did happen* to her. This is the powerful Truth of myth and this is why we need it so much today.

Recall above that many critics of religion today, both believers and skeptics, have argued quite well that it is the literal interpretation of religious texts that has thrown believers off the course of their respective religions. The above example of being baptized in the blood of Jesus clearly demonstrates that, even if we believe in the literal, factual, historical claims of the faith, we live in the mythical realm of faith, whether we admit it or not. If we, liberals and conservatives, move away from our literal slavery to the biblical text we might just find the truth we are looking for.

Myth, May suggests, builds community.[16] The Christians who have become frustrated with the church that is indifferent to their faith needs have left the fold but wish to have a religious community to attend. Where do they go? As of now they are underground or in the prayer closet, afraid to speak their ideas about Jesus to any but a select and trusted few. They are not welcome in their old faith communities because of their "liberal" or "pagan" or "heretical" ideas. And, ironically, some are not welcomed into liberal communities because their beliefs are still deemed conservative! People who believe in the same things tend to congregate together. As Christians reevaluate Jesus a new myth will form and those who believe in this particular myth will congregate together. And one central pillar of this community is a hero.

---

16. Ibid., 45.

Who Do You Say That I Am?

Justin Martyr, an early apologist for the Christian church, compared Jesus favorably to the mythical heroes of his Greco-Roman culture. In essence, the Church had its hero while the Greeks and Romans had theirs.[17] Today's theologians from both the left and right have reduced Jesus to a list of facts—born of a virgin, God-in-the-flesh, a real human yet also God, physically resurrected and one who one day will return physically—yet many Christians long for the mythical, heroic Jesus. The Jesus of old, the mythical one as portrayed by Mark, was a hero over evil but he has been replaced by rational denominational and doctrinal theorems and proofs. This reliance on creeds has destroyed the mythical Jesus. And, May suggests, the only way people can replace these dangerous rational proofs of a hero is to reinvent their own hero. This is what I have tried to do. Based on the book of Mark, I have looked again at Jesus with the eyes of doubt in order to retrieve the mythical Jesus he offered to his readers.

---

17. Jones, *Heroes*, 86.

Bibliography

Aesop's Fables, transl. V. S. Vernon Jones; Introduction and notes by D. L. Ashliman. New York: Barnes & Noble Classics, 2003.

Albanese, Catherine L. *A Republic of Mind and Spirit: A Cultural History of American Metaphysical Religion*. New Haven: Yale University Press, 2007.

Albright, W. F. and C. S. Mann. *Matthew: Introduction, Translation, and Notes*. Anchor Bible. New York: Doubleday, 1971.

Anderson, Hugh. *The Gospel of Mark*. New Century Bible Commentary. Grand Rapids: William B. Eerdmans, 1976, 1981.

Armstrong, Karen. *The Case for God*. New York: Knopf, 2009.

———. *A History of God: The 4,000-Year Quest of Judaism, Christianity and Islam*. New York: Ballentine, 1993.

———. *The Great Transformation: The Beginnings of Our Religious Traditions*. New York: Alfred A. Knopf, 2006.

Aslan, Reza. *Zealot: The Life and Times of Jesus of Nazareth*. New York: Random House, 2014.

Barna, George, and David Kinnaman. *Churchless: Understanding Today's Unchurched and How to Connect With Them*. Tyndale Momentum, 2014.

Barrett, C.K. *The First Epistle to the Corinthians*. Harper's New Testament Commentaries. New York: Harper and Row, 1968.

Bass, Diana Butler. *Christianity After Religion: The End of Church and the Birth of a New Spiritual Awakening*. New York: HarperOne, 2012.

Bauer, Walter. *Orthodoxy and Heresy in Earliest Christianity*. Philadelphia: Fortress, 1971.

Bauer, Arndt and Gringrich. *Theological Lexicon of the New Testament and Other Early Christian Literature*. Chicago: University of Chicago Press, 1957.

Bergler, Thomas E. *The Juvenilization of American Christianity*. Grand Rapids: William B. Eerdmans, 2012.

Bethke, Jefferson. *Jesus > Religion: Why He Is So Much Better Than Trying Harder, Doing More, and Being Good Enough*. Nashville: Nelson, 2013.

Black, C. Clifton. *Mark*. Nashville: Abingdon, 2011.

Bloch, Jon P. *The Everything Health Guide to Adult Bipolar Disorder*. Avon: Adams Media, 2006.

Bibliography

Borg, Marcus J. "Jesus Before and After Easter: Jewish Mystic and Christian Messiah," in Marcus J. Borg and N.T. Wright, *The Meaning of Jesus: Two Visions*. New York: HarperOne, 1999.

———. *Jesus: Uncovering the Life, Teachings, and Relevance of a Religious Revolutionary*. New York: HarperOne, 2006.

———. *Meeting Jesus Again for the First Time: The Historical Jesus & the Heart of Contemporary Faith*. HarperSanFrancisco: 1994.

Boring, M. Eugene. *Mark: A Commentary*. Louisville: Westminster John Knox, 2006.

Bridges, Linda McKinnish. *1&2 Thessalonians*. Smyth & Helwys Bible Commentary. Macon: Smyth & Helwys, 2008.

Brown, Raymond E. *The Birth of the Messiah: A Commentary on the Infancy Narratives in the Gospels of Matthew and Luke*, Updated Edition. New York: Doubleday, 1993.

Burridge, Richard A. *What Are The Gospels? A Comparison with Graeco-Roman Biography*, 2nd ed. Grand Rapids: William B. Eerdmans, 2004.

Camp, Claudia. *Wisdom and the Feminine in the Book of Proverbs*. Sheffield: JSOT, 1985.

Carcopino, Jerome. *Daily Life in Ancient Rome*, 2nd. ed. New Haven: Yale University Press, 2003.

Chance, J. Bradley. *Acts*. Smyth & Helwys Bible Commentary. Macon: Smyth & Helwys.

Chittister, Joan. *Called to Question: A Spiritual Memoir*. Lanham: Sheed & Ward, 2004, 2009.

Clingerman, C. "ok on the surface." Retrieved from https://www.amazon.com/The-Christian-Atheist-Believing-Living/product-reviews/031032789X/ref=cm_cr_getr_d_paging_btm_2?ie=UTF8&showViewpoints=1&filterByStar=critical&pageNumber=2 March 28, 2017.

Cohen, Shaye J. D. "Judaism Under Roman Domination: From the Hasmoneans Through the Destruction of the Second Temple," in Burton L. Visotzky and David E. Fishman, *From Mesopotamia to Modernity: Ten Introductions to Jewish History and Literature*. Boulder: Westview, 1999.

Collins, Raymond F. *The Many Faces of the Church: A Study in New Testament Ecclesiology*. New York: Herder & Herder, 2003.

Cotter, Wendy J. *The Christ of the Miracle Stories: Portrait Through Encounter*. Grand Rapids: Baker Academic, 2010.

Cousins, Ewert. *Christ of the 21st Century*. New York: Continuum, 1998.

Crossan, John Dominic. *Jesus: A Revolutionary Biography*. HarperSanFrancisco: 1994.

Crossan, John Dominic and Jonathan L. Reed. *Excavating Jesus: Beneath the Stones, Behind the Texts*, rev. and updated. New York: HarperOne, 2001.

Culpepper, R. Alan. *Mark*. Smyth & Helwys Bible Commentary. Macon: Smyth & Helwys, 2007.

Dunn, James D.G. *Unity and Diversity in the New Testament: An Inquiry into the Character of Earliest Christianity*, 2nd ed. Philadelphia: Trinity Press International: 1990.

Erhman, Bart D. *Lost Christianities: The Battles for Scripture and the Faiths We Never Knew*. Oxford: Oxford University Press, 2003.

———. *Misquoting Jesus: The Story Behind Who Changed the Bible and Why*. HarperSanFrancisco, 2005.

———. *The New Testament: A Historical Introduction to the Early Christian Writings*, 2nd ed. New York: Oxford University Press, 2000.

Fenton, John. *St. Matthew*. Pelican New Testament Commentaries. New York: Penguin, 1963, 1985.

Bibliography

Fitzmyer, Joseph A. *The Gospel According to Luke X-XXIV*. Anchor Bible. New York: Doubleday, 1985.

Fowler, James W. *Stages of Faith: The Psychology of Human Development and the Quest for Meaning*. New York: HarperOne, 1981.

Fowler, Robert M. "In The Boat With Jesus: Imagining Ourselves In Mark's Story" in Kelly R. Iverson and Christopher W. Skinner, eds., *Mark as Story: Retrospect and Prospect*. Atlanta: Society of Biblical Literature, 2011.

Fox, Richard Wightman. *Jesus in America: Personal Savior, Cultural Hero, National Obsession*. HarperSanFrancisco, 2004.

Fredriksen, Paula. *From Jesus to Christ: The Origins of the New Testament Images of Jesus*. New Haven: Yale University Press, 1998.

Freeman, Charles. *A.D. 381: Heretics, Pagans, and the Dawn of the Monotheistic State*. New York: Over Look, 2008.

———. *The Closing of the Western Mind: The Rise of Faith and the Fall of Reason*. New York: Vintage, 2002.

Freund, Richard A. *Digging Through the Bible: Modern Archeology and the Ancient Bible*. Lanham: Rowman & Littlefield, 2009.

Geldenhuys, Norval. *The Gospel of Luke*. New International Commentary on the New Testament. Grand Rapids: William B. Eerdmans, 1951.

Gibbs, John. "A challenging call to believe what you say you believe." Retrieved from http://www.amazon.com/The-Christian-Atheist-Believing-Living/product-reviews/031032789X/ref=dp_top_cm_cr_acr_txt?ie=UTF8&showViewpoints=1; last accessed May 18, 2016.

Goodman, Martin. *Rome and Jerusalem: The Clash Of Ancient Civilizations*. New York: Alfred A. Knopf, 2007.

Groeschel, Craig. *The Christian Atheist: Believing in God But Living as if He Does Not Exist*. Grand Rapids: Zondervan, 2011.

Guthrie, Donald. *Galatians*. New Century Bible Commentary. Grand Rapids: William B. Eerdmans, 1973.

Hanh, Thich Nhat. *Living Buddha, Living Christ*. New York: Riverhead Books, 2007.

Harpur, Tom. *The Pagan Christ: Is Blind Faith Killing Christianity?* New York: Walker & Company, 2004.

Harris, Sam. *The End of Faith: Religion, Terror, and the Future of Reason*. New York: W.W. Norton, 2004.

Hooker, Morna D. *The Gospel According to Saint Mark*. Black's New Testament Commentary. Peabody: Hendrickson Publishers, 1991.

Horne, Milton P. *Proverbs-Ecclesiastes*. Smyth & Helwys Bible Commentary. Macon: Smyth & Helwys, 2003.

Hubbard, Moyer V. *Christianity in the Greco-Roman World: A Narrative Introduction*. Grand Rapids: BakerAcademic, 2010.

Huffman, Daphne. "I Was Disappointed With This Book." Retrieved from https://www.amazon.com/The-Christian-Atheist-Believing-Living/product-reviews/031032789X/ref=cm_cr_getr_d_paging_btm_2?ie=UTF8&showViewpoints=1&filterByStar=critical&pageNumber=2 March 28, 2017.

Hunter, R. Lanny and Victor L. Hunter. *What Your Doctor and Your Pastor Want You to Know about Depression*. St. Louis: Chalice, 2004.

Jamison, Kay Redfield. *An Unquiet Mind: A Memoir of Moods and Madness*. New York: Vintage Books, 1995.

Bibliography

Jeffers, James S. *The Greco-Roman World of the New Testament: Exploring the Background of Early Christianity*. Downer's Grove: InterVarsity, 1999.

Jenkins, Philip. *Jesus Wars: How Four Patriarchs, Three Queens, and Two Emperors Decided What Christians Would Believe for the Next 1,500 Years*. New York: HarperOne, 2010.

Jones, Christopher P. *New Heroes in Antiquity: From Achilles to Antinoos*. Cambridge: Harvard University Press, 2010.

Keck, Leander E. *Romans*. Abingdon New Testament Commentaries. Nashville: Abingdon, 2005.

Keller, Timothy. *The Reason for God: Belief in an Age of Skepticism*. New York: Riverhead, 2008.

Kidd, Sue Monk. *The Dance of the Dissident Daughter: A Woman's Journey from Christian Tradition to the Sacred Feminine*. HarperSanFrancisco, 1996.

Koenig, Harold. *Is Religion Good for Your Health? The Effects of Religion on Physical and Mental Health*. New York: Haworth Pastoral Press, 1997.

Kolodiejchuk, Brian M.C., ed. *Mother Teresa: Come Be My Light: The Private Writings of the 'Saint of Calcutta.'* New York: Doubleday, 2007.

Lane, William L. *The Gospel of Mark*. The New International Commentary on the New Testament. Grand Rapids: William B. Eerdmans, 1974.

Leeming, David. *The Oxford Companion to World Mythology*. Oxford: Oxford University Press, 2005.

———. *The World of Myth: An Anthology*. Oxford: Oxford University Press, 1990.

Malbom, Elizabeth Struthers. *Mark's Jesus: Characterization as Narrative Christology*. Waco: Baylor University Press, 2009.

Mare, W. Harold. *1 Corinthians*. Expositor's Bible Commentary Vol. 10. Grand Rapids: Regency, 1976.

Marshall, I. Howard. *1 and 2 Thessalonians*. The New Century Bible Commentary. Grand Rapids: William. B. Eerdmans, 1983.

May, Rollo. *The Cry for Myth*. New York: W.W. Norton, 1991.

McDonald, Dennis R. *The Homeric Epics and the Gospel of Mark*. New Haven: Yale University Press, 2000.

Meyers, Carol. *Discovering Eve: Ancient Israelite Women in Context*. Oxford: Oxford University Press, 1988.

Michel, Otto. "The Conclusion of Matthew's Gospel: A Contribution to the History of the Easter Message," in Graham Stanton, ed., *The Interpretation of the Gospel of Matthew*. Philadelphia: Fortress, 1983.

Moltman-Wendel, Elisabeth. *The Women Around Jesus*. New York: Crossroad, 1993.

Morris, Leon. *The First and Second Epistles to the Thessalonians*. New International Commentary on the New Testament. Grand Rapids: William. B. Eerdmans, 1959, 1989.

———. *The Gospel According to Matthew*. Grand Rapids: William B. Eerdmans, 1992.

Nash, Robert Scott. *1 Corinthians*. Smyth & Helwys Bible Commentary. Macon: Smyth & Helwys, 2009.

Nerburn, Kent. *Neither Wolf Nor Dog: On Forgotten Roads with an Indian Elder*. Novato: New World Library, 1994, 2002.

New International Version NIV Study Bible. Grand Rapids: Zondervan, 2011.

Nineham, D.E. *The Gospel of St. Mark*. The Pelican Gospel Commentaries. New York: The Seabury Press, 1963, 1968.

BIBLIOGRAPHY

Noll, Mark A. *The Scandal of the Evangelical Mind*. Grand Rapids: William B. Eerdmans, 1994.
Oden, Thomas C. *The African Memory of Mark: Reassessing Early Church Tradition* Downers Grove: IVP Academic, 2011.
Oden, Thomas C. and Christopher A. Hall. *Mark*. Ancient Christian Commentary on Scripture, II. Downers Grove: InterVarsity, 1998.
Orr, William F. and James Arthur Walther. *First Corinthians: A New Translation*. The Anchor Bible. New York: Doubleday, 1976.
Ovid. *The Metamorphoses*, edited with an Introduction and Notes by Robert Squillace; transl. Frank Justus Miller. New York: Barnes & Noble Classics, 2005.
Perrin, Norman. *The Resurrection According to Matthew, Mark, and Luke*. Philadelphia: Fortress, 1977.
Pettengill, Mike. "The Author Seems Afraid to Commit to Biblical Absolutes." Retrieved from https://www.amazon.com/The-Christian-Atheist-Believing-Living/product-reviews/031032789X/ref=cm_cr_getr_d_paging_btm_1?ie=UTF8&showViewpoints=1&filterByStar=critical&pageNumber=1 March 27, 2017.
Ricci, Carla. *Mary Magdalene and Many Others: Women Who Followed Jesus*. Minneapolis: Fortress, 1994.
Rhoads, David and Donald Michie. *Mark as Story: An Introduction to the Narrative of a Gospel*. Philadelphia: Fortress, 1982.
Riley, Gregory J. *One Jesus, Many Christs: How Jesus Inspired Not One True Christianity But Many*. HarperSanFrancisco, 1997.
Rhoads, David and Donald Michie. *Mark As Story: An Introduction to the Narrative of a Gospel*. Philadelphia: Fortress, 1982.
Roetzel, Calvin J. *The Letters of Paul: Conversations in Context*. Louisville: Westminster John Knox, 1998.
———. *Paul: The Man and the Myth*. Minneapolis: Fortress, 1997.
Rohr, Richard. *Everything Belongs: The Gift of Contemplative Prayer*, revised and updated. New York: Crossroad, 1999, 2003.
Rubenstein, Richard E. *Aristotle's Children: How Christians, Muslims and Jews Rediscovered Ancient Wisdom and Illuminated the Dark Ages*. Orlando: Harcourt, 2003.
———. *When Jesus Became God: The Struggle to Define Christianity during the Last Days of Rome*. San Diego: Harcourt: 1999.
Sanders, E. P. *Jesus and Judaism*. Philadelphia: Fortress, 1985.
Simonetti, Manlio, ed. *Matthew 14–28*. Ancient Christian Commentary on Scripture: New Testament Ib. Downers Grove: InterVarsity, 2002.
Smith, Judah. *Jesus Is _____*. Nashville: Thomas Nelson, 2013.
Sordi, Marta. The Christians and the Roman Empire. Transl. by Annabel Bedini. Norman: University of Oklahoma Press, 1994.
Stark, Rodney J. *Cities of God: The Real Story of How Christianity Became an Urban Movement and Conquered Rome*. HarperSanFrancisco: 2006.
Steiger, Phillip. Retrieved from http://www.amazon.com/The-Christian-Atheist-Believing-Living/product-reviews/031032789X/ref=dp_top_cm_cr_acr_txt?ie=UTF8&showViewpoints=1; last accessed on May 18, 2106.
Stossel, John. *Myths, Lies, and Downright Stupidity: Get Out the Shovel—Why Everything You Know is Wrong*. New York: MJF, 2006.
Sugirtharajah, R. S., ed. *Asian Faces of Jesus*. Maryknoll: Orbis Books, 1993.

Bibliography

Tabor, James D. *The Jesus Dynasty: The Hidden History of Jesus, His Royal Family, and the Birth of Christianity.* New York: Simon & Schuster, 2006.

Talbert, Charles H. *Romans.* Smyth & Helwys Bible Commentary. Macon: Smyth & Helwys, 2002.

Taylor, Barbara Brown. *An Altar in the World: A Geography of Faith.* New York: Harper One, 2009.

———. *Leaving Church: A Memoir of Faith.* New York: HarperOne, 2006.

Torensen, Karen Jo. *When Women Were Priests: Women's Leadership in the Early Church & the Scandal of their Subordination in the Rise of Christianity.* HarperSanFrancisco: 1993.

Van Voorst, Robert E. *Jesus Outside the New Testament: An Introduction to the Ancient Evidence.* Grand Rapids: William B. Eerdmans, 2000.

Virgil. *The Aeneid.* Introduction and Notes by Sarah Spence; Transl. by Pearse Cranch. New York: Barnes & Noble Classics, 2007.

Watson, David F. Watson. "The Life of Aesop and the Gospel of Mark: Two Ancient Approaches to Elite Values." *Journal of Biblical Literature* 129 (2010) 699–716.

Weinberg, Steve. "Author goes undercover into world of evangelicals." *Raleigh News & Observer*, 8D, February 28, 2010.

White, L. Michael. *From Jesus to Christianity: How Four Generations of Visionaries & Storytellers Created the New Testament and Christian Faith.* HarperSanFrancisco, 2004.

———. *Scripting Jesus: The Gospels in Rewrite.* New York: HarperOne, 2010.

Witherington, Ben, III. *Matthew.* Smyth & Helwys Bible Commentary. Macon: Smyth and Helwys, 2006.

Wright, N.T. "The Mission and Message of Jesus," in Marcus Borg and N.T. Wright, *The Meaning of Jesus: Two Visions.* New York: HarperOne, 1999.

Wylen, Stephen M. *The Jews in the Time of Jesus.* New York: Paulist, 1996.

www.ingramcontent.com/pod-product-compliance
Lightning Source LLC
Chambersburg PA
CBHW051933160426
43198CB00012B/2131